C000258912

Raich Carter
The Biography
by Frank Garrick

SPORTSBOOKS

Published in Great Britain by
SportsBooks Limited
1 Evelyn Court
Malvern Road
Cheltenham
GL50 2JR

© Frank Garrick 2003
First Published October 2003
Reprinted November 2003

Front cover designed by Kath Northam.
Photograph by Hulton Getty of Raich Carter against Scotland
at Hampden Park in 1943.

A catalogue record for this book is available from
the British Library.

ISBN 1 899807 18 7

Printed and bound in England by
Creative Print and Design Ltd., Wales.

Contents

Foreword

by Sir Tom Finney

WHEN I was just starting my football career during the Second World War Raich Carter was an established superstar, although we did not use words like that in those days.

Like many of his generation he lost the prime years of his career to the war when for the obvious reasons you will read in this book football did not have an international or national league and cup structure.

Raich, of course, had several outstanding years in the game before the war. He captained Sunderland to League championship and FA Cup triumphs in the 1930s and he also won the FA Cup in 1946 for Derby County which made him the only player to collect winners' medals before and after the war.

But when I made my England debut alongside him in 1946 he was well into his thirties. I had replaced the injured Stanley Matthews for the match with Northern Ireland in Belfast and Raich was my inside forward partner. I was impressed by the way he delivered the ball to me, right to my feet, impeccably measured passes, even when he was under pressure.

He had a reputation for arrogance and not suffering fools gladly but he and Tommy Lawton, the senior figures in the England team, were consideration itself in helping the newcomers settle in. They kept talking about football, attempting I'm sure to help us keep our nerves under control.

Raich also had a successful managerial career but it is as a commanding inside forward that he will be remembered, his white hair helping him stand out on the pitch. I've always said that there were three inside forwards from which I would pick my ideal forward line from those I played alongside – Stan Mortensen and Wilf Mannion were two, Raich Carter was the other.

Dedicated to Harry and Nancy Garrick:
Sunderland born and bred

Introduction

MY EARLIEST football memory is the 1946 FA Cup final. I was ten and it was the first cup final since 1939 when the Second World War intervened. It was an eventful match: a player scored at both ends within a couple of minutes, the leather ball burst with only a few minutes left and extra-time was needed. We did not have a television set because the BBC had not yet resumed television broadcasting and I do not remember sitting through a radio commentary. Maybe we saw a few minutes of the final on the cinema news. For certain I studied the reports and photographs in the *News of the World* and in Monday's *Daily Express*: Derby County four, Charlton Athletic one.

It soon emerged that one of the cup winning players had also been a cup winner in 1937 for another club, Sunderland. This was important information to our family because we were all Sunderland supporters despite living 260 miles to the south. Unemployment in the shipyards in the 1920s had forced my parents to seek work, initially in London. The double cup winner was Raich Carter but we had to make do with watching St Albans City.

However, when all the family gathered for a reunion there was one legend about Raich Carter which was often repeated. It concerned a dribbling competition between Sunderland schools in the early 1920s. Young Raich had represented Hendon School while my father's younger brother, Uncle David to me, represented South Hylton. The surprising outcome of this contest was that David Garrick was declared the winner. The story was probably first told in 1934 when Raich Carter made his England debut. It was certainly retold when he led Sunderland to their first cup triumph at Wembley in 1937. The cup victory with Derby in 1946 would no doubt have given the story fresh significance.

Raich Carter went on to new challenges in Hull and Cork, in Leeds and Middlesbrough while I suffered the sad fate of all Sunderland supporters, especially since the first relegation in 1958. It was not until nearly 40 years later when I showed my son a book review of a biography of Wilf Mannion and suggested it would make someone a nice present. The following Christmas the book duly arrived. It set me thinking, 'could there be a similar work about Raich Carter?' There was nothing available, so tentatively I began to research about him. The material grew and grew. There was certainly enough for a biography and thanks to Mrs Pat Carter and my publisher Randall Northam it has become a reality.

Acknowledgments

MY THANKS go to the many people who generously gave me their time and expertise. The whole project would have been impossible without the support of my wife Franca who checked my first drafts chapter by chapter and gradually became a great admirer of Raich Carter. Also to my sons Robert and Andrew who took an active interest in the progress of the book.

I received the full and enthusiastic backing of the Carter family, especially from Mrs Pat Carter and her children Jane and Raich junior, from Raich's eldest daughter Jennifer and her husband Peter.

I am particularly grateful to Andrew Ward whose writing experience and first hand knowledge of Raich Carter and his family were invaluable, I greatly appreciated talking to John Charles, Sir Tom Finney, Terry Murray and Ian Hall. I am also indebted to the late Walter Winterbottom, to Tony Pawson, OBE, the late Charlie Mitten, JC Beal of Sheffield University, Elizabeth Rees of Tyne and Wear Archives Service, Val Craggs of the City of Sunderland Library, Cllr Eric Holt of Sunderland City Council, Suzanne Crosbie of the Irish Examiner Library, to Willie Cotter (Cork), Gordon Dreyer (Hull City), Brian Glanville, Tom and Walter Grendale, Rom Gormley, Tony Gavin, Jack Washington, Paul Taylor (Mansfield Town historian), David Orme, Mark Maunders (Fulham FC), Trevor Bugg (Hull City), Bernard Moore, Derek Norman, Jackie Jones, Archie Hunt, Charlie Nicholas, Paul Smith, N Hughes (Port Vale), G Chalk (Southampton FC), Paul Szczerbakowicz (Brentford FC), Tim Chapman (North Herts branch Sunderland Supporters' Club), Kevin Stirling (Aberdeen FC).

I would also like to thank Mrs June McDonald for all her word processing work.

Chapter One

The Young Horatio

FOOTBALL WAS in his genes. His father Robert 'Toddler' Carter, had played for Burslem (now Port Vale), Fulham and Southampton before the First World War. This included Fulham's first season in the Football League, 1907-8, when he played ten games, scoring seven times. The nickname derived from his small stature. He was a quick and enterprising winger who would shoot at every opportunity. In 43 appearances for Southampton he scored 12 goals. It is thought he suffered a serious knee injury at the end of the 1909-10 season and did not play again until the 13th November when he turned out for Southampton reserves at Salisbury City. He scored but never played for the first team again. At some point he received a severe blow to the head from which he never fully recovered. He returned to his birthplace in Hendon, Sunderland, to become licensee of the Ocean Queen in June 1912.

The Ocean Queen, in Tower Street Hendon, was in the dockland area of Sunderland. It had a 'beerhouse license' only, considered adequate for the needs of the local dockers. By the time he took over Robert Carter had married Clara Augusta. Their first child, a boy, died while still a baby. The second was christened Horatio Stratton Carter. The origin of the Stratton name was straightforward; it was his mother's maiden name. Carter, himself, said in 1949 that he did not know where the idea for Horatio came from but as his maternal grandfather was called Horatio the source of the name seems obvious. Whatever, the combined names would certainly have been an unlikely appellation for a lad born into Sunderland's East End in December 1913.

Horatio was undoubtedly an unusual name despite Shakespeare's use of it and Nelson's considerable fame but to young Carter it was a stimulus to excellence and achievement. He was determined to overcome his small size and fancy name by excelling at sport. So Horatio soon became 'Raich' and he determined to become a runner, a cricketer and a footballer. However, according to family legend, young Horatio, aged three, had been promised a trial by Leicester City. He had wandered into a neighbour's backyard to find someone to play with. The neighbour turned out to be George Metcalfe, who had played for South Shields and was by then a scout for Leicester. He is alleged to have told Clara that the boy would be given a trial when he reached 17.

While Raich undoubtedly inherited his footballing abilities from his father, he never received any coaching or encouragement from that source. The repeated headaches that the career ending injury caused had understandably destroyed Robert Carter's interest in the game. He never spoke about his own footballing experiences and never went to watch his son play. However, he put no obstacles in the way of his son's football progress. Probably he did not want a serious injury to blight Raich's life in the way his own had been affected.

In August 1916 the license for the Ocean Queen switched to Clara. At that time Robert was 35 and may have been involved in war-work for a couple of years because the license reverted to him shortly after peace was restored. Meanwhile Raich began to attend Hendon Board School in 1918. This was the school which could claim to be the birthplace of football in Sunderland. James Allen, a Scot, arrived in 1871 to take up a teaching post and introduced the Association code to Wearside where rugby had previously flourished. At a meeting in 1879, Allen helped found the Sunderland and District Teacher Football Club. They played at the Blue House Field in Hendon and soon became Sunderland AFC.

The First World War had kept Sunderland's shipyards busy and an immediate post-war boom continued to keep employment high. Sixty-seven ships totalling a third of a million tonnes were built in the 16 Wear shipyards in 1920. But the boom was brief and the great over-capacity in shipbuilding created by the war made its decline all the more dramatic. By 1926, unemployment in the town had reached

19,000 and half the yards launched no ships.

Thus schooling in Hendon in the 1920s took place in a tough area in a tough period. Children without shoes relied on the Mayor's Boot Fund, but some still went to school barefooted. The custom at the Ocean Queen was sufficient to protect the Carters from the worst of the recession and young Raich remained determined to make his mark in sport. Initially he took up running because only when you moved from the Junior Department to the Boys' Department was there any chance of organised games. He had some early sprinting successes which stimulated his Aunt Jen to make him some silk running shorts and a vest with a big 'H' on it from Uncle Ted's underwear. In 1923, aged nine, he won the 100 yards on sportsday.

Meanwhile, left-footed, left-handed and diminutive, Raich Carter picked up the basics of football and cricket in the streets. The lampposts acted as goalposts or wickets depending on the season. Alternatively a 'tanner' ball was taken to the beach for an improvised game. Wherever the game, Raich's natural talent was quickly apparent. Further inspiration came from following the fortunes of his local professional team, Sunderland. The club had long been one of the most successful in the country with five league championships. One of the stars of that team, Charles Buchan, was still playing at Roker Park in the early 1920s when Raich Carter first stood at the Roker End. The tall, angular Buchan, who had paid occasional visits to the Ocean Queen, was Raich's great hero. To get to the games Raich walked down the Hendon Road to catch the ferry across to the North Bank and on to Roker Park.

In order to maintain their top level status in the 1920s, Sunderland three times raised the British transfer-fee record without capturing their pre-1914 success. Warney Cresswell cost £5,000 from South Shields in May 1922, but failed to settle although he later won the championship twice with Everton; Bob Kelly, an ageing international forward, was acquired from Burnley for £6,000 and stayed for about a year before moving to Huddersfield, playing for them in two FA Cup finals.

Obviously Charlie Buchan was a more lasting role model for young Raich. He had returned from the horrors of the Western Front to take part in a Victory match in 1919, the only officer among the 22 survivors of World War One. Buchan scored more than 200 goals for Sunderland between 1920 and 1925. His transfer to Arsenal just before his 34th birthday involved an unusual fee. Sunderland valued Buchan at £4,000 but Arsenal would not agree, Sunderland claimed

Buchan would score 20 goals a season so Arsenal challenged them by offering £2,000 plus £100 per goal in his first season. The deal was done. Buchan scored 21 goals and Sunderland collected £4,100. However, even with Buchan, the club under-achieved in the '20s by their standards; runners-up in the top division in 1923 being their best.

Meanwhile, Raich Carter's football progress at Hendon School was a bit unusual. A football competition had been organised for school teams under the age of 13. Although he was only ten at the time and had never played in an organised match, young Carter put down his name. When the team selection took place, boys who had played before took all the places except left-half. For this position there was Raich and one other boy. The master in charge then checked the boys' legs and the young Carter made the team because his legs looked more like a footballer's.

In fact, Raich Carter was comfortable at left-half because he was a natural left-footer. But his ambition was to play at inside-right and in preparation had practised kicking with his right foot. By the age of 12 he was equally efficient with both feet. He maintained throughout his career that the game is played principally with the feet and anyone who could use only one foot was halving his potential.

The next stage in Carter's progress was to play for Hendon School's first team where he was chosen at inside-left. This move to the forward line was maintained throughout his career. Gordon Dreyer, six months younger and also from Sunderland's East End, remembers Raich as an outstanding schoolboy footballer. Dreyer, who attended James Williams' Street School, also went on to play professional football with Hull City, the club Raich was later to player-manage. The two boys were rivals at cricket when their respective schools met in the summer term. Walter Grendale, also a contemporary, remembers Raich as a natural footballer who was in the school team at ten years of age. He also recalls a school cricket cup match in which an enthusiastic Carter caught him in the slips.

Once established in the Hendon School first team, Carter was soon nominated for a trial with Sunderland Boys. His first mention in the local paper, the *Sunderland Echo*, was on 11th April 1925 when he played in the Pickering Schools' Cup final. Hendon beat Moor 2-0 to retain the trophy – Carter scoring a first-half goal – while Moor could not make an impression on a "sterling Hendon defence."

At the trial for Sunderland Boys, Raich was chosen at inside-left for one team while another talented football, Sep Smith, was at inside-left for the other. As Sep was two years older, Raich was not optimistic about winning a place in the town team. He had reckoned without the artfulness of the selectors because although Smith won the inside-left position they nominated H S Carter at inside-right. From that point Raich played regularly for Sunderland and Durham Boys at inside-right, his favourite position. But Sep Smith remained an obstacle to further honours if only one boy was to go forward from his team. Sep Smith would in future play for Leicester City so he was a formidable rival.

During the 1925-26 season the two boys represented Sunderland in the English Schools Shield. Both scored in a 3-0 first round victory over Durham and District. They then beat Spennymoor on 30th January 1926 which meant an away tie at Dearne Valley. Again, the Carter—Smith combination was triumphant but the fourth-round involved a difficult away match at Leeds. Victory was achieved on 17th April and within a week they met Grimsby in the fifth-round. It seems Grimsby were a "physical team" because Argus of the *Echo* referred to the match twice. Initially he wrote: "I hear our Sunderland lads had a rough experience at Grimsby. The ambulance men, I am told, were busy for a long while after the match attending to the Sunderland representatives." In June, when Grimsby had won the final against Liverpool, Argus wrote: "They had beaten Sunderland in an earlier round – well, they did more than beat them! Nine of the Sunderland boys were injured in the game!" He did not say whether Raich Carter was one of them.

Chapter Two
Schoolboy International

RAICH CARTER'S fears about the competition from Sep Smith proved to be well founded. In his final year at Whitburn School Smith was chosen for the England trials. This resulted in him winning a cap for his country against Scotland. At the time Raich did not take any comfort from being told that he would have been nominated but because of his age he had been kept back for the following year. In effect he was being told he was too young to represent his country. Raich resented the decision for a long time particularly when he realised that it had deprived him of a record. Had he played in the match against Scotland that year he would eventually have gained three schoolboy caps. At the time, only two internationals were played per season, against Wales and Scotland. Of course, the record, had it been achieved, would not have lasted long because later Ireland joined the competition. More than 20 years later Raich continued to be bitter that his age, over which he had no influence, had lost him a cap.

The following season, 1926-27, the frustrated Carter got his opportunity. He was chosen to play for the North against the South in a boys' international trial match at Newark. As a result of a good display Raich was selected for a further trial at Bournemouth the following week. He remembered this game well because it was the first occasion he received payment for playing. At the end of the trial, as the players walked off, a spectator hurried out of the crowd, patted Raich on the back and said, "Well played sonny!" and pressed half-a-crown (worth about £5 on current value) into his hand. This generous gesture reinforced Raich's view that he had played well but he wondered whether he would be chosen for England because the South's inside-right, Ronnie Dix, was the man of the match. Dix would eventually play for six League clubs, including Tottenham, and also for England. It was a tense wait for Raich but once again the selectors found a way to accommodate both players. Raich was chosen at inside-right while Dix was switched to centre-forward. A photograph of the North's team at Bournemouth (*see illustrations*) shows the 11 players in a single line so that their relative heights are clearly visible. Raich Carter is obviously the shortest player and several of his teammates are more than a head taller, nor does he appear to be particularly strongly built. Nevertheless, the dream of international honours was to be fulfilled and eventually the great day arrived. Raich had travelled down on the Friday evening to stay overnight with the rest of the England team at the Royal Hotel. The match against Wales was played at Bristol Rovers' ground on the 23rd April 1927. Raich was 13 years and four months old.

For the first time he experienced pre-match nerves. The preliminaries added to the tensions of the occasion. Photographs, anthems and pulling on the white shirt of England were new experiences. Happily all forms of nervousness disappeared with kick-off as they always would throughout Raich's career. The combination of Ronnie Dix and Raich Carter proved too much for the Welsh defence. Dix scored four while Carter scored one in the final minutes in a 6-2 victory. To score on his England debut was a great thrill. International caps were presented that evening back at the Royal Hotel. One of the features of this schoolboy international was the number of players who went on to play professional football. Eleven were to play for league clubs and seven won international honours – altogether a very memorable weekend for the diminutive Hendon schoolboy. Still to come though was the triumphant homecoming and the big welcome from everyone at Hendon School. Any remaining derogatory views on the name Horatio were now completely banished. However, Raich was very uncomfortable being paraded round the school wearing his England cap for all the boys to see.

Despite his England duties and various international trial matches, young Carter continued to play for his school, for Sunderland boys and for County Durham boys. At every level he was a regular maker of goals and a prolific scorer. For example, he scored twice for Sunderland against West Stanley, three times against Newburn and another two against Kelloe. He also scored Durham's only goal in a county championship match which Lancashire won 4-1. Carter was "the best inside forward on view but Durham had no luck in front of goal."

The next season, 1927-8, Sunderland Boys made an impressive start with four wins, scoring 21 goals with only three conceded. Carter was still eligible to play and he was joined by Alf Young from Bishopwearmouth Church of England School. Young later went on to play centre-half for Huddersfield Town and England. Also challenging for a place was Jack Washington, a goalkeeper too small to win a regular game. Nevertheless, he would go on to play in three Amateur Cup finals for Bishop Auckland, the third of which was played at Wembley in 1950. Thirteen years earlier Jack had been an enthusiastic supporter at a tremendous FA Cup Final, also at Wembley. Now, at the age of 87, Jack still clearly recalls the sporting encounters with Raich Carter at football, cricket and athletics. Looking back over 70 years he clearly remembers Carter's lightening shots at goal. He believes the exceptional power of this shooting was the result of marvellous natural timing. The same timing, he believes, that made Carter such a powerful hitter when batting for Hendon or Durham. Incidentally, Jack Washington still wonders whether at 5 feet 6¼ inches he was the shortest adult to play in goal in a Wembley cup final.

Carter was chosen to play for the North in a trial at West Ham. Although his father was ill in hospital, no one prevented him travelling to London for the match. However, he intuitively felt that all was not well and this contributed to him having a poor game. Another trialist from Sunderland, George Farrow, was injured in the game and so lost his chance of an England cap. The two unhappy schoolboys returned north together. As Raich was responsible for getting George back home he did not get off at his usual station but continued for one more stop from where George could get home to Whitburn. This change of station meant that Raich missed the uncle who had arranged to meet him with the bad news. Instead, Raich Carter walked home alone and as he approached Ocean Queen he saw the blinds pulled down. So he knew before he entered that his father had died. An altogether wretched and dismal occasion. On 14th March 1928 Argus, writing for his Sports Review column in the *Sunderland Echo*, wrote, "Nearly a quarter of a century ago when

Royal Rovers were probably the best local team in the district, two of their promising players were George Souter, a fine goal keeper and Robert Carter, a fine inside forward, who made a name for himself with Southampton. By strange coincidence both have been laid to rest today. Souter was a man with a wonderful personality of whom I could relate many a good story, while Carter was the father of the present promising schoolboy footballer."

In May 1928, the license of the Ocean Queen reverted back to Clara Augusta Carter. Although Toddler Carter had talked little to his son about football, one of his comments so impressed young Raich that he recalled it throughout his life. He had been playing a game for Hendon boys on Sparks Farm. When he arrived home his father asked him how he had got on. Raich said his team had lost but that they were the better side. His father smiled and said, "You are wrong, son. My experience taught me, and it will teach you, that the best team always wins." Many times after that advice was given the words were recalled by Raich and he completely agreed with them. He put it in this way. "I fail to see how any losing team can be said to be the better side. The objective of the game is to score goals, so however achieved, the team scoring most must be the better team. When a player hits the post or the bar he is said to be unlucky. I say it's a bad shot. You cannot score when the ball goes higher then eight feet or wider than eight yards." He felt so strongly about it that when he was shown a newspaper report of the match Hull City v Sunderland in which the journalist criticised him for being too harsh on an "unlucky" losing team, he wrote to the newspaper to insist that teams which control games but fail to score must be playing negative football. The players who played in such teams should be criticised as they had been in the 1930s.

Despite the bereavement and his poor form in the trial, Raich Carter retained his place in the England Schoolboy team until the end of the season. The first international was reported by Argus in the *Echo* on 24th April 1928. "Young Carter, the Hendon schoolboy was, I am told, the best forward on the field in the match against Scotland on Saturday at Leicester which England won five to one." Raich's schoolboy international career was completed when he captained England against Wales at Swansea. He celebrated the occasion by scoring twice in a 3-2 victory. The *Echo* reported, "This young Hendon product is one of the best all-round athletes Sunderland has produced for many a day, and his future career will be watched with interest." Years later, in 1954, Bishopwearmouth school produced a centenary booklet which looked back to the 1927-8 season. It reported that the team they feared most was Hendon whose captain Raich Carter dominated the scene. Bishopwearmouth had managed to win by the odd goal, but it was a case of Bishops versus Carter, who seemed to be playing in every position at once. Bishops almost expected him to head the ball into the net from his own corner kicks.

For schoolboy international Carter there was one more campaign in season 1927-8 to be concluded. It was the climax of the first division league programme and Sunderland AFC, without much warning, were in trouble. Relegation was unthinkable for a club with 38 years continuous membership of the top division. With only one game remaining Sunderland were second from bottom despite having 37 points, usually enough for safety. Equal on points but with a better goal average were local rivals Middlesbrough and against the odds the fixture list matched the two clubs at Ayresome Park for the final match. Raich was there to see Middlesbrough dominate the first half but the biggest cheer was for the injured Sunderland goalkeeper, Albert McInroy, who inspired his team to a 3-0 victory. Top-flight status was preserved for the club and its future recruits. Also of significance for the future was a change in management. After a reign of 23 years as secretary-manager, Bob Kyle stepped down to be replaced by 'Wee' Johnny Cochrane from St Mirren. It would be Cochrane who would play an influential role in Raich Carter's future footballing career. In the meantime, the cricket season for the summer of 1928 was about to begin.

Chapter Three
Too Small for Leicester City

EARLY SUCCESS at football did not distract young Raich Carter from developing his cricketing talents. He wished to succeed as a sportsman and so all options had to be kept open. His reputation as a schoolboy cricketer was secured in the final of the Swan Cup. Batting for Hendon School, Carter scored 111 runs in 25 minutes – a considerable achievement for a lad of 13. He clearly had a talent for both games but which should it be?

In 1928 he was invited to the Sunderland Cricket Club at Ashbrooke for coaching along with other promising players. One of his outstanding abilities was as a fielder. It was said that he was worth his place for that alone. Looking back 20 years later, Carter said it would have been great to play professionally at both games as Denis Compton had done, but that it would have involved divided loyalties. He believed that a professional should give his full and undivided commitment to one employer. He reckoned he could make it as a professional in both games and ultimately the decision was made on practical grounds. Sunderland AFC played professionally in the top division of the Football League whereas County Durham then played amateur Minor Counties cricket. First Class cricket would have involved a move away from his widowed mother and setting up home elsewhere. The obvious solution was to concentrate on football.

Carter remained at school for the summer term of 1928. He was 14 and old enough to leave elementary education, but the chance of another season of school cricket was too appealing. However, football was never far away. Cochrane proposed that Raich should sign for Sunderland as an amateur until he could turn professional at 17. Meantime he would be given a job in the club office. Raich was delighted with the offer but his uncle, Ted, a detective sergeant in the Sunderland police force, was not impressed. He had been acting as Raich's guardian since his father's death and he insisted that Raich should learn a trade to fall back on should the football career not work out. Raich was disappointed but his uncle used a further argument which was that Raich was still too small and light for the tough world of professional football. This line of reasoning made more sense to Raich. In fact, he would never be a tall man, eventually making just under five feet eight.

Therefore, the Sunderland offer was declined. Instead it was arranged that Raich would be apprenticed as an electrician with the Sunderland Forge and Electrical Company. Meantime, school-leaving day arrived and did not go unmarked. Staff and boys of Hendon Elementary School united to present Raich Carter with a gold medal inscribed with his football and cricket achievements. Mr R Dodds, the Headmaster, wrote the school's final report which said that in English, Maths and Drawing Carter, "always showed neatness and painstaking effort," while in school sport, "he was exceptionally brilliant." In later life, however, Raich Carter confessed that his school studies had taken second place to sport. He regretted this fact and used every opportunity in adulthood to make good any gaps in his education.

With school football over, Raich Carter joined the juniors of Whitburn St Mary's, to whom the best of Sunderland schoolboy footballers were recruited at that time. In fact, the quality of the junior team was soon revealed in a cup-tie. Whitburn St Mary's were drawn against their own juniors in a Divisional Cup match. To the embarrassment of the older players the juniors, "ably marshalled by young Carter" won 3-1. The juniors completed the season unbeaten, with a goal ratio of 50 for, two against. Looking back, Raich believed that this competition against boys of roughly his own age was better preparation for his career than playing against older and professional footballers at Sunderland AFC. Similarly, the next season he played for his works team, Sunderland Forge, against the apprentices of other companies where an age limit also applied.

As his 17th birthday approached, Raich began to consider his football career. It was already clear that he had no enthusiasm for becoming an electrical engineer but there were still four years remaining on his apprenticeship. The prospect of starting a football career at 21 did not appeal to him. His one great passion was football, except, of course, for cricket in the summer. He had other interests of course. Gordon Dreyer remembers regular visits to the billiard hall in Fawcett Street with Raich and their friends. Often the prize was a tuppenny bar of chocolate and Raich was a regular winner.

Carter was 17 on 21st December 1930. He did not take long to further his football career. Leicester City were due at Roker Park for a league fixture on Christmas Day. He looked up his old neighbour, George Metcalfe, the Leicester scout, and reminded him of the long-standing promise to arrange a trial. Such was Carter's persistence that George arranged a meeting with the Leicester team and the journey back with them for a trial. Raich looked forward to the trial with confidence. His footballing progress to date had been smooth and uninterrupted. He was sure he would make the grade. Little did he know the fates were conspiring against him. The bad weather had turned Filbert Street into a "veritable quagmire" according to the local press. The fact that matches had been played on it on Christmas Day and Boxing Day only added to the problems. Carter was selected for Leicester reserves at outside left against Watford reserves on 27th December, a position he had never played in before.

The game proved a disaster for the undersized trialist. The ball got heavier and greasier and the pitch got churned and boggy. Crossing the ball from the left became more difficult. The harder he tried the worse he seemed to play. Despite a 3-2 score line, Carter left the pitch frustrated and full of disappointment. All he could hope for from the Leicester manager was a second chance to show his true potential. Instead, Willie Orr said in kindly manner, "Son, you're too small to play football. You want to go home and build yourself up physically. Get some brawn and weight on you. And gain some more experience of the game." So Raich Carter returned home from Filbert Street, scene of one of his schoolboy international triumphs, with a heavy heart. Would his lack of height exclude him from the professional game? How much longer should he have to remain an electrician? It was back to the works team on Saturday afternoons. Leicester's rejection, he admitted later, was "a bit of a blow to my ego," but when that door closed another opening at his own home town club was not far away. With the benefit of hindsight, Leicester's decision could be seen as a blessing in disguise.

Chapter Four
Signing for Sunderland

DURING THE summer of 1931 Raich Carter recovered from his disappointment at Leicester. There were other clubs around, including Sunderland, who had been prepared to sign him as an amateur when he was even smaller. Accordingly Raich presented himself at the office of Johnny Cochrane at Roker Park. Once again amateur forms were offered and a trial organised when the season began to determine whether professional terms would be available. Raich left the ground full of hope and excitement but the trial on the first day of the season proved to be another flop. This time the mediocre display was attributed to an inability to train because of work commitments and to over-anxiety following the Leicester experience. Predictably, a professional contract was not forthcoming.

However, Raich remained on the books as an amateur but no games were offered. He needed to resolve the situation himself. His response was to join Esh Winning, a village about seven miles west of Durham, in the Northern Amateur League. Before long confidence was restored and fitness regained. Interestingly, Carter found his form playing at inside-left. As the north east was well known as a breeding ground for potential professional footballers, league club scouts were regular visitors to clubs like Esh Winning. Very soon Huddersfield were taking an interest in the young inside-left. Inevitably a trial was offered but in his excitement Raich overlooked to mention that he was on Sunderland's books as an amateur. He really had not appreciated just how ensnared he was for the rest of the season. Obviously, it in no way compared with the virtual servitude which signing as a professional involved. However, there was still the Sunderland manager to be faced over Huddersfield's trial offer. Johnny Cochrane may have been smaller than Raich but he made up for it in the fierceness of his temper. He let Raich know of his displeasure in no uncertain terms while he put a call through to the Huddersfield manager Clem Stephenson. Carter knew that both the club and its manager were innocent of illegally poaching him so while the telephone conversation continued Raich slipped quietly out of Roker Park.

Much to his surprise and delight the reaction of the Sunderland manager to this incident was to pick H S Carter for the second team in the North-Eastern League. A match programme for the fixture between Sunderland reserves and Walker Celtic on the 10th October 1931 contains the name of Carter at inside-right at the age of 17 years and ten months. Despite the standard of football being higher than any he had played before, Raich must have done well because he was chosen again the following week. After that came the offer he had been seeking for nearly a year, a professional contract.

This time Uncle Ted, now an inspector, was no longer insistent on him learning a trade. It was much clearer at 17 years of age that Raich had a future in the game. But equally important to the decision was the state of the local economy. The Sunderland Forge was typical of Wearside: most of Raich's colleagues were on short time. In the five years 1930-1935 Sunderland shipyards built as many ships as were built in six months in 1914. Wearside could claim to be the hardest hit area in the country with 11,800 ship builders unemployed and only 2,380 at work. That meant 75 per cent of the workforce were idle. For the town as a whole 1934 was the worst year when unemployment peaked at 29,000 – about half the working population. In that year Lady Astor, MP, visited the town and reported to Parliament that it was, "The most derelict and depressing spot I have ever seen in my life."

In this economic climate Raich and his uncle met Johnny Cochrane in the boardroom at Roker Park. It was agreed that Raich would be paid £3 per week plus £1 for a reserve team appearance. Although this was a vast increase on the nine shillings (45p) he received as an apprentice it still disappointed Raich because he was anxious to support his widowed mother and two sisters as generously as possibly. He was conscious that since his father's death the family had been helped out by his uncle and his grandfather. The date was 12th November 1931 and Raich remembered it for the rest of his career. He also remembered, as he signed the form, that he was in the same room where Charlie Buchan had signed for Sunderland 20 years before. He hoped to do as well as his great hero.

All that was left to be done was for Johnny Cochrane to count out the ten £1 notes which Raich received as his signing-on fee. To celebrate the occasion he went to an afternoon performance at the cinema with the notes still tightly held in his hand. Eventually he returned home triumphantly to his mother. He was ready to shoulder the responsibility of the main breadwinner.

The professional status did not immediately secure a regular game for Sunderland's reserves. Despite an early hat-trick Raich Carter featured in only about one third of the games. No doubt there was considerable competition for places and probably Cochrane did not wish to place too much responsibility and pressure on his diminutive inside forward. Later in the season a second hat-trick, against league leaders Workington, did generate a cautious assessment that progress was being made and if it continued there was the possibility of first team football next season. That prospect would be a considerable achievement as it was rare for an 18-year-old to establish himself in the top division of the football league. But that was the target which Raich Carter set himself in the summer of 1932.

Chapter Five

Debut in the Top Division

THE CARTER Plan was aimed at the pre-season trial matches which most clubs in the 1930s held. Pre-season friendlies against other clubs or foreign tours in August were unheard of. Normally players were required to report back to their clubs about a month before the season began. So far Carter had been employed as a part-time professional continuing to serve his apprenticeship during the week. Training at Roker Park had been confined to two evenings a week. As his wages had been increased by £1 a week, Carter applied to his employers for leave of absence in the summer to allow him to commence a vigorous training programme. His request was granted and that was the last Sunderland Forge would ever see of Raich Carter. His apprenticeship was subsequently amicably cancelled. In the meantime a six-day a week schedule of pre-season training was started. So dedicated was the young professional that he decided not to smoke or drink. As a result of this preparation Carter was in peak condition for the practice matches. Along with the rest of the reserve players he was determined to give the first team players a severe test. In fact, such was Carter's aggression and competitiveness in the match that he was a bit reluctant to turn up for training next day in case any first team players had taken offence at his whole-hearted display. There was no reaction. They had probably been in the same position earlier in their own careers.

This time Raich Carter did not have to wait long before his form was recognised. Late in September 1932, when he checked the team sheets, he found he had been selected as travelling reserve for the first team to play Blackburn Rovers on 7th October. The man he was challenging for the inside-left position was Scottish international Patsy Gallacher. Raich secretly half-hoped Patsy might be called away on urgent business. Instead they shared a room in a Manchester hotel and Patsy talked way into the night until both fell asleep. Despite the lack of sleep, Patsy Gallacher had a fine game the next day and scored three goals. His third goal was particularly memorable because his clever side-step caused the oncoming goalkeeper and fullback to collide and crash to the ground. Patsy had time to calmly slot the ball into an empty net. The Blackburn fullback was Jimmy Gorman who later became a Sunderland player. He was not allowed to forget that Patsy Gallacher goal. As this was 30 years before substitutes were first permitted there was no prospect of the young reserve having any part in the match. Nevertheless, valuable experience was gained and Carter was gaining confidence in the company of the first team. He found the older players more than willing to help and advise the newcomers. At no point was he to find any hostility from senior players seeking to preserve their first-team positions. Indeed, the club he had joined was cheerful and good-humoured with a great relish for practical jokes.

Another feature of the Sunderland playing staff was the number of Scots on the books. This was not a recent trend introduced by Johnny Cochrane. There was a long tradition dating back to the 19th century for Sunderland teams to be reinforced from north of the border. In Raich Carter's view the Scots not only provided international quality football but also good-humoured rivalry which contributed to the harmonious dressing-room atmosphere.

The next stage in Carter's career was not long in coming. Two weeks after the visit to Blackburn, Sunderland were due to play Sheffield Wednesday and Gallacher was injured. His place, at inside-left, was given to local boy Bob Gurney while Carter was chosen for the reserves. However, on Friday morning Gurney was found to be suffering from influenza. That day the *Sunderland Echo* reported the club's directors had decided to bring in Horatio Carter for his debut in league football. It is interesting to note the influential role of the directors in determining the team selection in that period. Clearly Cochrane did not have the free hand enjoyed by his successors. It is worth noting also that the full name of Horatio was generally used by the press when referring to the young local lad.

For the Sheffield Wednesday game Carter was chosen at inside-left. Today the distinction between the inside forward positions has lost its significance. But from the '20s to the '50s the formation was pretty well fixed – 2-3-5. Of course, there were notable examples of players who mastered more than one position like Tom Finney, who played on both wings and late in his career at centre-forward, and John Charles, equally at home at centre-forward and centre-half, but they were the exception. While Carter's natural left-footedness would normally lead him into the inside-left slot he always believed he was more dangerous operating from the inside-right channel.

Despite the fact that his selection was fortuitous, relying on the withdrawal of Gurney, it did not diminish the thrill which Raich experienced. He knew that in 11 months since signing professional he was about to make his debut in the top division. He was still only 18 years old.

Meanwhile things in the town of Sunderland were deteriorating. The police had to make two baton charges in Ryhope as an angry crowd attacked the escort of a non-striking miner. The local press was particularly disturbed by the screaming women who encouraged the riotous gathering. The deepening depression in the town was souring industrial relations.

By the time of the Saturday morning journey to Sheffield, Carter's elation had turned to apprehension. On route he was subdued despite the friendly gibes about his youth. When he ran out on to the pitch he was struck by the vastness of Hillsborough and the biggest crowd he had every played before. Nerves and misgivings affected his stomach and legs. Fortunately as the players lined up, left-half Joe Devine quietly reassured him that there was nothing to worry about. "You'll be OK," he said, "I'll be right behind you." Devine's assessment proved correct for the evening headline said, 'School International's Excellent Form.' The Sunderland team for that day was Thorpe; Murray, Shaw; Thomson, McDougall, Devine; Davis, Beach, Yorston, Carter, Connor.

Carter immediately struck up a promising partnership with left winger Jimmy Connor. Carter became a great admirer of the skilful Scot and rated him the best outside left he had ever seen. This was high praise because Carter would later play with two great left wingers, Dally Duncan, a colleague at Derby, and Eddie Burbanks of Sunderland and Hull. It must have been a close call between Connor and Duncan, one which the Scottish selectors usually resolved by picking Duncan.

Despite Carter's encouraging debut and his instant rapport with Connor, Sunderland lost to Wednesday 3-1. Argus reported that it was not a bad first appearance and certainly as good as any of the Sunderland forwards. Most of his failings were entirely due to youthfulness: "You can't put an old head on young shoulders." Carter himself recognised the pace was faster but felt that he had coped with it. Clearly, experience and physical strength would need more time. Most important for the debutant was the fact that he was selected for the next game – a local derby at Middlesbrough. That game brought his first victory 2-1 and it was reported that Carter and Connor were undoubtedly the best wing on the field. However, Argus was concerned that Carter was being brought along too early, perhaps a year too soon, due to the circumstances.

The next match was against Bolton Wanderers and meant much more to Raich than the previous two because it was at Roker Park. This was where his dreams and hopes had first been inspired on the terraces. This was where Charlie Buchan strode across the turf, and other legends from 'the team of all the talents' of 1912-13. What a remarkable match it turned out to be! Not only was the home debut crowned with Carter's first league goal but the team's 7-4 victory broke all records for a first class game at Roker Park. One reporter wrote, "Carter showed all the skill of a veteran and placed the ball with a deftness of a player twice his age to pave the way for practically every successful Sunderland move. He used the cross pass to find the opposite wing regularly and this lightening moving of the point of attack accounted for the early Bolton reverses." A further comment proclaimed, "A grand footballer this Hendon lad, one who will make his name in the old colours, playing for the club which to a Sunderland boy should be regarded as the greatest of all." It is interesting to note that the average age of the Sunderland team for that match was 23 years. The forward line included four players, Gallacher, Gurney, Connor and Carter, who would play together for the next six remarkable years.

A fortnight after the Sheffield debut, Argus, writing in the *Echo*, noted that, "Carter is improving every time he turns out with the seniors. I think he should be brought on slowly and he should not be overworked. It is many years since I saw a more promising pure footballer." However, the writer warned Carter of the dreaded disease which affects young footballers, that of "an inflated idea of their own abilities and importance." Fortunately, he added, there was not the slightest indication of any such symptoms in Raich who remained the same quiet, unassuming boy who had arrived in Roker Park.

Argus returned to the subject of Raich Carter a week later. He was again concerned that the youngster was being overworked. He admitted that the stamina was there all right because he had been nourished in a good home and his father, Robert, had been a good footballer with grit and staying power, much needed in those days. Argus thought that as Raich gained experience he ought to become one of the best forwards in the game. His advice was "early to bed and no smoking."

Carter continued to keep his place through until Christmas 1932. One particular game during that period must have given him a special thrill. On 17th December Sunderland met Leicester at Roker Park. This was the club which had rejected him and revenge took the form of a 2-0 victory for Sunderland, with Carter scoring both goals.

By the close of 1932 Sunderland had played 19 matches winning eight and drawing seven, which was their best start for years. Carter, who had played in more than half those games, was now an established member of the team. Argus in the *Echo* in January 1933 was speculating about the reason for the team's improvement. His theory was, "that it began with the introduction of Carter and Thomson. Both these lads became players by keeping them in the team and both of them are a couple of years from reaching their peak. Carter had made Connor his best partner since he joined from St Mirren."

One further highlight of Carter's first season in the top flight was Sunderland's cup run. Sunderland had already won the league title five times and had 42 years' continuous membership in the top flight. But it was the FA Cup that everyone in Sunderland desperately wanted to win. Since their first entry into the competition in 1884, when they lost a preliminary round match at Redcar, Sunderland had made one unsuccessful appearance in the final in 1913. Each season the supporters wondered if this was to be the cup-winning year.

In December 1932, the third-round draw for the cup paired Sunderland against Hull City, the tie to be played on 14th January 1933. The week before Sunderland played the mighty Arsenal at Roker Park. Every Arsenal player was a household name: Moss; Male and Hapgood; Hill, Roberts and John; Hulme, Jack, Lambert, James and Bastin. Despite going 2-0 down, Sunderland fought back and Carter scored the winner with less than five minutes left. This was excellent preparation for the Hull match which Sunderland duly won 2-0. Writing in his newspaper column Sunderland's former star, Charlie Buchan, predicted that Raich Carter would one day play for England. Argus had already made this assessment of "the Hendon lad's potential." He was pleased to report that Carter was as unspoiled today as when he made his debut. He is as he was – "It doesn't cost you half-a-crown to speak to him as the saying goes."

The fourth-round produced a difficult away tie against bogey team Aston Villa, who Sunderland had never beaten in a FA Cup-tie. Bob Gurney scored three goals in a magnificent team performance on a treacherous surface. A great left wing of Connor and Carter was a decisive factor in the 3-0 victory.

In the fifth-round Sunderland had a home draw against Blackpool. In blizzard-like conditions Blackpool made a great fight of it and Sunderland were saved by a brilliant display by goalkeeper Jimmy Thorpe. Charlie Thomson gave one of the best performances of his career in a narrow 1-0 win. Now Wearsiders everywhere were taking note of the club's progress. A sixth-round draw against Derby County meant thousands of hearts and minds turned to the question, "is this Sunderland's FA Cup Year?" The team was stronger than the one which had reached the semi-final two years earlier. Johnny Cochrane was beginning to build a team with the potential of making its mark in English football. Certainly journalists in various parts of the country were beginning to take note of Sunderland's young inside forward. London-based sports writer Jack Howcroft had suggested that Raich Carter might be the man the England selectors had been looking for to fill the inside-left position. Argus in the *Echo* begged to differ with Howcroft insisting that Carter was not ripe for international honours.

Meanwhile 4th March duly arrived and the cup run continued at the Baseball Ground. Appropriately for the keenly awaited tie, both the crowd and the receipts were records. Reaching the last eight in this competition was a real tonic to Sunderland supporters, especially those worst hit by the depression, but the opening 20 minutes saw Derby take a 2-0 lead. To say that the game was a thriller would be an understatement, because within 36 minutes six goals had been scored and the teams were level. Within four minutes of the second half Sunderland took the lead from a Gurney header. Then goals temporarily dried up, although frenetic goal-mouth incidents continued. In the final minute Derby's left winger Dally Duncan, already a goal scorer, prepared to make his final cross. Raich Carter watched helplessly from some distance as the ball left Duncan's foot and took a freak curve into the net. Raich stared in disbelief as Sunderland's victory was snatched away. It was no consolation to know that Duncan had sliced his kick. Nevertheless, it represented a magnificent achievement to come back from a two-nil deficit and to force a replay.

It seemed that practically every man, woman and child in Sunderland and Derby wanted to see the replay. Roker Park groaned with the strain of accommodating a record crowd of 75,118. This was on a Wednesday afternoon, there being no floodlights at that time. The Ryhope and District Wednesday League cancelled its programme and Sunderland Council deferred a meeting. Masses of unemployed men invaded the unemployment exchange to sign on in the morning rather than the afternoon. No doubt many imaginary grandmothers had their funerals arranged for that Wednesday. Inside the ground the crush was so great that the small and the endangered were passed down over the heads to the cinder track. Soon the track was overflowing and the pitch encroached. One such spectator was Walter Grendale who found his fingers trapped under a policeman's foot. He was told to get back off the grass. There was certainly no space for wingers like Connor, Duncan and Crooks to take their corners. Commenting 15 years later, Carter described the conditions inside the ground as pandemonium and wondered if the game should ever have been allowed to start. He recognised that with so many inside and thousands more outside to have postponed the game would have caused a riot.

The game itself was something of an anti-climax. No goals after 90 minutes so extra-time was required. The match was settled in the 101st minute with a goal scored by Derby's Peter Ramage. For another season the Sunderland cup dream was over. Derby gave thanksgivings to Jack Kirby, their goalkeeper, for their place in the semi-final. But it was not to be their winning year either. That would have to wait for another 13 years by which time Raich Carter's career would have taken a new turn.

The season 1932-3 had been a great start to Raich Carter's career. He had made 29 cup and league appearances, the 'glamour boys' of Arsenal in their prime had been beaten and revenge had been extracted from Leicester City. Sunderland finished 12th in the League and the feeling was that the club was on the way up. As an added bonus the club agreed to pay Raich £8 per week, acknowledging his status as a first team player.

Chapter Six

Building a Championship Winning Team

JUST BEFORE the close of the 1932-3 season Sunderland widened their football experience by inviting Racing Club of Paris to play a friendly match at Roker Park. They had just achieved third place in the French league which had only just introduced professional football. In this respect the French league was about 50 years behind their English counterparts. This may partly explain Sunderland's 5-2 victory. Two weeks later on 10th May 1933 a return match was played in Paris. The match was noteworthy because of two innovations for Sunderland. It was the first time the club had played under floodlights with a fresh white-coloured ball every 20 minutes or so (also, the posts were painted yellow). Secondly the teams played in numbered shirts, something which was being experimented with in England. The kick-off was not until 9.15 p.m. which meant the game did not finish until 10.55 p.m. Some travelling supporters wondered if it might not be too cold in north east England to watch that late. The Sunderland players coped admirably winning 3-0. Raich Carter was reported to be playing like his old self.

Despite the undoubted attractions of Paris in the spring, Carter was keen to return home in order to resume his cricket career. He remained an enthusiastic cricketer hoping to make the same progress as he had in football. His club, inevitably, was Hendon; the competition was the Durham Senior League. His attacking batting on the 3rd June resulted in a brilliant 90 out of 186 against Durham City. It was a great performance for Hendon, from Sunderland's East End, to beat "the mighty citizens of Durham" (as the *Echo* put it) by three wickets on their own ground. It was unlikely that the Durham attack would be so ill-treated again that season. By 17th June Raich Carter topped the Senior League's batting averages with 62.3. By scoring over 50 on four consecutive Saturdays he was beginning to draw the crowds to Hendon. Most cricket supporters loved to see his crisp driving. The Durham selectors must have sat up and taken note of the Sunderland footballer's batting form. On 22nd July Carter scored 91 against Whitburn and the selectors must have been convinced because he was chosen to play for Durham in the Minor Counties championship against Yorkshire seconds. The match was to be played at Headingley on 26th July, a midweek game. Carter's chance came because three regulars were not available.

The headline in the *Sunderland Echo* read, 'Horatio Carter Makes Bright County Debut. Hendon Batsman to Rescue at Leeds.' In fact, Carter had batted at number ten and had top scored with 44. This had taken him an hour and had included six boundaries. Carter wrote later that he had been much impressed by the batting of one Yorkshire opener, Len Hutton. His batting was stylish and correct and he took two hours and ten minutes over his 48 runs. It was the difference between Carter's knock and Hutton's innings. For Carter it was a relaxation away from the demands of football while for Hutton it was the foundation of a full-time professional career. Carter aimed to hit every ball to the boundary whereas Hutton chose his shots carefully.

Raich Carter retained his place in Durham's team against the West Indian tourists. This was to be played at the Ashbrooke ground, home of Sunderland Cricket Club. It meant that Carter's return to Roker Park for pre-season training was delayed by a couple of days. Eight of the tourists' team had played in the Test match against England at Old Trafford the previous week. They must have seriously underestimated the strength of the Durham side because they were beaten, having been forced to follow on. Their great batsman George Headley was out twice in a day for a total of four runs. A brilliant running catch by Cyril Merry accounted for Carter for a duck. The tourists were delighted, however, with the enthusiastic reception they received on Wearside.

Raich Carter returned to Roker Park to join the 28 players who had signed on. Details of the playing staff were released on 12th August 1933 and 19-year-old Raich was measured at 5 feet 7 inches and weighed 9 stones 6 pounds. There must still have been some growth in him because later in his career he claimed to be 5 feet 8 inches!

For the opening fixture of the 1933-4 season Sunderland were away to Huddersfield. Their team was at full strength: Thorpe; Murray, Shaw; Thomson, McDougall (capt), Hastings; Davis, Gallacher, Yorston, Carter, Connor. The Huddersfield game was lost but more important for Raich Carter's career was the fact that he suffered a bad ankle strain which kept him out of action for eight weeks. There were other injuries for the Sunderland squad during this period so that, by the time Carter was fit, the inside forward positions were held by Patsy Gallacher at inside-left, Bob Gurney at centre-forward, and Ben Yorston at inside-right. Gallacher was playing so well that Carter's return seemed likely to be delayed. Fate intervened because Yorston was injured and Carter was brought in at inside-right. This was the position Carter had always favoured as a schoolboy and it would be the position in which he would have his greatest triumphs. In fact, he soon found that he was a more effective player at passing, shooting and beating defenders in his new position. At Sunderland it also gave the inside forwards, Gallacher and Carter, the option of switching positions during a game, as both were comfortable in the other's position. Critical to such a changeover was a player's ability to kick with both feet. The match for Carter's return was the local derby at Newcastle. Although Sunderland had more of the play and created more chances, Newcastle won 2-1. As Carter missed three of the chances, the switch of position was not seen as an immediate success. Assessments must have been revised the following week when Sunderland beat Leeds 4-2 and Carter scored twice.

However, Argus in the *Echo*, under the headline, 'Why Not Play Carter at Inside Left?' in November 1933, re-opened the debate. He was convinced that Carter was 25 per cent less effective when selected at inside-right. Argus was sure that Gallacher and Carter should revert back to their original positions. He also felt that Carter's busy cricket season followed by his long injury had affected his form. He need not have worried: on 9th December Arsenal, the league leaders, were over-run in brilliant style. There was not a weakness in the Sunderland team and the 3-0 victory could have been doubled. Apparently the London press were astounded by the Sunderland performance but the truth was that they would have beaten any team on that day's form.

At the same time observers were beginning to admire Johnny Cochrane's astute team building. Five of the team had been signed by the manager as juniors and had cost the club nothing. Other players like Jock McDougall and Jimmy Connor were bought at bargain prices. Argus confided, "I have confidence in him. Cochrane is a bigger force in football than most people think." In some quarters Sunderland FC were being seen as championship possibilities but first there was the FA Cup third-round draw. The annual pilgrimage towards Wembley began with a home tie against Teesside rivals Middlesbrough. The game was played on 13th January 1934 and the headline in the local press was 'Carter's Header Forces Replay.' Sunderland had 80 per cent of the play but a stubborn Middlesbrough defence held out for a 1-1 draw. While Sunderland won the replay the following Wednesday, the biggest football news of the week was the death of the great Arsenal manager Herbert Chapman. There was speculation in the press linking Johnny Cochrane with the post.

The fourth-round draw once again matched Sunderland with old rivals Aston Villa. The match at Villa Park crushed Wearsider's cup dreams emphatically by 7-2. Villa forwards were on excellent form, especially Dai Astley who scored four. Sunderland struggled without Gallacher while Carter played better back at inside-left. Nevertheless, Argus continued to argue that Carter should be nursed during the remainder of the season in order to revive his true potential. He also recommended a complete rest during the summer but would the young cricketer be prepared to miss out on a whole season? Argus warned that Raich was in danger of falling between two sporting stools. In fact, he proved capable of a lot more cricket.

Revenge for the cup defeat was immediate. The two teams met in a league fixture at Roker Park the following week and Sunderland produced their true form. In a 5-1 victory, Carter and Gallacher each scored twice. Two weeks later Sunderland had a free Saturday because it was the fifth-round of the cup. The club therefore arranged a friendly match against England's premier amateur club, the Corinthians. Although they hardly compared with the great teams they had fielded 30 to 40 years previously, they could still turn out an attractive side. Such a friendly contest has long since disappeared from a modern Premiership club's arrangements. Another feature of the game, which places it firmly in its period, was the decision of the Sunderland directors to allow the unemployed in at the reduced rate of six old pence (2p). The Corinthians put up a creditable performance, losing to a full strength Sunderland team 2-0.

From the league victory over Aston Villa early in February until the end of the season Sunderland played 12 games, winning five and drawing three. They collected 44 points in total and finished in sixth place. The main blemish on an encouraging season was the away record which produced only ten points. Of those away fixtures, the most dramatic was the visit to The Hawthorns where West Bromwich Albion were the victors 6-5. In slippery conditions Sunderland were judged to have been unlucky while Carter was described as the greatest player on view. The season was summed up by Argus; "There has not been a post-war season at the end of which we could look forward to the next with such bright hopes." He had been confident for some time that Sunderland had the potential to challenge for the league title within two years. In the completed season 1933-34 Raich Carter made 29 appearances in the league and three in the cup. In total he scored 19 goals, 13 more than his first season.

Chapter Seven

England Trials and Triumphs

AS EARLY as February 1933 Raich Carter's name was being mentioned in the national press as a prospective international candidate. Despite being only 19 and the rigours of his first league season, some commentators saw him as a solution to England's inside-left problems. Other observers closer to Sunderland urged caution. They felt he might be rushed into international honours when he was too young and inexperienced. In particular, the only remaining international fixture was an away match against Scotland, always a very demanding contest.

Nevertheless, the selectors arranged a trial match at Portsmouth for late March. Earlier in the month, Carter bought an evening paper on his way home from the ground and to his shock and amazement found his name included in the England team to play the Rest at Fratton Park. He was chosen at inside-left alongside the Arsenal winger Cliff Bastin. The occasion caused Carter a lot of nervous tension trying to adjust to a new group of colleagues and their various styles of play. Of course there was no team manager to organise tactics as control was in the hands of a committee of selectors who could number as many as 12. Inevitably, perhaps, Carter found the style of play too individualistic and he never really settled down. Then, after a dull opening 20 minutes, the Rest scored three goals in five minutes undermining any confidence England had begun to acquire. Eventually they won the match 5-1 helped by injuries to goalkeeper Ted Sagar of Everton and to Derby right winger Sammy Crooks. Even in this non-competitive match substitutes were not permitted but one innovation, for a match in England, was the use of numbered shirts. Although the experiment was deemed a success, traditional forces within the Football League rejected its introduction the following season.

As the teams left the field Carter was convinced that he was not about to win his first cap as his opposite number in the Rest team, John Pickering, of Sheffield United, had scored and had generally played better. Nevertheless, few people were prepared for the selectors complete about-turn as they decided to dispense with the whole England forward line and replace it with the Rest attack.

During the following season, 1933-34, several factors conspired to revive Raich Carter's international prospects. Firstly Carter was now playing mostly at inside-right and his form had been consistently good. Secondly, the performance of the whole Sunderland team had improved as was demonstrated by the sixth place they achieved that season in the League. Thirdly, and perhaps most importantly, the 1934 trial was to be staged at Roker Park. In fact, the selectors chose two Sunderland players for the match including both Bob Gurney and Raich Carter. The two were together in the Rest team and the Sunderland club were delighted to have both players challenging for an England place. They had the added advantage of the bulk of the crowd cheering them on.

Even more significant for Carter's career was the partner the selectors had chosen for him on the right wing. Just a few months his junior and already a big favourite in his home-town of Stoke, it was 19-year-old Stanley Matthews. This was to be the first of very many occasions when Carter and Matthews formed a right-wing partnership. Carter wrote about 15 years later, that he knew at once Matthews would make a great name for himself in the game. His superb ball-control, speed and cleverness marked him out as a star of the future.

At lunchtime on match day Carter arrived at the hotel where the rest of the players were staying. He took the opportunity to discuss with Matthews what tactics they should adopt in order to produce an effective right-wing partnership. Only by such improvised exchanges could any tactical approach to such trial games be agreed. But Raich Carter would quickly discover that Stan Matthews was also a great individualist and it was difficult to play alongside him.

Once you passed the ball to him you could never predict when, if ever, it would come back.

From Matthews' perspective the trial match was the biggest break of his relatively brief career. Roker Park was packed and Carter put on a masterly show before his home crowd. According to Matthews, Carter was "bewilderingly clever, constructive, lethal in front of goal, yet unselfish. Time and again he'd play the ball out wide to me and with such service I was in my element." In these circumstances, the Rest gave England a 7-1 trouncing. Carter scored four while teammate Bob Gurney got two. Would the selectors follow the precedent of the previous year and replace the whole England forward line by the Rest's? Argus argued that while Carter had been unready the previous year at Portsmouth he had now matured sufficiently to represent his country. He added that everyone in the town would be delighted if he got his first cap against Scotland at Wembley on 14th April.

Raich Carter awaited the announcement anxiously. Everyone else was confident that he would be chosen and they were right. But only two of the Rest's forwards were chosen, Raich Carter and outside left Eric Brook of Manchester City. Sammy Crooks was chosen ahead of Matthews, probably on the grounds of his international experience. Matthews was disappointed of course but he reasoned that at his age there would be many more opportunities. How right he was.

For the match against Scotland the players travelled down on the Friday in time for dinner in the evening at their Harrow hotel. In 1934 there were no pre-match training retreats which have become commonplace in recent decades. Nor was there any rearrangement or postponement of the league fixtures. In this instance, Sunderland faced Middlesbrough in a local derby without Carter and also Jimmy Connor, who had made the Scottish team. The England team that day was: Moss (Arsenal); Cooper (Derby), Hapgood (Arsenal); Stoker (Birmingham), Hart (Leeds), Copping (Leeds); Crooks (Derby), Carter (Sunderland), Bowers (Derby), Bastin (Arsenal), Brook (Manchester City). *The Daily Telegraph* predicted an England victory but warned that Hughie Gallacher, Chelsea's centre-forward, would have to be watched.

Raich Carter's first impression of the great stadium was one of disappointment as the changing rooms were nothing special, no bigger or better equipped than the average club. However, it was possible to get from the changing rooms round to the back of the stand behind the goal. Although the great stadium was only half full at this time, it seemed to a new player like Raich that there was a mass of movement and noise. There was singing and cheering and the shrill cries of the programme sellers. There was an atmosphere of excitement and anticipation added to which there was the pitch, so well manicured and so accurately marked. It looked ideal for football. Carter and his companions remained unrecognised. They returned to the dressing room with another hour to kill before the 3.15 p.m. kick-off. Carter was taken under the wing of Sammy Crooks, also from the north east and his right-wing partner. The Derby County player was a natural comedian and an extrovert who could take the tension out of the situation. Tom Cooper, the captain, had a word with each player, not concerned with tactics but with how the players should line up before the Royal Box. At the entrance to the tunnel the English met their Scottish counterparts. Raich had the chance to exchange a joke with Sunderland teammate, Jimmy Connor. Then it was out into the mass of sound and the bright sunshine, a short walk to the point opposite the Royal Box, a slight delay before the band played the national anthem and then a wait before the captain introduced the team, one-by-one, to the Duke of York, later King George VI. There was a great sense of relief once the referee had blown his whistle. The attendance was 92,963, then a record for an international. The result was a 3-0 win for England but the press felt the score flattered the English as Scotland had dominated the second half. With the help of the excellent pitch and the support of Sammy Crooks, Carter felt he had played well but the critics were disappointed because he had not reproduced his trial match brilliance.

Back in the dressing room members of the Football Association and other well-wishers crowded in. The buzz of chatter included the rumour that the whole team would be included in the party to tour Europe in May. However, the immediate travel arrangements were for Raich Carter and Jimmy Connor to join manager Johnny Cochrane on the overnight train to Sunderland. Cochrane, who had come down to watch his two international players, had booked all four berths in the sleeper so that they would be on their own. It was just as well he had because 'wee Johnny' had been celebrating the caps of his two boys rather excessively. In fact, he repeatedly referred to the empty bunk as "that fellow Jones." "What's wrong with the fellow" he asked?"He isn't saying a word."

Chapter Eight

Summer 1934: Continental Tour and Aussie Tourists

FOLLOWING THE victory at Wembley, Raich was included in the England party to tour Hungary and Czechoslovakia in May 1934. This meant he was unable to accompany his Sunderland teammates on a three-match tour of Spain. The club remained unbeaten despite the fact that all their opponents were representative teams, as even the Madrid club teams were not considered strong enough to compete. Sunderland were given wonderfully warm receptions in Bilbao, Valencia and Madrid despite the tense political situation which eventually led to the Civil War.

Meanwhile the England party crossed by ferry to Calais and then made a 30-hour train journey to Budapest. The Hungarian capital made a great impression on the 20-year-old visitor from Sunderland. The weather was fine and the Danube was at its best. The cafés, cabarets and swimming pools made it a fairy-tale city so utterly different and preferable to grey, depressed Sunderland. The only complaint of the English players was of the condition of the pitch for the international, which was grassless and rock hard.

They immediately thought it was going to be difficult to play football on that surface. It proved to be worse than predicted with the ball bouncing much higher than it would in British conditions. The hosts adapted without problem to the surface, mastering the lively ball with skilful control and keeping their passes as low as possible. The Hungarians won 2-1 and so became only the third continental team to beat a full English side. The hosts were full value for their win and if their finishing had been as good as their approach play the score would have been doubled. Only gallant defending by Tom Cooper and Eddie Hapgood and brilliant goalkeeping by Frank Moss saved England from humiliation. Raich Carter always remembered the Hungarians as the best continental team he played against.

After five days in Budapest the England party departed for Prague. Although Carter was able to train at the stadium, his place in the international team was taken by Joe Beresford of Aston Villa. The match proved to be an exact copy of the Hungarian game down to the score of 2-1 to the Czechs. From the stand Carter was able to admire more clearly the skilful ball control and accurate passing of the continental players. A comparison between the successful Sunderland tour of Spain and England's ineffectual visit to south east Europe gave an indication of things to come. Clearly the Hungarians were well on the way to producing their marvellous team of the early 1950s, the first from outside Britain to beat England at home. Whereas the Spanish national team was underachieving, despite the strength of their club teams who would dominate the late 1950s.

By the time Raich Carter was safely back in Sunderland, the local headlines were concentrating on the town's 'terrible housing legacy' as revealed in an inspector's report. 'Human cattle sheds rushed up in the industrial revolution' was another comment. In Sunderland's East End there was a five-bedroom house containing 24 inhabitants. "Scandalous!" observed the Town Clerk on behalf of the Borough Council. By the outbreak of war the Council had built 5,000 houses.

As the football club completed their tour to the praise of their hosts, being described as "excellent teachers" and as a "team of gentlemen", Raich Carter was into the new cricket season with two wickets for 27 runs against Chester-le-Street. More memorable was his 135, including three sixes, which he scored out of a Hendon total of 231 for 5. This was a record total for the 30-over Saunders Cup. During the innings, Carter scored off all 11 opposition bowlers including the wicket keeper who removed his pads in order to bowl an over. More exciting for the crowd was the fact that four neighbouring windows were broken by this inspired hitting.

A story was told that Carter had a friend who was a glazier and a cricket supporter and that he arrived at one match with a pane of glass in his hands. He had come straight from work and very soon his services were required as Raich had broken a window. The householder was amazed to find a glazier on his doorstep so quickly. Raich got a huge thrill out of his club cricket especially the cut and the thrust of 30-over cup matches. Probably, if he had been seriously coached, his technique would have improved but the uninhibited enjoyment of attacking the bowling from the first ball might have been lost. Such was his instinct to hit every ball that the local press identified him as the 'Gilbert Jessop' of Durham Cricket. Carter's cricket was so carefree that he never bought his own bat but simply used the first one that came to hand. Certainly the crowds who watched Hendon in the 1930s appreciated the exhilarating cricket played by Raich Carter. What better distraction from the miseries of the dole and overcrowding?

Again the Durham selectors chose Carter to play against Yorkshire Seconds, this time at Ashbrooke in Sunderland. The match, in July 1934, showed that Carter was an all-rounder because, to the delight of the crowd, he was brought on to bowl and took a Yorkshire wicket with his fifth ball and another in his second over. He finished with figures of 5 overs, 1 maiden, 22 runs and 4 wickets. He became the hero of Ashbrooke and even more renowned in Hendon. Of course, his innings of 10 runs was disappointing and Argus in the *Echo* maintained that a good bowler could make Raich Carter get himself out. In particular, county bowlers could not be treated like club bowlers. Patience was needed and a curb on his attacking instincts. Raich would almost certainly have agreed. Nevertheless he was selected for Durham's prestigious fixture against the Australian tourists. This was the highlight of his cricket career and, in preparation for the game, Carter travelled to Leeds to watch the England v Australia Test and to study the visitors' bowling.

On 25th July the weather in Sunderland smiled on the Australians, although the crowd was disappointed to hear that Don Bradman was in London receiving treatment for an injury. By lunchtime the ground was almost full, with 9,500 in attendance. Raich Carter was quite clearly the idol of the crowd but things were not going well for Durham. Carter came out to bat at number eight to face the spin bowler Leslie Fleetwood-Smith, who had already taken several Durham wickets. Carter struck the first ball for four which produced the biggest cheer of the day but the bowler took his revenge in the next over with a 'Chinaman' which wrecked the stumps. Fleetwood-Smith went on to take seven wickets for 21 runs and Durham were all out for 73. The tourists made 314 for 3 declared and Durham dug in for a draw. Within two days Raich Carter was reporting back to Roker Park for the new football season 1934-35. Andy Reid, the trainer, soon had the players hard at work.

Chapter Nine

Challenging for the Title

SUNDERLAND ENTERED the new season with much brighter prospects than at any other time in the previous ten years. It was hoped that Johnny Cochrane's policy of building from youth would come to fruition in the forthcoming campaign. The team had already shown evidence of craft, ability and blend but lacked consistency. In particular, the away record had been disappointing. This would be helped by an improved partnership between the fullbacks and further development of key defender Bert Johnston at centre-half.

Pre-season checks revealed that Raich Carter now stood at almost 5 feet 8 inches while his weight was 10 stones and 7 pounds. The preparations went well and Sunderland were at full strength for their opening fixture against Huddersfield. The team was: Middleton; Murray, Shaw; Thomson, Johnston, Hastings; Davis, Carter, Gurney, Gallacher, Connor. Critics were hopeful that the younger players would have benefited from the increased experience they would bring to the new season. These early season hopes were entirely fulfilled by Sunderland's impressive start. The first three games were won with ten goals for and only one goal against. Argus observed that "no team in the country can play more attractive football than Sunderland – not even Arsenal at their best." He was prepared to predict after three weeks that if they remained free from injuries, Sunderland would have one of their best seasons.

The good form continued throughout October, culminating in a 2-1 home victory over Arsenal. This was the best game at Roker Park thus far and it featured two second-half headed goals by Raich Carter. Curiously, it was at home where Sunderland's form faltered. As Christmas approached, Sunderland were unbeaten away from home with convincing wins at Wolverhampton, Leicester, Stoke and Leeds. It was lapses at home which dented the title challenge. The press were particularly impressed with Carter's display against Leeds late in November. He was picked as the best inside forward on the pitch, recapturing the form which won him international honours the previous seasons. His energy was prodigious, allowing him to support the halfbacks while always being in position when an attack was launched. In the victory at Stoke, Stan Matthews had been marked out of the game by Alex Hall while Bob Gurney scored a hat-trick in the first 23 minutes. In this outstanding performance, Carter was the best forward on the field. In December, Sunderland had further away success at Portsmouth and Huddersfield. It therefore came as a considerable shock to both players and supporters to be beaten 6-2 by Everton on Christmas Day. However, in one of the greatest reversals of form in football history, the two clubs met on the following day with Sunderland taking revenge by 7-0.

Improbably the two league fixtures were only a prelude to further hostilities between the clubs. Early in January, Sunderland were drawn at home in the third-round of the FA Cup against Fulham. Another Gurney hat-trick was needed to dispose of the determined Londoners. Once again Sunderland were on the cup trail but awaiting them in the fourth-round were Everton. The match was played at Roker Park before 45,000 supporters. The game was spoilt by treacherous weather but it was a hammer and tongs battle. Everton were captained by their legendary centre-forward Dixie Dean. A replay was necessary after a 1-1 draw with Carter scoring for Sunderland and Jimmy Cunliffe equalising for Everton. The game at Goodison Park on 30th January 1935 is now regarded as one of the FA Cup's classic contests. Because the first game had been unruly and had got out of hand there was a general view that a different referee should be appointed. Consequently, Ernest Pinkston of Birmingham was allocated the replay. Tall and burly he was known as 'the sergeant major' but in spite of his formidable presence he never dismissed a player.

Pinkston's appointment made a classic game possible. Nearly 60,000 spectators crammed into the ground where 12 internationals were on view. It was a full-blooded cup-tie with enough excitement and passion to fill ten lesser games. After 30 minutes Everton were two goals up, both scored by left winger Jackie Coulter. Sunderland's right winger Bert Davis pulled a goal back before half-time, but a third goal for Everton seemed to assure them of victory. Not as far as Sunderland were concerned: they poured forward and Jimmy Connor scored. Into the final minute and Bob Gurney scored his most memorable goal. With his back to the goal he hooked a shot over his shoulder and past Everton's international 'keeper Ted Sagar. That meant extra-time and Coulter quickly completed his hat-trick for Everton. Once again, Sunderland fought back with an equaliser from Connor. It now seemed that Sunderland might take the lead for the first time and Gallacher actually got the ball into the net, only for referee Pinkston to rule it offside. That seemed to set Sunderland back on their heels and Everton scored two more goals.

Geoffrey Green, of *The Times*, described the match as "the pinnacle of football" while Bob Gurney believed it was the greatest game in which he had played. Argus wrote in the *Echo* that if Sunderland ever won the cup it would "not be in a better game of football than this one." He was worried because although Sunderland were the better footballing side, all six Everton goals were scored by forwards completely unmarked.

For the remainder of the season Sunderland continued to chase Arsenal for the title, meeting at Highbury on the 9th March. The game attracted Arsenal's record crowd of 73,295 but produced no goals. The Arsenal side included most of the stalwarts who won three successive League titles for the club. They included Eddie Hapgood, the left back and England captain, Ted Drake, Cliff Bastin and the great Scottish inside forward Alex James. Sunderland maintained their pressure on Arsenal for the title until the second week in April when they lost 1-0 to Manchester City. By the 22nd April Arsenal were proclaimed League champions for the third successive season: only the second club to do so in the history of the Football League. The feat was first achieved in the 1920s by Huddersfield, also managed by the legendary Herbert Chapman, who had died early in the new year. At the end of the season Sunderland had to settle for second place in the league, four points behind. Sunderland gained the same number of away points as the champions but too many lapses at home cost them the title.

For Raich Carter the season 1934-35 had been a successful one. He made a major contribution to the club's best challenge for the title in 20 years. Early on in September he had been chosen to represent the English League against the Irish League, an annual fixture being played for the 36th time. The selectors were a separate body from that which chose the England team. Technically all the Scots, Welsh and Irish playing in the Football League were eligible for selection but in practice they were rarely picked. On this occasion the selectors produced an all-northern team for the visit to Belfast. This meant that once again Raich Carter linked up with Stan Matthews following their exceptional performance for the Rest in the England trial six months earlier. Argus, in the *Echo*, congratulated Carter on his selection and predicted that if he played well with Matthews then he ought to go straight into the national side. The English League finished up easy winners by 6-1 after the Irish had taken the lead after seven minutes. All the forwards, apart from Carter, scored and generally he had a disappointing game. Certainly neither set of selectors called on Carter for the rest of the season, although for the final game against Scotland he was chosen as reserve. This was the match when Bob Gurney was selected, so Sunderland's fine season had not gone unnoticed by the selectors. This was his first cap and all Wearsiders were delighted by his selection because he had been a loyal player for ten years. They only regretted that Carter was not chosen to partner him especially as the inside-right position went to Cliff Bastin, the Arsenal left winger. Such an experiment with the national team was seen as hazardous and unnecessary, especially in the north east.

As the football season came to a close the news from Europe was disturbing. The Nazi government in Germany was found to be re-arming in defiance of League of Nations' resolutions. Particularly alarming to the British government was the revelation that German Fuehrer Adolf Hitler had begun a programme of submarine building. Meantime, in football circles, the main concern was the possible impact on club gates of the broadcasting of the cup final on radio. It certainly seemed to have contributed to the low attendance at Roker Park on that Saturday.

Early in May, Raich Carter was chosen for an FA party to tour the continent. Unfortunately, Sunderland would already be on their own tour of Spain. One proposal was that Carter should fly from Spain to join the FA party when it arrived in Amsterdam. Eventually that solution was abandoned and the FA simply released Carter from their squad and replaced him by George Eastham of Bolton Wanderers. En route for Spain, Sunderland officials and players stopped over in London in order to accept Arsenal's invitation to their celebration dinner. At the Holborn Restaurant the Sunderland party watched the Arsenal players receive their championship medals and thought to themselves, "That will be us next year." To his considerable embarrassment the Arsenal director, JJ Edwards, had to admit that he did not know where Sunderland was.

While Sunderland were completing another successful Spanish tour, Hendon cricket club were anxiously awaiting the return of their star player. Disappointingly, it proved to be a much less successful summer for both club and player. Carter's best score was 58 and he was only 12th man for Durham's match with the South African tourists. There was, however, more cheerful news on the local economy. Recovery from the depths of depression was evidenced by the lowest unemployment figures for five years. These figures were followed by the announcement of the biggest shipbuilding contract on the Wear for 12 years. Nevertheless, economic recovery on Wearside between 1935 and 1939 would be slow compared with the rest of the country as the region was believed to be unattractive to potential employers. There can be no doubt that the depression was a catastrophe to the area, blighting the hopes and wrecking the lives of thousands especially those depending on the shipbuilding trade.

Chapter Ten
Championship Number Six

ON 1st August 1935 the Sunderland players reported back for the new season. All 31 players were pronounced fit and well. Manager Johnny Cochrane declared that prospects for the coming campaign were good. To prove their fitness and versatility the football club arranged a cricket match against the Sunderland club. The footballers triumphed in a 25-over game with Raich Carter and Jimmy Thorpe, the best batsmen and bowlers.

In the event it proved to be a season of mixed fortunes both for Sunderland and for Raich Carter. For the player, personal loss came just before the season started. On 13th August 1935 his maternal grandfather, Horatio Stratton, of 17 Norman Street, died, aged 75. He and his wife Fanny had been very close to their grandson and his sisters. At this time Raich Carter's mother was suffering from serious ill-health and he was very involved in helping to nurse her. He always believed that man's best friend is his mother. As her condition worsened he arranged for a makeshift bed to be put into the corner of her room so that he could sit up with her through the night. She died in November, a second bereavement for Raich in three months; later in the season there would be a tragic third. What really perplexed Raich during this first half of the season was his brilliant form on the pitch despite the domestic worries. He was so concerned by this unlikely combination that he consulted a doctor and was reassured to be told that his football commitments provided the mental relief he needed from his personal worries.

What a tremendous autumn it was for the club. By the end of October they led the division by a point from Derby County. Carter scored in almost every game and it was no surprise when he was again selected to represent the Football League at Blackpool. Carter's old hero, Charlie Buchan, now working as a journalist, witnessed a superb away victory by 5-1 at Brentford. "I cannot hope to see anything finer," he wrote. "The forward line – Duns, Carter, Gurney, Gallacher and Connor – made the ball do everything but talk." Brentford manager Harry Curtis, whose team so far were making a good impression in their first season in the top division, said he believed Sunderland could win anything they entered that year. Patsy Hendren, the great test cricketer, said Sunderland were the best team he had ever seen.

Argus and Charles Buchan were in agreement that the 1935-36 team was as good as the great team of 1913 in all respects, except physique. The team Buchan himself had graced was bigger and stronger. However, he rated local boy Raich Carter as the inspiration of the great forward line. "His wonderful positional sense and beautifully timed passes made him the best forward of his generation." By the end of November, Argus was claiming a record for Raich Carter, playing as an inside forward, as the League's highest goalscorer with 19 goals. He was well ahead of the 21 centre-forwards the other clubs selected and it was his own centre-forward, Bob Gurney, who was running him closest.

In December, Sunderland beat Bolton 7-2, but Scottish international left-half Alex Hastings was injured, forcing Carter to cover his position. This was the match in which Bob Gurney broke his personal record by scoring five goals. This gave the club a five-point lead at the top of the league. The following week, with Hastings still unfit, Raich Carter was given the honour of captaining the team. It was believed that he was the first Sunderland-born player to captain the club since Fred Gale in 1888.

As the Christmas programme approached many observers were confidently predicting a championship title for Sunderland. Between 21st December and 28th, Sunderland were due to meet Derby, Leeds and Arsenal at Roker Park, a demanding schedule. The first two were dispatched comfortably but the Gunners, reigning champions and hailed as the greatest club side in the world, were determined to cut back Sunderland's lead at the top of the table. Raich Carter remembered this game as one of the two great encounters of his

Sunderland career (the other the cup replay with Everton). Arsenal were described by Carter as, "a very special, powerful side but we could match them." In an epic encounter Sunderland swept to a 4-1 half-time lead but gradually Arsenal edged their way back with two goals. At 4-3 the tension was beginning to show; then Jimmy Connor, with a diagonal run from the halfway line, exchanged passes with Raich Carter and shot home from 25 yards. Arsenal were still not beaten and brought the score back to 5-4 in the 75th minute. They laid siege to the Sunderland goal but the confidence Sunderland had built up sustained them to the end. One of Sunderland's first half goals was scored by Carter with a low, hard shot which goalkeeper Frank Moss appeared to dive over. When asked for his view Carter responded, "Oh, I don't know about goalkeeping error. Any goal I score is a good one." Sunderland were now seven points clear at the top of the League.

In this confident form Sunderland looked forward to their annual saga to bring the FA Cup back to the north east. Prospects seemed particularly good when the draw for the third-round brought a home tie with Port Vale who were struggling at the foot of the second division. True to its reputation the cup produced a surprise on 11th January 1936, when Port Vale held Sunderland to a 2-2 draw. The Sunderland display was described as "too bad for words." Surely Sunderland could not play so badly in the replay at Vale Park the following Monday? Even the weather turned against them over the weekend with a heavy frost which made the Port Vale pitch hard, bumpy and dangerous. Such conditions are great levellers and Port Vale had every incentive to exploit the situation. They threw themselves into the fray with daredevil rashness. Raich Carter was one of the first to take a tumble, splitting his chin on the unforgiving surface. Sunderland's preoccupation was to try to avoid a long injury list and as a result they lost 2-0. The players soon realised what it was like to be the victims of giant-killers in the cup. Port Vale were through to the fourth-round but they remained bottom of the second division and were relegated at the end of the season.

Despite this upset, Sunderland maintained their grip on the title chase but they were to suffer more misfortunes on the way. The only regular change this season was the promotion of Jimmy Thorpe to goalkeeper in place of Matt Middleton. There had been concerns about Thorpe's health in the previous season but he seemed to have made a full recovery. When Raich Carter first met Thorpe he recalled a big, strong lad. However, it was apparent during the season that he was losing weight but his form was good and his health was not discussed. His 26th match was at home against Chelsea who seemed determined to upset the team heading the table. During a generally rough game which the local paper believed was to the discredit of the Chelsea colours, there was a protracted goalmouth tussle around Thorpe, as he held the ball on the ground. Thorpe was injured but managed to complete the game although in that time Chelsea scored twice to draw the match 3-3.

After the game, as the players set off for home, Thorpe appeared to be alright and did not complain of any illness. Therefore, it was a tremendous shock to players, staff and supporters to hear on the following Wednesday that he had died in hospital. He was 22 years old and had been a diabetic. There was a deep sense of loss among supporters and a strong feeling about the general conduct of the match. The referee had a most unfortunate game in which it was surprising only one Chelsea player was sent off. As a result of this tragedy the FA made changes to the laws of the game to protect goalkeepers who had the ball in their hands.

The extraordinary contribution which Raich Carter had made in the first half of the season is measured by the 24 goals he scored in the opening 22 games. Such a prodigious scoring rate could not be maintained for the remainder of the season and he finished with 31, joint top scorer for the club with Gurney.

But in this season of fluctuating fortunes, triumphs and tragedies, Sunderland's seven-point lead was under threat from a poor spell of form in March in which two games were lost and two drawn. To put the club back on the winning road there was a derby fixture at Middlesbrough who were languishing in the bottom half of the division. Sunderland were at full strength with Middleton replacing Thorpe and Carter back after an England trial. None of this mattered to Middlesbrough who were determined to turn the Tees–Wear match into a battle. They stormed into a 3-0 lead in a vigorous and physical style which delighted their supporters. This in turn led to a loss of tempers and frequent fouls. The referee was at full stretch to keep the game under control. In the second half the game resumed in much the same fashion with Middlesbrough continuing to dominate the lighter Sunderland team.

With less than 15 minutes left and with Middlesbrough leading 5-0, Carter and the other Sunderland forwards were just hoping to survive unhurt until the final whistle. Then Carter received a pass and set off for goal, beating two defenders, but lost control of the ball so that it was a 50-50 ball between him and the Middlesbrough fullback. Carter, at full stretch, tried to hook the ball away as the defender sought to control it with his body. The result was that Carter did not reach the ball but came into contact with the defender's knee, who fell to the ground. A foul had been committed but there was no premeditation as far as Raich Carter was concerned. Unfortunately the referee judged that the foul merited a dismissal. So Carter, who had not been involved in any of the incidents earlier in the game and who had never been cautioned never mind sent off before, was the referee's scapegoat in what must be judged a belated attempt to get the game under control. Carter was bewildered; even Bob Baxter, the opposition captain, appealed against the referee's decision, to no avail. A desperately disappointed Raich Carter left the field confused and chastened. In the dressing room he was explaining his predicament to reserve, Sandy NcNab, when he heard the voice of right winger Bert Davis as he too entered the dressing room. "Surely it could not be full-time yet?" Raich wondered. Perhaps Bert had come to bring him back on to the field to rectify the mistake by the referee? In fact, Davis had been dismissed for arguing Carter's case too persistently. It is necessary to recall how relatively rare sending offs were in the 1930s to understand how severe and arbitrary the referee's decision seemed to the Sunderland camp. Johnny Cochrane did his best to console Raich and the club requested the FA to hold an enquiry into the incident. This took place in Darlington three weeks later and Raich Carter knew he had no chance when he heard in the referee's evidence that he saw "intent in Carter's eyes to foul the defender." So the enquiry did not rescind the referee's decision but they did impose only a one-week suspension (Davis got two weeks).

Fortunately, on the Saturday following the Middlesbrough game, Sunderland recovered their best form and Portsmouth were dismissed 5-0. There was a confident performance in goal by Johnny Mapson, secured from Reading, who would become Thorpe's long-term replacement. Sunderland's lead at the top of the table was now eight points and they seemed certain to win the title as neither Derby nor Huddersfield had taken advantage of Sunderland's set-backs in March. By the time Easter Monday, 13th April, arrived, Sunderland needed only a draw at Birmingham to clinch the title. Their captain, Alex Hastings, was unfit so Raich Carter was appointed to the position. For the Birmingham game there was absolutely no intention of defending for a draw. Sunderland had attacked all season and scored far more goals than anyone else and that would continue at Birmingham under the youthful leadership of Raich Carter, aged 23. The result was a 7-2 victory. That season Sunderland became the first club to score 100 goals, eventually reaching 109, nearly twice as many as second placed Derby County. They did, however, concede 74 goals that season, more than any other club in the top half of the League. Nevertheless the attacking style produced 25 victories that season and only 11 defeats.

The league trophy was presented to captain Alex Hastings after a 4-3 victory over Huddersfield at Roker Park on 18th April. At the close of the season Aston Villa and Blackburn Rovers were relegated so Sunderland became the only club never to have played outside the top division, a record they would retain until 1958. Also, by winning the title for the sixth time, Sunderland drew level with Aston Villa with the most championships to their credit. A telegram was received from George Allison, manager of Arsenal. It read, "The ex-champions hail you as the champions of the season and wish you prosperity and good luck."

It had been a remarkably eventful season for Raich Carter. He had suffered two bereavements; the loss of a young colleague; a first and only dismissal and an early, embarrassing exit from the elusive FA Cup. Consolation could be derived from the league title, the joint top goal scorer position, the team captaincy and a recall to the England colours. To become captain, even temporarily, at the age of 23 was a special achievement because in the past the position had been based on seniority. Also, the appointment rarely went to a forward because halfbacks were believed to be better positioned to do the job. However, Carter had the great advantage of being the local lad and, therefore, Johnny Cochrane knew he would be a popular choice. In fact, for the odd few games when Raich Carter stood in for Alex Hastings, the Sunderland team was operating so well that he felt he was only nominally doing the job. The real responsibility lay ahead when he would be appointed on a permanent basis, incidentally while Hastings was still captaining Scotland. In fact, Carter became a strong supporter of the captain's role both on and off the pitch. He should set an example by his own play; he should foster team spirit and he should be a persuasive spokesman for the team in any dispute with the management. The extra quality which would characterise Carter's leadership was his emphasis on attack. He could not tolerate any tactics which were based on defensive priorities. He believed the manager's role should end with the pre-match talk about the opposition's style and strengths, and the captain should take over from the kick-off adapting the team's tactics as the game progressed. Later in his career Carter became notorious for maintaining that if you gave him two able inside forwards he could build a successful side around them.

Raich Carter's recall to the national side was short lived. In September he had been chosen for the Football League against the Irish League. This was the match in which the legendary Irish goalkeeper Elisha Scott made his debut for the Irish League, having already won many international caps since 1920. Carter was partnered by Freddie Worrall of Portsmouth who, like most of the English side, had a poor game. Scott inspired the Irish to a 2-1 victory. Because of this disappointing result Carter did not figure in the full international between the two countries played in October. He had now missed seven internationals since his second cap against Hungary. Over that period five different inside-rights had been chosen only one of whom played in more than one match. Such was the fickleness of the selection committee. However, by December, the form of Sunderland and Carter was so outstanding that the selectors were obliged to turn to County Durham again for their inside-right. The opposition was Germany and the venue was White Hart Lane. The England team, including four players from Arsenal, was: Hibbs; Male, Hapgood; Crayston, Barker, Bray; Matthews, Carter, Camsell, Westwood, Bastin. Inevitably, the fixture generated a good deal of political interest since the visitors represented Nazi Germany. Hitler had already passed his anti-Jewish laws so the choice of Tottenham, a club long supported by north London's Jewish community, was particularly inappropriate as a venue. However, the two Football Associations were on cordial terms and the Foreign Office was determined the game should go ahead.

The Germans were the first European team to travel to an away game by plane and 10,000 German supporters also arrived for the match. Surprisingly, Germany was one of the few countries in Europe where professionalism was not permitted. Stan Matthews was a last-minute replacement for the injured Ralph Birkett and so joined Carter to form the right wing. Both players would be winning their third caps. England for the first time wore blue shirts and their superiority was evident from the kick-off. The game should have been won in the first 15 minutes but the Germans concentrated hard on defence as if determined to keep the score down. England's forwards, especially Matthews, were having an off day. For 20 minutes Carter gave him wonderful service but nothing was made of it. Matthew's bad game apparently affected Carter who began to fade. The *Daily Mail* concluded that Matthews did not have the big match temperament while Carter was only a shadow of the brilliant Sunderland man we knew. The Mail added that Carter, "must have begun to wonder why he cannot do himself anything like justice in a representative match." Consequently, Raich Carter missed the next five internationals and had to wait 11 months for his next cap. Argus in the *Echo* expressed his misgivings over Carter's international performances. He dismissed the London journalists' view that Carter lacked the big match temperament. He felt he had been dragged down by Matthew's poor performance. Argus also thought that the tendency to individualism in representative games undermined Carter's best form. He continued to be concerned with Carter's left-footedness when playing at inside-right. His tendency "to drift to the left" was accommodated at Sunderland but not in internationals. He was also critical of the 'amateur' FA Selection Committee and favoured the use of professional club managers.

All that was left in the 1935-36 season was the victory dinner with 350 guests at the New Rink. It was one of the most brilliant occasions seen in the town. The players received their medals for winning the title. Jimmy Thorpe's medal was presented to his family. A benefit match was to be arranged for the following season to support his widow and child.

The cricket season was soon in full swing and Raich Carter found several clubs keen to employ him as their cricket professional for the summer. Seaham Harbour CC were the front runners but Carter was reluctant to be lured away from his roots in Hendon. There was also the danger that the additional responsibilities of a cricketing match professional would interfere with his duties as a professional footballer. In fact, Raich Carter remained a Hendon cricketer and he had a very modest season with the bat. Meanwhile over at Roker Park the new clock stand was being constructed with covered terracing for 10,000 and was expected to be ready for the new season.

Foreign news in July and August was dominated by the outbreak of civil war in Spain and the developing struggle for Madrid. This event would curtail Sunderland's developing relationship with the Spanish footballing authorities until after the Second World War.

Chapter Eleven
The FA Cup at Last

AT THE beginning of the 1936-7 season Raich Carter was appointed captain of Sunderland AFC at the age of 23; a great honour, especially as ex-skipper Alex Hastings continued to feature on the left side of midfield. For the new season, Johnny Mapson was fully established in goal and the only change among the forwards was the emergence of Len Duns to challenge Bert Davis for the right-wing place. The main area of concern for Johnny Cochrane was at fullback where £4,000 had been spent but no settled combination had been achieved. This was highlighted in the first three away games in the league all of which were lost with eight goals conceded. The distinguished career of Scottish fullback Bill Murray was coming to an end although his connection with the club would be re-established later as a replacement for the manager.

Fortunately, during the autumn, home form was consistently good although Carter was injured in September, causing him to withdraw from the English League team to meet the Irish League. He was back in the news in October when rumours, originating in north London, suggested that Carter might join Arsenal at a cost of £10,000. Argus in the *Echo* was swift to quash such speculation, stating "Carter could not be replaced in England because his equal to fit into the Sunderland team is not to be found."

Fully fit after his pulled muscle, Raich Carter led Sunderland into a great derby battle at Middlesbrough. He may have been especially determined as he had been omitted from the England team to play Wales that day. There were ten goals scored in the opening 65 minutes with Middlesbrough taking a 3-1 lead only to be overhauled as Sunderland went 4-3 ahead. Eventually this thriller resulted in a 5-5 draw with Duns scoring twice and Carter once.

By the end of October there was concern in the town that the Sunderland team did not seem ready for a strong cup challenge. Nobody was relinquishing the league title publicly but everyone knew the number one objective was the FA Cup. A morale boost came on 28th October from the success in the Charity Shield over cup holders Arsenal. Carter scored a late winner although it was a generally disappointing game. Within a fortnight, Carter was recalled to the England team to play against Northern Ireland where he would again be partnered on the right wing by Portsmouth's Worrall.

By 14th November Sunderland had reached second place in the league following away wins at Chelsea and Manchester City. In the game at Maine Road, Carter contributed one of Sunderland's four goals while at the other end Peter Doherty, a talented Irishman, scored for City. The careers of these two great inside forwards were destined to cross memorably over the next 20 years. But in the short term they met again at Stoke in the England v Northern Ireland game. Raich Carter was again on the winning side by 3-1 and he also headed a magnificent goal.

This performance led to another cap as Carter retained his place for the fixture with Hungary early in December at Highbury. He was initially selected for his customary position at inside-right but injuries caused the withdrawal of Cliff Bastin and Ray Westwood. Consequently, the selectors moved Carter across to inside-left and recalled Raymond Bowden to inside-right. The Hungarians were rated as one of the top continental teams mainly because they spent long periods together touring other countries and establishing an understanding usually found at club level. The visitors were looking forward to playing in England, the home of football.

'Arbiter' of The Daily Mail welcomed Carter's positional switch because the player was naturally left-footed and he believed that Carter had only switched to the right to accommodate Patsy Gallacher. The Mail's report of the game praised the quality of the Hungarian football which excelled England in all aspects except shooting. In particular, Arsenal's Ted Drake capitalised with three goals while Carter added a headed goal. The Mail did not believe that Carter revealed his best Sunderland form. He probably needed the roving commission he had back at Roker Park. Additionally, the heavy conditions may have favoured England who won comfortably 6-2.

At the end of November the league table showed Sunderland leading Portsmouth but only because of a better goal average. The next away game was in London and coincided with the huge blaze which destroyed the Crystal Palace. Ten days later there was further sensational news from the capital as Edward VIII abdicated the throne in favour of his brother, the future George VI. While the national news spoke of crisis, on Wearside the vital shipbuilding industry had its best year since 1930 with 36 launches. The important football news in December 1936 was the FA Cup draw which required Sunderland to travel to Southampton. Prior to that there was an important home fixture in the League against arch rivals Arsenal. Duns scored a late equaliser which preserved Sunderland's unbeaten home record. In a tough game both Jimmy Clark, who had outplayed Ted Drake, and Alex Hastings were injured. It was their misfortune that efforts to retain the championship meant they would miss the cup run. Raich Carter, also hurt in the Arsenal match, was compensated with a benefit cheque of £650 for five years' service with the club.

Never to have won the FA Cup was a terrible thing for the north east and Sunderland went into their latest campaign replacing Clark with Bert Johnston and Hastings with Alex McNab. This did not seem to seriously deplete the team as both reserves had a lot of first team experience. The bigger worry was: would Raich Carter recover in time to play at The Dell? He was desperately keen to do so because Southampton was one of the clubs his father had played for. He travelled south with the club and undertook an unorthodox fitness test by running down the platform at Waterloo station. He could feel the injury and declared himself unfit so Cyril Hornby was the late selection. It is difficulty to imagine Michael Owen or Sol Campbell assessing an injury in this informal way!

Southampton were situated in the lower half of division two but a record crowd of 30,380 turned out to encourage them. In fact, they were outclassed by a Sunderland team, inspired by Gallacher in attack and by Johnston in defence. They built up a three-goal lead but Southampton staged a rally in the last 20 minutes which reduced the deficit to one goal.

The fourth-round looked like an away match at Second Division Blackpool who had drawn at Third Division Luton Town. But against the odds Luton won the replay 2-1 which meant an awkward visit to Kenilworth Road where the home team were unbeaten that season. Sunderland's newly signed right back, Jimmy Gorman from Blackburn, was eligible for this tie. The conditions on match day, 30th January 1937, were very difficult for the players as the ground was frozen, and frustrating for spectators because of fog. Raich Carter was fit to captain Sunderland but like the rest of his team he failed to cope with the hard surface. By contrast, Luton players took the risks and dominated the first half in which they could have scored four or five goals. The Luton attack was led by Joe Payne, who had created football history the previous April by scoring ten goals against Bristol Rovers, and by half-time Luton were two ahead. Sunderland desperately needed some luck and it came in the form of rain which made the pitch softer to play on. Gradually their play improved and two second-half goals gave them a fortunate replay. Carter was convinced that the softer pitch had allowed Sunderland to play to their full potential and he was an advocate of watering hard surfaces before matches to encourage good football.

The replay was held on the following Wednesday afternoon and 53,200 made their way to Roker Park. Len Duns gave Sunderland a lead after five minutes but 'Ten-goal' Payne soon equalised. He was one of the best centre-forwards seen at Roker that season and clearly Luton were not going to give up without a fight. Jimmy Connor restored the Sunderland lead but later suffered an injury which virtually ended his career. Few players had been such a delight to watch, combining amazing dribbling with accurate centres and powerful shooting. Sunderland continued the contest with ten fit men and it was not until three minutes before the end that Carter made the match safe with a third goal. Connor's tragic injury has been likened to that suffered by Brian Clough on the same ground 25 years later.

When the draw for the fifth-round gave Sunderland a home tie with Swansea, the bookmakers made them second favourites for the cup at 5-1 behind Arsenal at 9-2. The match with Swansea was eventually won comfortably 3-0 but it was a poor game spoiled by windy conditions. Sunderland were helped by having such a capable replacement for Connor in Eddie Burbanks, signed two years earlier for £500.

In the quarter-finals Sunderland were drawn away to Wolves, like themselves strongly placed in the top division. Before the cup-tie there was an extraordinary league game at West Bromwich Albion on 27th February. The ground was heavy and the game was full of thrills and goals. Raich Carter was involved in much of the brilliant attacking play in which he hit the cross bar and scored a goal but also missed a penalty in a 6-4 defeat.

For the match at Molineux, as at Southampton, there were record receipts and a record gate of 57,731. The Sunderland team was: Mapson, Gorman, Hall; Thomson, Johnston, McNab; Duns, Carter, Gurney, Gallacher, Burbanks. Wolverhampton were led by centre-half Stan Cullis who would also captain England and in attack they had Bryn Jones who would later break the British transfer record in a move to Arsenal. It turned out to be a wonderful game, despite the muddy conditions, with Jones giving Wolves a first-half lead and Duns equalising in the second half. Sunderland's defending had earned them a replay at Roker Park. The winners of that match faced a semi-final against the season's great giant-killers, Millwall, of the Third Division South. Sunderland supporters may have believed the road to Wembley was clear, except that, on Wednesday afternoon 10th March, Wolves were in determined mood.

Although the pitch and the weather were greatly improved for the replay, it was not such a good match apart from the drama of the last five minutes of normal time. Until the 86th minute the game was goalless and Wolves resisted all Sunderland's pressure. Then, in a breakaway, Tom Galley scored for Wolves, silencing the vast crowd of 61,800. Then in the final 30 seconds Charlie Thomson rushed to take a throw in which Carter received and passed back to Thomson. The wing-half centred to Bob Gurney who, in a crowded goal area, had escaped from Cullis and brought the ball down, and swinging, almost on his knees, hit a low, weak shot. It did not seem possible that it could find its way through a mass of legs but, with the goalkeeper Jim Gold unsighted, the ball entered the net. It was a miraculous escape for Sunderland and there was uproar at Roker Park. In extra-time Sunderland took the lead through Duns but Wolves levelled the scores within two minutes.

Raich Carter and four teammates were unfit for the Saturday league game at Portsmouth. The much-rearranged team fought back from a 3-0 deficit but lost 3-2. The second cup replay was due at Sheffield on Monday 15th March. The London and north eastern Railway organised excursions from Sunderland at a cost of seven shillings (35p) for a third class return ticket. Those supporters who took advantage of this left Sunderland at 10.09 and helped to swell the crowd to 48,960. Raich Carter was doubtful but it was decided to play him with his injury strapped. The decision was the right one because the young Sunderland captain inspired a brilliant display. On a treacherous surface and only 75 per cent fit, he played as if his life depended on it. He scored Sunderland's second goal just before half-time followed immediately by Gallacher scoring the third. Wolves, five times finalists and twice FA Cup winners, were defeated. Sunderland added a fourth goal near the end to secure a semi-final place.

The following Saturday, 20th March, Sunderland lost their unbeaten home record to Chelsea and the strain of the cup run was beginning to tell. The following week they lost 5-3 to Stoke City which meant they were unlikely to retain the League title. The *Echo* advised "the need to judiciously rest key players to preserve them for the Cup."

The players took no comfort from meeting Millwall in the semi-final. In their cup run the club from the Third Division South had disposed of three top division clubs: Chelsea 3-0; Derby 2-1; and Manchester City, the eventual champions, 2-0. They were the first club from the Third Division to reach the semi-final. The match was scheduled for Huddersfield's Leeds Road ground. Sunderland had their first selection problem of the cup run because both Jimmy Clark and Alex Hastings were fully fit again. As far as Argus was concerned there was nothing to choose between Clark and Johnston, so the incumbent should be retained. As far as the left-half position was concerned, Argus maintained that "admirable as McNab is, Hastings fit and in form has neither superior nor few equals in England or Scotland." The dilemma for the club was temporarily resolved when McNab was declared unfit for the semi-final and Hastings returned to the side.

Just before the semi-final the London press was reporting that Millwall considered that reducing Carter to an ordinary level would get them to Wembley. Argus wondered if Raich Carter should wear armour and a dozen pairs of pads. On the day, Leeds Road was packed with 62,813 spectators. More than 20,000 had travelled from the north east and their colours and cheers predominated. It was 10th April 1937 and Wembley awaited the winners. Within 10 minutes Millwall had taken the lead with a brilliant goal from their dangerous centre-forward Dave Mangnall. However, this Sunderland team had shown already their capacity to recover from such a setback. Millwall held out until the 29th minute when Gurney hooked in a shot from a narrow angle to equalise. Millwall goalkeeper Duncan Yuill kept them in the game until mid-way through the second half when Patsy Gallacher scored a wonderful winner which he later described as "the greatest and most important goal I ever scored." From then on Sunderland had all the play and made every effort for a third decisive goal. There was terrific pressure on the Millwall defence and Carter was given a clear chance but he shot wide.

Back in Sunderland a crowd of between 4-5,000 had gathered in the streets around the *Sunderland Echo* offices to follow the progress of the semi-final. The winning goal brought a great cheer from the throng and it became necessary for the police to control the crowd and make a passage for the traffic. Nothing but Sunderland's victory was talked about in the town that night. The burning question soon became how to get a ticket for the final at Wembley.

Chapter Twelve
4th May 1937: Wembley Final

A WEEK before the semi-final victory the *Echo* revealed that Raich Carter would be married in the week before the cup final. Argus understood that there was a superstition among brides that it was unlucky to marry in May. Therefore the date for the wedding was fixed for Monday 26th April. On 6th April the paper published a photograph of Raich Carter and his bride-to-be Rose Marsh. The couple had met when the Marsh family lived in Hendon. They had attended the same Sunday school but then lost touch for ten years. The bride and her family subsequently moved to Chaddesden on the eastern side of Derby so the marriage would take place at Spondon near Derby. The best man would be Bob Gurney. The aim was a quiet wedding away from the football-frenzy in Sunderland.

Three days after the semi-final success Raich Carter had more good news. He had been restored to the England team against Scotland at Hampden Park. He was back at inside-right and his partner on the right wing was Stan Matthews who was making his first appearance against the Scots – he was still to be there 20 years later. The match was played on 17th April and the Scots were strong favourites, having home advantage. The crowd was an extraordinary 149,693, many of whom could see little of the match. This was unfortunate as it turned out to be a great international in which England dominated the first half and took a 1-0 lead. Carter's approach work was admired, especially the way he brought Matthews into the game. However, his shooting chances were blocked. While Matthews was having his best international, his club colleague, Joe Johnson, on the left wing, was even better. In the second half the Scots were revitalised and equalised but the England players battled all the way. With 11 minutes to go it was anyone's game but then Scotland scored two glorious goals. England would play 18 more internationals before the outbreak of the Second World War and Raich Carter would not feature in any of them. However, Madam Tussaud's in London had more confidence in his future success as they arranged for him to sit for his wax image three days after the international match.

Meanwhile, back at Roker Park, Cochrane was overturning long-established Sunderland AFC policy. Recognising early in April that Sunderland could not retain their league title, he decided to rest a number of players from league games prior to the cup final. Two days after the semi-final victory only three members of that team, Mapson, Duns and Burbanks, turned out against Grimsby. The cup finalists were outplayed 6-0. Not until 24th April, the week before the final, was a full-strength team selected and they lost 3-0 at Leeds.

Sunderland were by no means clear favourites to win the cup. Preston North End had had a splendid cup run, culminating in a 4-1 victory over West Bromwich Albion in the semi-final at Highbury. Their Scottish international centre-forward Frank O'Donnell had scored in every round, totalling ten goals. He was regarded as the most dangerous forward in the final.

Both teams travelled south to spend the last week before the game at hotels near London. They needed peace and quiet away from the tension and the incessant stream of badgering callers that infested Preston and Sunderland. Raich Carter was particularly upset by the pestering which came by 'phone, by letter, by callers to his home and by people in the street. Even the players' families, as well as ordinary supporters, were subjected to the pressures of professional ticket touts.

According to their plans, Raich Carter and Rose Marsh were married in Derby on the Monday before the big match. Immediately after the reception, Raich, together with Bob Gurney, left the bride and other guests to join up with their teammates at the Bushey Hall Hotel. There they could relax in their training together with swimming, golf and even croquet. On the Wednesday it was announced that Sunderland had drawn the lucky number one changing room. Both teams took a traditional view and decided against wearing numbered shirts. In the *Echo* on Friday 30th April, Raich Carter sent a message to the people of Sunderland, "I think we will win. I am proud to captain the Sunderland team in the final, and the finest wedding present I could possibly get would be to receive the cup from His Majesty tomorrow and to bring it to Sunderland on Monday. Sunderland expects, and our boys won't fail for the want of trying." Letters and telegrams poured into the club. One came for Cochrane from South Africa. It said, "Best of luck in the cup from Sunderland men and lasses in Durban."

Trainer Andy Reid announced that the players "could not be fitter than they are now." This meant there was one selection issue: Alex McNab or Alex Hastings for left-half. It was decided that McNab, who had played in seven cup-ties so far, should be chosen ahead of the unfortunate Hastings. Therefore, the Sunderland team would be Mapson; Gorman, Hall; Thomson, Johnston, McNab; Duns, Carter, Gurney, Gallacher and Burbanks. All the team apart from Mapson and Gorman had come up through the club's reserve team. It included five Scots but Preston would outdo that by fielding seven. Only Carter was born in Sunderland, although Gurney came from Silksworth, a nearby mining village, and Duns was a Tynesider. Burbanks was a Yorkshireman from Doncaster. A new set of shirts was provided but the superstitious Reid rejected them, preferring to retain the shirts used in the earlier rounds. As a compromise he allowed the coat of arms to be transferred from the new shirts to the old.

Finally, the 1st May arrived and the towns of Sunderland and Preston appeared deserted. Thousands of Sunderland supporters who had been following the club since their only other final appearance in 1913 arrived in London to find the capital hit by a bus strike. Transport and General Workers' Union leader Ernest Bevin, later a Foreign Secretary, had chosen the symbolic May Day to call out 30,000 drivers and conductors. Fortunately for the travelling fans, the tube services, the tramcars and the trolley buses were still running. The Sunderland team coach left Bushey Hall near Watford en route for Wembley stadium. The players were absolutely astounded by sheer numbers of supporters from County Durham who had turned the streets of the capital into a mass of red and white. Patsy Gallacher recalled the tremendous team spirit and the happy atmosphere as the coach made its way across north London. The positive approach continued into the changing room, which was cheerful and optimistic. The Sunderland team knew their opponents quite well as they had played them twice already in the league. Some possible tactics were discussed but no master plan of campaign was adopted. In fact, Raich Carter was vehemently opposed to so-called 'victory plans.' He remained deeply sceptical about the value of coaching, even after he became a full-time manager in the 1950s.

Once inside changing room number one, Carter felt at home. He had used it before in his England matches. Furthermore, in all his subsequent visits to Wembley this was the only changing room he would use. The preliminaries were similar to those at an international. This time, because it was coronation year, both the new King George VI and Queen Elizabeth were guests of the Football Association. As captain, Raich Carter introduced the Sunderland players to the King. Soon the referee called the captains together to toss up and Carter lost the toss. There was, however, nothing in the conditions to give Preston an advantage in the first half.

From the kick-off it was clear that the players were suffering from nerves. In the opening exchanges passes regularly went astray. The Sunderland team took longer to settle down than Preston but gradually they came more into the game. Bob Gurney missed a difficult chance from an Eddie Burbanks cross and then put the ball in the net only to be judged offside. In the 38th minute, Frank O'Donnell combined with his brother Hugh, on the Preston left wing, to split the Sunderland defence and score the opening goal. This meant the Preston striker had scored in every round in the competition. More significant to Sunderland players and supporters was the knowledge that no team in a Wembley final had won the cup having conceded the first goal. However, this was the fourth time in five ties that Sunderland had fallen behind, so they knew they could come back. At half-time the score remained 1-0. In the dressing room one player claimed that O'Donnell must be stopped at all costs. This provoked Raich Carter into a forceful response: "We have got to be more in the game. We have got to make the ball work more, find the man more. Let's play football as we can play it, and we shall be alright." It is interesting that there does not seem to have been any significant comment from the manager or the trainer.

With the captain's words in their ears, the Sunderland team equalised within six minutes of the restart. Burbanks took a corner which Carter headed forward to Gurney who had his back to the goal and back-headed the ball into the net. This goal further revived the Sunderland players, confidence flowed and the football was transformed. Sunderland were really playing now and they laid siege to the Preston goal. Next Carter missed what the *Echo* described as "an absolute sitter" when, on receiving a pass from Burbanks, he topped his shot into the side netting. The moan from around the stadium reinforced Carter's sense of disappointment. A chance had come and he had missed it.

At the other end of the pitch one of the great battles of the match between Sunderland's centre-half Bert Johnston and the Preston number nine O'Donnell continued to rage. Johnston had only prevented his opponent from scoring a second goal by bringing him down. The referee administered a stern warning but no caution or dismissal as would be the case today. As the duel continued Johnston gradually achieved mastery. At the same time Charlie Thomson, in midfield for Sunderland, was playing more and more impressively. He gave support to the defence and was involved in the moves which led to the goals.

In the 72nd minute, Raich Carter was given a chance to atone for his missed chance. He was in the inside-left position when a bouncing pass came over from Gurney to his right. Carter beat the fullback, raced the goalkeeper to the ball and lobbed it out of his reach into the net. Both players finished in a heap on the ground and Sunderland were in the lead.

Carter was mobbed by his teammates and the cheering lasted for several minutes. Choruses of the song 'Blaydon Races' echoed around the stadium. Within six minutes Patsy Gallacher created a third goal with a skilfully judged pass to Eddie Burbanks who shot home from a very narrow angle. As Preston strove to narrow the margin they found Jimmy Gorman strong and cool in defence. His form was brilliant by this stage. When the final whistle sounded it pierced Raich Carter's concentrated mind and took him by surprise. This was followed by a thrill of delight in the knowledge that the cup was on its way to Sunderland after 53 years and 140 cup-ties. The Sunderland players shook hands and congratulated each other while commiserating with the Preston team. Probably the most disappointed among them was right-half, Bill Shankly, who would eventually become Liverpool's legendary manager.

Next the Sunderland team was marshalled into order with captain Raich Carter at the head to file up to the Royal Box. He recalled the broad smile of King Farouk of Egypt and then he was taking the cup from the Queen who said, "That is a nice wedding present for you." Immediately he recalled he was a married man who had left his bride right after the reception. Events quickly brought him back to the current situation: with the cup in one hand and its stand in the other, he needed to receive his medal from the Queen. Fortunately, Alex Hall, Sunderland's left back, took hold of the stand. Next the King added his congratulations, as did Lord Derby and Stanley Rous of the Football Association. So Raich began his way down the steps, clinging to the trophy as supporters pounded his back and grabbed at his arms. Jack Washington, the future Bishop Auckland goalkeeper, was one of them, leaning over to try to slow Raich down so that a photographer opposite could get a good picture. Once Raich was back on the pitch his teammates lifted him on to their shoulders while he clung on to the cup for a circuit of the stadium.

Much to Raich Carter's relief the dressing room was eventually reached without dropping the cup. The directors soon had it filled with champagne and everyone had a chance to drink out of it. Eventually the Sunderland party was ready to board the coach back to the Russell Hotel.

From there, Raich Carter was rushed to Broadcasting House where he was due to take part in the popular radio show 'In Town Tonight.' Raich was happy to play football in front of thousands but in front of a microphone he was less comfortable. Despite this nervousness the interview went well. After the broadcast he was immediately reunited with his new wife for the first time since the wedding. They were supposed to be staying in the Russell Hotel with the rest of the Sunderland party but Raich had overheard some of the plans that the team had in store for them and decided to make alternative arrangements by booking into the Strand Palace Hotel.

The next morning *The Daily Sketch* had laid on a car and a reporter to show the honeymoon couple around the sights of London. The capital was in the midst of preparations for the coronation in ten days' time. Rose Carter's first comment about the Londoners' efforts was that they were 'skimpy.' Back in Sunderland she said every house had already put its flags out, proving to her a much greater loyalty to the monarchy. Westminster Abbey, Buckingham Palace and Hyde Park followed but the highlight came at the Zoo when a chimpanzee put his arm round Mrs Carter's neck. After lunch it was off to Windsor Castle for another chance to meet the King and Queen. Rose felt it had been the perfect start to a girl's honeymoon.

The triumphant return to Sunderland had been arranged for

Monday. This was a day Raich Carter would never forget. It began at Kings Cross Station where crowds had gathered to give the special Pullman, decorated everywhere in red and white, an impassioned send-off. The further north the train sped the bigger the crowds which packed the station platforms until Newcastle was reached. There the Mayor and town band gave their biggest rivals a civic welcome. A sporting gesture by the 'Magpies.' The next stop was Monkwearmouth station, Sunderland. As the train approached from Fulwell the whistle of the huge engine rang out in shrill triumph. When it ceased, the vast crowd outside the station began a tremendous roar of 'Ha'way the Lads.' Raich Carter climbed off the train with the FA Cup in his hands to be greeted by the chief constable, but he was quickly drawn into a small office by a BBC local reporter to say a few words about the game to listeners in the north east.

Out in the station yard the coaches awaited and as players appeared there was a thunderous roar of applause followed by another chant of 'Ha'way the Lads.' After a four-mile tour of the town, the team were warmly welcomed by the mayor at the Town Hall. He said that this was the day the town had waited for since the club was formed in 1879. Next Raich Carter thanked the crowd for their marvellous reception. It all meant so much to him as this was his home town and he had led the club to victory.

From the Town Hall the next stop was Roker Park, which had been thrown open to the public. More than 30,000 were in attendance and there was no football match! But there were costumes, songs and dancing. Even a crate of beer which had been taken to the unsuccessful final of 1913 and not used was now produced and consumed eagerly. The celebrations went on until well past midnight, but not for the Carters who had slipped away to their new home. Can anyone doubt that had the Footballer of the Year award existed in 1937 that Raich Carter would have been the outstanding candidate? The League title and the Charity Shield had now been followed by the FA Cup and an England cap against Scotland. Raich Carter had won all the honours available at the time and he still had not reached his 24th birthday. As far as the 1936-37 season was concerned Raich Carter had played in 37 league games and scored 26 goals while in eight cup-ties he had scored three goals making him the club's top scorer.

Chapter Thirteen

The War and Fire Fighting

THE SUMMER of 1939 was dominated by the threat of war. Late in June, German pressure on Danzig in Poland caused anxiety across Europe. By early August Hitler was intensifying his threat to Danzig in what the *Sunderland Echo* described as "a war of nerves." Meanwhile, Wearsiders were enjoying their best summer for years and the beaches were packed. The football club held a trial match on 12th August between the stripes and the reds. This traditional preparation for the new season attempted to defy the bleakness of the international situation. Raich Carter scored for the stripes but only played in the first half. The week between 22nd and 29th August was entirely dominated by frantic negotiations with Hitler to avert war and culminated in the commitment that Britain would stand by Poland. In the midst of these momentous negotiations Sunderland opened their league programme with a 3-0 victory over Derby County with Carter scoring twice. This fine performance delighted the spectators who needed some good news. The Sunderland team was Mapson; Gorman, Hall; Housam, Lockie, Hastings; Duns, Carter, Robinson, Smeaton, Burbanks. Argus, in the *Echo*, felt the shadow of a crisis like that of 1914. He predicted that the new season would not last beyond the first week, which proved to be very prescient.

Sunderland played a second fixture on the following Thursday, 31st August, which they lost to Huddersfield 2-1. The following day Sunderland travelled to London for a fixture with Arsenal on the Saturday. However, on Friday 1st September Germany invaded Poland, and Warsaw was bombarded. The British government invoked the Anglo-Polish treaty. The Sunderland party found the capital digging trenches and preparing for war. On Saturday the kick-off was delayed until 5.00 p.m. in order to allow the evacuation arrangements to proceed efficiently. The crowd was unusually low at only 5,000: clearly both Londoners and those from the north east had more important things on their minds. Raich Carter could recall, ten years later, only the result of the game which Arsenal won 5-1. He could remember the feeling that something significant could happen at any moment. In an atmosphere of unreality all the players wondered if it would be their last game together. For the first time in Raich Carter's career, football seemed immaterial.

The Sunderland party were staying at the Russell Hotel and, at 11.00 a.m., the team gathered together to hear a radio broadcast by Prime Minister Neville Chamberlain. The news everyone had feared for months was announced: Britain was at war with Germany. Within a few minutes of the broadcast an air-raid siren went off which immediately ended players' speculation about their futures in a country without football. After a period spent sitting on the carpets of the third floor, the all-clear siren sounded. It had been a false alarm. The immediate effect of the Declaration of War was a ban on the assembly of crowds.

Back in Sunderland on Monday morning, Raich and the rest of the players collected their wages but there was no training. In fact, there was no training for the rest of the week and the fixture for Saturday was cancelled. On 11th September the Football Association announced that, "All football under the jurisdiction of the association would be suspended until further notice." All players' contracts were suspended, so, like many thousands of others, they were out of a job. However, the football clubs retained the players' registrations which meant they continued to control their careers even though they no longer paid them. Not surprisingly, the system has been described as feudalism or serfdom.

For those players who had already volunteered for the territorials or the militia, call up to the colours was immediate or very swift. However, for the remainder, conscription would take longer. Faced with the prospect of no income in the short term and with only half a week's wages from Sunderland plus instant termination of contract, Carter took one of the most crucial decisions of his life. He joined the Fire Service. Ted Smith, his uncle, was still a senior police officer in Sunderland, which would have streamlined entry into the Fire Department. Nevertheless, this option was one that Carter came to bitterly regret.

The fact of the matter was that Raich Carter was a public figure, especially in the north east, and therefore his decisions excited a lot of comment. In this case mostly unfavourable because it was interpreted as being a tactic to avoid military service. With the benefit of hindsight, Raich Carter wrote later that he should have waited and used any influence he could muster to get into one of the services as quickly as possible. Instead the Fire Brigade would pay £3 a week and enlistment was straightforward. Nevertheless, his income was cut by more than 60 per cent.

On 21st September the Football Association, after consultation with the Home Office, announced that it would lend its full support to the organisation of competitive and friendly matches so long as they were confined to local or district areas on Saturdays and public holidays, and as long as there was no interference with the war effort. However, there would be a limit to the number of spectators set at 8,000, or half the capacity of the stadium. They also set a 50-mile limit on the distances clubs could travel.

The Football League were planning to introduce regional leagues late in October. One of the first clubs to announce it would not take part in the regional leagues was Sunderland. They consequently closed down for the season 1939-40. In the *Echo*, Argus appealed to the Sunderland directors to reconsider their position even if it meant the club would get further into debt. As this plea went unheeded, the Sunderland team began to migrate. Raich Carter, for example, travelled to Huddersfield early in October where he had been invited to play. Meantime, Alex Hastings and Bert Johnston were guesting for Hartlepool. The *Echo* wondered how Huddersfield could be regarded as "a reasonable distance" in accordance with Football Association guidelines. As far as Carter was concerned, there was £1.50 to be earned, which he needed. It was a hectic arrangement for the player who had to arrange to do night duty on Friday night so that he could leave at 8 a.m. for Huddersfield and then dash back for duty after the game. On 7th October Raich Carter scored a hat-trick for Huddersfield in a friendly with Blackburn and he followed that with another hat-trick at Sheffield Wednesday.

In their first north east regional league match, he completed a hat-trick of hat-tricks at Bradford Park Avenue. The other goalscorer for Huddersfield was Willie Watson, who would become a double England international at football and cricket.

On 25th October it was announced that a match between the Football League and an All-British XI would be played on 4th November at Goodison Park. The League team would consist entirely of international players including a formidable forward line of Matthews, Carter, Lawton, Doherty and Brook. It was one of three games arranged in November in aid of the Red Cross. Many observers thought it the best match seen in ten years and Carter distinguished himself with a fine display, scoring once, and was involved in a move which led to former club mate Alex McNab, scoring. While Raich Carter and Peter Doherty had played against each other more than once before the war, this occasion was a prelude to their fantastic combination after the war.

Huddersfield's form in the north eastern regional league was outstanding and they eventually won the competition with only one defeat in 20 games. Carter made 11 appearances, his contribution restricted by his fire duties and his selection for representative teams. His games for Huddersfield were concentrated into the first half of the season. Late in November he was chosen to play for the England XI against a Scottish XI at Newcastle on 2nd December 1939. Eight of the England team were full internationals including all the forwards: Matthews, Carter, Lawton, Westwood and Brook. However, Ray Westwood withdrew before the game while Eric Brook and Sam Barkas were injured in a car crash en route for Newcastle. Consequently, the match earned a permanent place in football history for two reasons. It was the first international played between two countries in time of war and secondly the England team included a Scot, Tom Pearson of Newcastle. He was one of two Newcastle players (the other, Joe Richardson, was English) who replaced the accident victims. *The Times* wrote "The victory, in the circumstances, was a thoroughly worthy one and England owed a lot to the genius of Matthews at outside right." Certainly, he made the England goals for Tommy Lawton and Henry Clifton but Argus' comment was more critical, "What a treat to see Matthews in possession but oh how he can hold up the forward movement by retaining possession. Unquestionably one of the cleverest post-1918 players, but he generally gives the impression of playing for himself. He seldom gives the ball back to the man who gave him the pass." Raich Carter's most glaring contribution to the game was to miss a late penalty.

Into the New Year of 1940, the weather deteriorated and there was widespread cancellation of fixtures. This was the period of so-called 'phoney war' after the speedy fall of Poland when nothing much happened on the western front. In particular there was none of the widely predicted bombing of British cities. Instead, in this lull before the storm the British Expeditionary Force took up positions at the northern end of the Maginot Line.

By the end of January 1940, Raich Carter was once again selected for a Football League team to play an all-British XI in aid of the Red Cross to be played at Bradford. The League team was a powerful one: Sagar; Sproston, Catlin; Willingham, Cullis, Mercer; Matthews, Hall, Lawton, Carter, Beasley. Among the opposition were Matt Busby, Wilf Mannion and Peter Doherty. Carter's selection at inside-left was a reversal to experiments made by Johnny Cochrane several years before.

In February, the comment in the *Echo* was that Carter seemed to have transferred his affection from Huddersfield to Hartlepool. It was more a question of convenient travel than a change of sentiment. In fact, Raich Carter played only six times for Hartlepool. Meanwhile Sunderland were beginning to take an interest in a proposed national cup to be played towards the end of the season. The main difficulty for the club was the availability of Roker Park. They decided to enter the new competition (Football League War Cup) along with 82 other entries and began negotiations with Newcastle to use St James' Park for any home matches. The Football Association agreed to extend the season to 8th June because of the cancellations caused by bad weather, the coldest recorded since 1894. It would also allow the new cup competition to be completed.

Raich Carter had now completed six months in the Auxiliary Fire Service. He found the work interesting and took his training seriously. The war had shown him how precarious a career in football could be, especially for a married man. He was prepared to give up the life of a footballer, which he loved, in order to enjoy the security offered by the Fire Service. In pursuit of this plan, Carter applied to join the regular Fire Brigade and was appointed on 19th March 1940. In the *Echo*, Argus lamented the loss to Sunderland AFC not only in the short term but also when peacetime returned. He noted that Carter was only one year away from ten years' service at the club, which would have qualified him for his second benefit of £500. It was hoped that, if the chief constable gave his permission,

Carter would be able to help Sunderland in the forthcoming cup-ties but, after the war, he certainly could not sign a professional contract while a full-time member of the Fire Service.

However, the transfer to the full-time Fire Service did not proceed as smoothly as the parties might have wished. On the 11th April, Raich Carter found himself the subject of an article in the local press away from the usual sports pages. The report concerned a meeting of the Sunderland town council at which questions were asked about the procedure adopted for filling vacancies in the Fire Brigade. Alderman Taylor, Chairman of the Watch Committee, answering questions from councillors, stated that: "Horatio Carter was one of the best auxiliary firemen we ever had," and was chosen by the chief constable as being the most suitable man for the vacancy in the Fire Brigade. That was the usual procedure followed by the Committee. In answer to another question about public feelings in the town about the appointment, the Alderman said that Horatio Stratton Carter had been an auxiliary fireman for seven months. "He can be up a ladder like a monkey."

This newspaper report of the council's proceedings provoked some lively correspondence to the editor over the next few days. The writer of a letter from Hood Street was not at all satisfied with the council's decision to promote Raich Carter to the full-time Fire Brigade. He suggested that favouritism was at work in selecting him out of 239 others. He also hinted that Carter was pursuing this path to avoid conscription, as the Fire Service was 'a reserved occupation.' This sort of disparagement had already come Carter's way and it would pursue him throughout his Fire Service career. As the months went by he became increasingly resentful, especially when he had just got off a long and dangerous shift. It was little comfort to know that thousands of other young men, also in reserved occupations, were getting similar treatment.

In the meantime, new manager Bill Murray, the club's former left back, had the difficult task of reassembling a Sunderland team after a seven-month break. He was hopeful that despite his changed status Raich Carter would be available to the club. Three friendly matches were organised early in April prior to the cup-tie with Darlington on 20th April. The competition was played on a two-leg basis and Sunderland's first competitive match since the declarations of war ended one each. With Roker Park not available the second leg was scheduled for St James' Park, Newcastle.

The background to the birth of the wartime cup was not propitious.

The latest German invasion had taken place against Norway. Britain and France were determined to respond rapidly. Unfortunately, the allied landings in Norway were followed by reversals which led to their hasty withdrawal. This setback was the forerunner of a bleak spell for the allies facing the German war machine.

Raich Carter was among those required to register for military service on 27th April. Despite this Carter scored twice in Sunderland's second-leg tie with Darlington which secured a place in the next round against Leeds United. Again Sunderland drew the first leg away but were victorious in the second, 1-0.

While Sunderland took on Blackburn in the next round, events in Europe dominated the nation's attention. The Allies had rushed to the aid of Holland and Belgium, the latest victims of Nazi invasion, early in May 1940.

Sunderland's exit from the cup, beaten 3-2 by Blackburn, was completely overshadowed by the retreat and surrender of Belgium. Within days the British Expeditionary Force was retreating towards Dunkirk and a dramatic appeal for hundreds of little ships to cross the channel was made. Around 300,000 men were rescued from the beaches of Dunkirk.

Remarkably, a large batch of the survivors was at Wembley on 8th June for the League War Cup Final, at which West Ham beat Blackburn 1-0. The whole competition of 137 matches had been completed within nine weeks. So the first wartime season came to a close with the country deprived of her European allies and deserted by the new French government. There had been talk for some weeks of football closing down for the duration of the war. After all, an invasion was anticipated at any time that summer.

Early in July, in the *Echo*, Argus was very pessimistic about the prospects for football in the season 1940-41. The directors of Sunderland AFC loaned Roker Park to the government for a physical training scheme. Whatever proposals the League came up with, Sunderland would not be competing in the near future. Eventually the League proposed a division between north and south with clubs permitted to choose their own opponents within their sector. It was hoped clubs would play at least 20 matches each. There would be no points awarded for wins or draws and league tables would be compiled entirely on goal averages. This would overcome the problem of some clubs being able to complete more games than others. Along with 20 other clubs Sunderland did not participate in these arrangements.

Consequently, footballing opportunities for Raich Carter as a regular fireman were severely limited. In August he played for a Sunderland Police team against Bill Murray's XI in aid of the Spitfire Fund. Guests included Jimmy Connor and Hughie Gallacher and a very satisfactory £200 was raised. In November Carter played for the Sunderland Police in a match against the Gordon Highlanders' XI in aid of the Mayor's Boot Fund for Children. The police proved too strong for the soldiers at Roker Park but the Highlanders were sporting opponents. The chief constable announced that £30 would go to the Mayor's Fund. The chief and his deputy, Ted Smith (Carter's uncle), were both keen football enthusiasts and encouraged any opportunity for the police team to play. In December there were several games against army teams; unfortunately, against the Royal Engineers, Carter was injured with a suspected broken arm.

As far as Britain was concerned, since July 1940 the war had to be waged in the air. The Luftwaffe tried to establish air superiority in order to allow Hitler's invasion plan, Operation Sea Lion, to succeed. By mid-September, as the Battle of Britain reached its climax, the invasion plan was abandoned. However, throughout late autumn and winter, bombers continued to attack London and the larger industrial cities. The German bombing campaign put the Sunderland people into the front line. In all, the town suffered 42 air attacks which caused damage or casualties, the first on 27th June 1940 and the last nearly three years later. While there was nothing like a blitz as in Coventry or Plymouth, Sunderland was the most heavily bombed town north of Hull with 267 civilians killed and more than 1,000 injured.

During early 1941, the long hours of the fire brigade routine began to tell on Raich Carter's health and he suffered from a series of abscesses. He began to feel increasingly unhappy with his life in the fire service. The biggest fire that he had been involved in was that at Binns, a large department store hit by an incendiary raid on 10th April 1941. The fire was so bad that every brigade in the district was called out. At one point, after one building had been evacuated, Raich Carter and a colleague were ordered back into the building to recover a length of hose left on the second floor. The smoke was acrid and the heat was more intense as they climbed stair by stair. Raich reached a point where he could go no further but his mate attempted to continue only to collapse a couple of stairs ahead. Then Raich felt really apprehensive. He struggled to carry his mate to safety and managed to stagger to the street with him. They were later informed that the hose had not been left behind after all. The heroics had been for nothing. Despite these efforts Carter continued to be subjected to taunts about his fire service career and they were increasingly difficult to stomach.

On 8th February 1941, England played Scotland at St James' Park in support of the Red Cross. Carter's lack of match practice gave the selectors the opportunity to give a debut at inside-right to the startlingly blond Wilf Mannion, who had been plucked from the beaches of Dunkirk the year before. The Scots had a glimpse of a potentially dangerous opponent although, on this occasion, the Scots won 3-2. The match produced more than £2,000, to the delight of the Football Association and the Red Cross.

The repeated question in the opening months of 1941 said the *Sunderland Echo* was, "When will Sunderland AFC return to competitive football?" It was pointed out, just before the annual meeting in April, that if Newcastle and Middlesbrough managed to compete, why not Sunderland? The directors were thought too apprehensive about possible small losses during the war compared with the large cost of completely rebuilding a team in peacetime. Murray sought to reduce the club's deficit by playing a friendly at St James' Park on Monday 14th April. Sunderland won 4-3 and Carter and Gurney were among the scorers, but more importantly the club made £100. A week later Winston Churchill, now Prime Minister, made a whirlwind visit to Wearside, touring five shipyards, and praised the grand spirit of the town. Early in May, the Royal Northumberland Fusiliers came to play a Sunderland Police team which included four Sunderland players with Raich Carter at inside-left. A week later Murray played a friendly against Middlesbrough and was again successful 4-3. Carter was man of the match scoring three goals, making chances and helping the defence out from time to time.

More serious news from London was the bombing of the House of Commons. This was quickly followed by the bombing of Sunderland's Victoria Hall which, for 70 years, had played a unique role in the town's social life. It had housed many memorable moments including politicians: Herbert Asquith, Randolph Churchill and Stanley Baldwin plus musicians like Edward Elgar, Sir Thomas Beecham, Dame Nellie Melba, Clara Butt and John McCormack.

In early June 1941, the Sunderland club announced it was prepared to resume football in the new season 1941-42. One reason for the director's decision was to help the manager who was unable to sign anyone while the team was not playing. On 1st

July the Football League said that for the next season 73 clubs had entered and that they would be divided into two sections, north and south. Sunderland had joined the northern section and their opening fixture would be against Sheffield United. The two leagues would conclude by 25th December. Bill Murray was banking on the chief constable releasing Arthur Housam, Ralph Rogerson, Harry Thompson and Raich Carter from duties wherever possible. Meantime, Raich was hoping to play cricket for the police against the Northumberland Fusiliers who were expected to include Major Herbert Sutcliffe, the former England opener.

In the latter part of August the usual two trial matches were played at Roker Park. Of the old brigade Alex Hastings showed that he was still one of the best wing halves in the game and Carter, while taking it easy, showed all his old skills. For the opening game against Sheffield, Len Duns, back on leave, was included alongside Raich Carter at inside-right. League football returned to Roker Park after nearly two years and to celebrate Sunderland won 7-1. The 10,000 gate was considered excellent for a wartime match. The Duns-Carter wing operated with all its old skill and Raich Carter helped himself to a hat-trick including the opening goal of the season. A week later the return game ended 1-0 to Sunderland with Raich Carter outshining Sheffield's star inside forward, Jimmy Hagan.

After two years at war the town of Sunderland had lived up to its motto 'Nil Desperandum' (never despair). It had survived some heavy bombing and its courageous seamen fought out the Battle of the Atlantic. Within days of the Dunkirk evacuation several thousand men from 16 to 80 had joined the Home Guard. Also, among the 'immortal few' who fought and won the Battle of Britain, there were Sunderland men.

In the match at Bradford Park Avenue Raich Carter scored both Sunderland goals in a 2-2 draw. The first was described as "as good as anything seen for years." The second was more fortunate, being a sliced shot which went in off a post. It was reported that Raich said it did not matter how you got them so long as you did get them. Playing for Bradford that day was a future Sunderland star Len Shackleton. On 22nd September the *Sunderland Echo* warned that the club might soon lose the services of Raich Carter for a while. He had applied to be released from the Fire Service in order to join the RAF. His request to the fire chief was granted without fuss. His medical was passed in Newcastle and, on 2nd October 1941, he reported to Blackpool for basic training.

Chapter Fourteen
The War and the RAF

THE RAF station at Blackpool was the biggest in Britain. There were 60,000 airmen and women passing through at any one time. During the War, 770,000 RAF personnel were posted to the resort. The Air Ministry had taken over 5,000 hotels and boarding houses and 40 shops plus offices and sea front buildings to accommodate its servicemen. Even the famous Winter Gardens were commandeered. AC2 H S Carter, number 1546973, was relieved to have escaped from unfair taunts received while in the Sunderland Fire Service.

Surprisingly, AC2 Carter was released at the first weekend and dashed back to play against Leeds. The 6-1 victory was easier than anticipated and it was Carter's best game for months. The brilliance of this play could be interpreted as a celebration of his entry into the RAF. It was no secret to Argus that Raich Carter had been longing to get into a service uniform for some time. The journalist asked who was the greatest Sunderland inside forward – George Holley, Charlie Buchan or Raich Carter? Certainly, he concluded, Carter is a great footballer.

For the next four or five weeks it was impossible for Carter to get to Sunderland for kick-off time and then back by 10.30 p.m. He made three guest appearances for Huddersfield and scored five goals for them. As soon as he was entitled to a long weekend, early in November, Carter was back in the Sunderland side against Bradford City. The following week, Sunderland were expecting him to be available for the return game at Valley Parade but ten minutes after the kick-off a telephone message was received from Carter to say that he could not reach Bradford. Instead, he asked permission from manager, now Captain, Bill Murray to play for Huddersfield.

This incident illustrates the problems of wartime transport and the regulations imposed by military stations. Ironically, the next weekend, 22nd November, Carter was in the Sunderland team to play Huddersfield at Roker Park and missed a penalty. Early in December he was posted to a unit in Yorkshire and it was hoped that this would make it easier to get to Sunderland for matches. In fact, for his first game in January 1942, Raich Carter guested for York City – the third club he had played for as a guest. This decision would not disqualify him from turning out for Sunderland in the Wartime Cup because that competition had not yet started.

Raich Carter was also called upon to play football for the RAF. Later in January he was chosen to represent the RAF against Scotland. The strength of the team the RAF could field is shown in that eleven: Marks (Arsenal); Turner (Charlton); Hapgood (Arsenal); Shankly (Preston), Jones T G (Everton), Paterson (Celtic); Kirchin (Arsenal), Carter (Sunderland), Dodds (Blackpool), Soo (Stoke), Brown (Charlton). Practically all were internationals. Soon, of course, Carter would be lining up with another airman available to the selectors, Stan Matthews.

At the end of January 1942, Raich Carter reported to RAF St Athan in Wales to take a course which would qualify him as a Physical Training Instructor (PTI). This was a familiar choice of trade for former professional footballers. Sceptics wondered whether footballers were necessarily the best recruits for this soft option. After all, Wilf Mannion was in the infantry with the Green Howards.

The news from the war fronts was mixed. The German blitzkrieg against the Soviet Union had gained them 600 miles of Russian territory before the tide was turned at Leningrad. In the Far East the Japanese advance was also rapid and they succeeded in capturing Singapore, but the attack on Pearl Harbour had serious repercussions. Before long the world's greatest neutral power, the USA, joined with the Allies against the Axis, transforming a primarily European struggle into a world war.

For Raich Carter the months of February and March 1942 were dominated by the PTI training course at St Athan and the logistics of getting home to Sunderland, especially as a new cup run was close at hand. For the first round proper 32 clubs qualified via the League Cup Qualifying Competition.

Sunderland were drawn against Oldham who they beat 5-2 over two legs. This brought a tie against Bradford City, the first leg of which Bradford won 2-1. At half-time in the second leg Sunderland were a further goal behind and immediately after the interval went another goal behind. Then Carter scored twice to bring Sunderland back into contention only for Bradford to score again. All seemed lost until centre-forward Cliff Whitelum hit three goals in 12 minutes. Result 6-4 and a place in the next round against the other Bradford team, Park Avenue.

For the second leg Sunderland benefited from the guesting system because the great Newcastle centre-forward Albert Stubbins played. A crowd of 15,000 turned up at Roker Park to see the man who was in prolific form for the Magpies, totalling 33 goals by the end of the season. Sunderland progressed by the odd goal even though Carter missed a penalty. In the semi-final Sunderland prevailed over Grimsby who were assisted by Manchester City's Peter Doherty. Within a year Raich and Peter would be posted to the same station where a fruitful partnership would develop. Sunderland's positional play meant the Grimsby defence was run ragged but in the Final (Northern) Wolves would be a different proposition.

In the first leg against Wolves at Roker Park Sunderland fielded both Stubbins, Newcastle's top scorer, and Whitelum, their own top scorer. Stubbins was accommodated at inside-right while Raich Carter moved across to inside-left. Also in the Sunderland line-up were Jimmy Gorman and Alex Hastings from the cup final year. Although Wolves were without their rising young star Billy Wright they still matched Sunderland's two goals scored by Stubbins and Carter. In the return match the Molineux held 43,038 spectators and they cheered Wolves on to a 4-1 win. Raich Carter again scored but Jack Rowley, guesting from Manchester United, scored twice for Wolves.

Since the completion of his PTI course, Raich Carter had been posted to RAF Usworth, a fighter operational training unit at Washington near Sunderland. This posting obviously allowed him to play for Sunderland much more regularly and in total he made 27 appearances. It also meant a new rank for the qualified PTI, temporary corporal.

During the summer of 1942 Raich Carter was able to make occasional appearances for the Sunderland Police cricket team in the Durham Senior League. The police were a strong side and, late in August, stood second in the league table. By that time

Sunderland AFC were holding their traditional public trial matches in preparation for the new season. The opening fixture was away to Bradford City and wartime conditions set manager Murray some problems. The Sunderland goalkeeper Albert Heyward lived and worked in West Hartlepool. His usual routine for away games was to meet the team at Darlington station. On this occasion the train was late and the team left for Leeds without him. Both Leeds and Bradford offered to lend Bill Murray a goalkeeper and he chose the Leeds player. However, Heyward had caught a later train to Leeds where, instead of the bus, he found a taxi ordered and waiting. So Heyward played having eaten only a single biscuit since working all night. Carter scored but Sunderland lost. The return game a week later, 5th September, was won by Sunderland 3-1. The local press noted that Raich Carter was carrying much more weight than before the war and that he did not show the burst of speed through defences that was a feature of his play. But, it added, "it would much sooner he played for Sunderland than against them."

At the end of September Raich Carter was chosen for an all-international RAF team to play Wales: Marks (Eng); Hardwick (Eng), Hapgood (Eng); Shankly (Scot), Joy (Eng), Paterson (Scot); Matthews (Eng), Carter (Eng), Dodds (Scot), Doherty (Ire), Smith (Eng). A fortnight later Carter was selected for a Football League team which included Tom Finney and Len Shackleton. Later in October the England team were beaten at Wolverhampton by a gallant Welsh team. Argus was concerned about the England selectors for choosing three centre-forwards (Rooke, Lawton, Gibbons) in the attack and went on to say they should not be allowed to pick another international team because they had diminished the honour of playing for England by their choices. In fact, the only irrational choice they made was that of Jack Gibbons who had so far played as an amateur in the 1930s and for the RAF in peacetime. Argus' real complaint was that Raich Carter had been overlooked again even though he remained one of the best players in the country.

The war was beginning to swing decisively towards the Allies by October 1942. In North Africa, General Montgomery, Commander of the British Eighth Army, routed Rommel's Afrika Korps at the battle of El Alamein. Meanwhile, on the Eastern Front, the Russians had begun a counter offence at Leningrad while, to the South, they had repelled an all-out Nazi attack on Stalingrad.

Raich Carter returned to the Sunderland team for the fixture with Leeds on 31st October. In the *Echo* match report it stated that

Leeds had become rattled and had beaten themselves by resorting to questionable tactics. They seemed determined 'to get at' Carter but, although he was not a big man, he could mix it with the rest and he was not so easy to foul when he was expecting it to come. That was why Carter was the complete clubman because you could have pure football if you wanted it, but if the opposition wanted to play rough then Carter wouldn't run out of the way. This description gives an insight into why Raich Carter became such a legendary player.

Around this time, two stars of the future, Bill Nicholson of Spurs and Harry Potts of Burnley, began to guest for Sunderland. Between them they made 24 appearances for the club. In November, Sunderland played Middlesbrough and the player who stood out head and shoulders above the rest, not in stature but in skill, was Raich Carter. He was the master craftsman behind most attacks and his display was of international standard. However, the England selectors had ignored him since the match against Scotland at Newcastle in December 1939. Since then, 13 wartime internationals had been played and the inside forward positions had been held by such talented players as Jimmy Hagan (7), Wilf Mannion (4), Len Goulden (4) and Maurice Edelston (5). Meanwhile, Carter had to be content with representing the RAF and, on 21st November, he linked up again with Stan Matthews against a Football Association XI. The Sunderland press remained sceptical about Matthews as a partner to Carter because he was too much of an individualist and did not exploit Carter's ability to create space. Early in December Carter was again forming a right wing with Matthews at St James' Park, Newcastle. Carter scored three out of four RAF goals but also contributed to the success of Matthews by taking the Scots defenders away from the Stoke winger. More importantly, the crowd of 28,000 boosted significantly the RAF Benevolent Fund.

It was at this time that PTI Corporal Carter was promoted to temporary sergeant. The country in general was welcoming the Beveridge Report, 'Making Britain a better place to live in.' The question of whether the country could afford it was answered in the report itself: "We cannot afford not to afford it." The other answer was that the scheme was remarkably cheap at £75 million, about the cost of one week at war.

Raich Carter was not available to play for Sunderland on Boxing Day because of a representative match. He had begun to notice, while playing regularly for the RAF with mainly the same players, a greater understanding and improved team work. Service matches were much more frequent than peacetime internationals so the standard of play improved considerably. The same was true of the Army team where Lawton, Mercer, Cullis and Swift played regularly together. Therefore, when the selectors met to pick the international team instead of dealing with 22 clubs, they simply looked to the Army and RAF teams.

As 1942 closed, the news from North Africa and the Eastern Front was very encouraging. The Eighth Army was pursuing Rommel across the desert while the Russians were breaking through into Latvia and the North Caucasus.

In January 1943 Sunderland met Middlesbrough in a League Cup match. Middlesbrough defensive tactics kept Sunderland down to a 1-0 lead at half-time. In the second half they conceded six more goals as the close marking of Carter was broken down by Carter taking his marker on two or three 'walks.' However, Sunderland's results between 26th December 1942 and 27th December 1943 in the cup qualifying competition were not good enough to go into the knock-out stages. Better news from the international front came when Raich Carter was chosen for the England team against Wales at Wembley on 27th February 1943. It was three years and three months since his previous appearance and his teammates were: Marks; Bacuzzi, Hapgood; Britton, Cullis, Mercer; Matthews, Carter, Westcott, Hagan, Compton D.

Chapter Fifteen

The War and International Football

THE MATCH between England and Wales in February 1943 was England's 17th wartime international. In total they would play 36 wartime and victory internationals and call on 78 players. No caps were awarded and no victories or defeats credited to their careers. The official view ranged from pretending they did not happen to dismissing them as meaningless friendlies. Such an assessment is a grave injustice, especially to the players, 40 of whom did win full caps either before or after the war. In fact, the war years produced dramatic and accomplished matches featuring many gifted and charismatic players. It also saw the development of a very fine England team which dominated its opponents from 1943 to 1947.

For Raich Carter's return to international duty, England faced an unchanged Welsh side which had done so well the previous November at Wolverhampton. This time the match was to be played at Wembley and the 75,000 tickets sold was a wartime record. Despite the November result England started the match as firm favourites mainly because of the four changes made in their attack. The predictions proved accurate and England's class told in one of the best internationals ever played at Wembley. The score of 5-3 created a record aggregate of goals, beating England's 5-2 win over Scotland in 1930. The Welsh put up a great defensive fight in the first half when England scored two rapid goals and threatened to run away with the game. However, it was always a losing battle because the left side of their defence was "outclassed by Matthews and Carter, the cleverest right wing England have fielded for many years," according to *The Daily Telegraph*. All the England goals were beautifully taken but Carter's two volleys were hit when he had only split seconds to shoot. All the press agreed that he had played himself into the England team for the match with Scotland in April.

As Sunderland were out of the cup there were several clubs seeking Raich Carter as a guest to improve their cup prospects. Sunderland left the decision to him and he decided not to go elsewhere when his own club had a fixture. This decision would have earned the appreciation of Sunderland supporters. On the 27th March Carter was chosen to play for the RAF against the Royal Netherlands Forces in the Inter Allies services cup at Brentford. Before that game took place Carter became a father for the first time with the birth of daughter Jennifer, on 19th March 1943. The next day he played against Middlesbrough and although Sunderland scored eight he did not get one. In that match he worked as a maker of chances for others. Middlesbrough's gloom was deepened by the news from the middle east that Wilf Mannion had received leg injuries in a German raid. While Raich Carter helped the RAF team dispose of the Netherlands XI, Sunderland floundered without him, acting like a ship without a rudder.

Early in April, the England team to play Scotland on 17th was announced. The brilliant attack remained unchanged but there were two new fullbacks, George Hardwick and Leslie Compton, and a new goalkeeper in Frank Swift. It was not thought that these changes would weaken the side, although it was sad to lose Eddie Hapgood after 13 wartime internationals. Hardwick's main memory of the game was that it was the only time he saw Carter shed his normally nonchalant attitude and crack his poker face in a game.

A corner by the Scots crossed into the England penalty area where it was brilliantly headed towards the top corner of the net. Hardwick, positioned on the line, managed to spring high enough to deflect the ball over the bar. To his amazement Carter ran from the edge of the area, threw his arms around him and kissed him on the cheek and said, "Well done son." Never again did he see him show any outward sign of emotion even when he scored from 25 yards.

Behind England's handsome 4-0 win was the triangle formed on the right-hand side by Cliff Britton, Matthews and Carter. During the first half Carter's fierce drives forced saves from the Scots' goalkeeper, but two goals were also struck by the inside-right. The *Sunderland Echo* was at last convinced that Raich Carter and Stan Matthews could strike up a partnership which would keep them both in the England team for the next few years.

The pair were due to play together again on Easter Monday for the RAF against the Army. Then, on 8th May, England took an unchanged team to Cardiff to play the final international of the season. The game was disappointing from England's point of view as they equalised Wales' first half goal only eight minutes from the end. For Dennis Westcott, the Wolves centre-forward, this was his fifth goal in four games for England. Nevertheless, he lost his place in the team and was not chosen again mainly due to the competition from Tommy Lawton. The Welsh tactics were to crowd out the England right wing and whenever Matthews received the ball he was surrounded by three or four opponents.

In contrast to the large crowds which international matches attracted, more modest contests might be pleased to have 300 or 400 in attendance. One such game at Eppleton Colliery Welfare, Hetton, took place just before the Cardiff match between an RAF XI led by Raich Carter and the local Air Training Corps. The RAF won 10-4 with Raich scoring six, but, more importantly, the proceeds went to Wings for Victory Week.

By 21st May, Raich Carter had switched to his favourite summer game. He played for the Sunderland Police cricket club against Wearmouth at his old home ground in Hendon. In June he played against Seaham, Burnmoor and Chester-le-Street. Unfortunately, it was evident that the Hendon Cricket Club was now defunct.

Further evidence of the progress of the Allies came from the news that the King had paid a visit to the Allied Armed Forces in North Africa. At the same time the RAF made its heaviest bombing raid on Germany, dropping 2,000 tons on Dortmund. Such success prompted Winston Churchill to hint that a second front was being contemplated. By mid-June he became more specific, forecasting an invasion of France in the autumn.

In the spring of 1943, the German airforce again turned its attention to the north east. A photograph from the Luftwaffe archives showed how dangerously close Roker Park was to military targets like the shipyards. On 14th March a stray bomb landed on the pitch, but an air raid on 16th May damaged the main stand and destroyed the old clubhouse on the corner of Roker Baths Road. Again pitch was damaged. Tragically, an auxiliary policeman was killed in this attack. The estimated cost of repairing the damage to Roker Park was between £4,000 and £5,000. However, at that time, the club had the authority to spend only £500 for emergency repairs.

Of more immediate concern to Raich Carter was the fact that his own house had been damaged by enemy action. Fortunately, his wife and daughter had already moved out and were living in Chaddesden, Derby. The move was considered advisable because Rose Carter had not enjoyed good health since the birth of her daughter, and Derby was where her parents were now based. It also removed them from the bombing attacks on Sunderland's shipyards.

After scoring 75 for Sunderland Police against Whitburn on 10th July, Raich Carter played little other cricket that summer. The Allies continued their advance and, on the same day as the Whitburn match, they invaded Sicily by moonlight. The attack was said to be going as planned. Just over a fortnight later Mussolini, the Italian dictator, was forced out of office and replaced by Pietro Badoglio who maintained the alliance with Hitler until September.

The new football season, 1943-44, was due to open on the last Saturday of August. Raich Carter was expected to be available when the RAF did not need him. Along with Alex Hastings he made an impressive contribution to the pre-season practice games. However, Sunderland's hopes that the RAF would not prove too demanding were not fulfilled. In the opening match at Roker Park, Leeds were defeated 7-0 without Carter scoring. Nevertheless, the press were unstinting in their praise for his contribution to the victory. He was all over the pitch in a manner which was a tribute to his fitness. One minute he was initiating attacks, the next he was taking throw-ins and the next he was passing back to the goalkeeper. After the game the Leeds chairman Ernest Pullan went into the dressing room and shook hands with Raich Carter and is reported as saying, "If we'd had a man to run about as you did, we might have done better."

The new international season opened on 25th September when England opposed Wales at Wembley. The Welsh, despite all their traditional fervour, were not expected to be strong enough to hold England despite having ten of the players who had achieved a draw four months earlier.

The Daily Telegraph described the England forward line as prolific and believed the rediscovery of Horatio Carter had created the most effective right wing for years. Matthews' unorthodox ways left many of his former partners "in the air." But Carter understood how to play up to him. In addition, Carter was an exceptional finisher himself. The left wing was considered to be almost as powerful. Jimmy Hagan was the best inside-left in the country while Denis Compton had rapidly developed Matthews' self-confident ball control. The match produced a new Wembley record for goals as England won 8-3. However, for most of the game, it was probably too one-sided to maintain spectator interest. Except for a quarter of an hour after the interval when Wales pulled back from 4-1 down to 4-3, they were outclassed. It might have been worse for Wales had not an Englishman, Stan Mortensen, come on as a substitute for Ivor Powell, who had broken his collarbone. This was the first time a substitute had been used at Wembley. England limited their service to Matthews because they anticipated a Welsh plan to heavily mark him. Raich Carter was England's best forward scoring two splendid goals. Hagan also scored twice while centre-forward Don Welsh got three.

Immediately following the Wembley international, Carter was posted to RAF Innsworth Lane, Gloucester. Obviously, this move would significantly affect his availability for Sunderland AFC. The new posting involved PTI Sgt Carter in much basic PT classes with both airmen and WAAFs. From his point of view, while the work was light-hearted and enjoyable, it did not seem to be making any tangible contribution towards victory. At this point Carter received permission to guest for Derby County despite an offer from West Bromwich Albion, which was closer to Gloucester. However, with his wife and baby daughter in Derby, he was able to make a strong case for guesting there. The *Sunderland Echo* lamented on 11th October that Carter had scored three goals for Derby and that he had scored two or three goals in every game that season, except when he was playing for Sunderland. Then he became the provider of goals for others.

For the international against Scotland on 16th October at Maine Road, Manchester, England restored Frank Swift, Joe Mercer and Tommy Lawton to their team. *The News of the World* declared, after the Scots were swamped 8-0, that this was England's perfect soccer team. It went on that old timers could say what they liked, but this was a wonderful England team. In fact, old timers agreed, led by Charles Wreford-Brown, ex-selector and former Corinthians and England player in the 1890s, who wrote, "This England team showed perhaps the greatest combination and teamwork in the whole history of international football. I myself have never seen anything like it before." Another veteran, Ivan Sharpe, agreed, saying he thought it "England's best team since 1907. For this there was a reason, services football brought them into action more frequently than is possible in normal times. They developed understanding."

It was an irresistible display of power and precision which won the approval of both players and spectators. The England captain Stan Cullis who gave a glorious display of attacking centre-half play said: "This was the finest football I have ever seen." The halfback line of Britton, Cullis and Mercer equalled any England had chosen for 30 years. Mercer said: "It was the greatest game I can remember," while Frank Swift, the goalkeeper, said: "It was the finest team I ever played in."

The Rangers right half Adam Little had been chosen in place of Bill Shankly but he had to sit an exam in medicine the day before the match, then travelled through the night to play. Shankly claimed that he was relieved not to be selected against such an England XI. He went on to say that "this was a great England team. They had wonderful players in the team and just as many waiting to get a game." Tommy Lawton wrote: "I can honestly say that I have never played in a better side than the England one on that day. Furthermore, despite that 1953 Cup Final, I don't think 'the old maestro', Stan Matthews, had ever played better.' Frank Swift paid tribute to the courage of the Scots team while *The News of the World* wrote that the Scots goalkeeper, Joe Crozier of Brentford, could not be blamed for the result: he even saved a penalty by Raich Carter!

Both Swift and Lawton and others have described how, when England were already 3-0 up after an hour, the team tried to set up a goal for Stan Matthews. Raich Carter had waltzed through the Scots defence, then paused with his foot on the ball until Matthews arrived to shoot home. In fact, he mis-kicked and the ball flew to Lawton, who sent it in the net to complete his hat-trick. However, Matthews was not to be denied. It was his game and he strolled through the complete defence on his own and side-footed the ball past Crozier. The whole crowd rose and roared for minutes. Even the Scots applauded! There seemed to be only one dissenting voice amongst the chorus of approval. That was 'Gentleman George' Hardwick, the England left back. He felt many of the claims made about England's display were invalid because of the quality of the opposition. That day he believed the Scots fielded a weak team.

Following the classic Manchester international, Raich Carter returned to a diet of league and cup games for Derby County intermixed with matches for the RAF. He scored six goals for Derby in eight games before the end of 1943. Unfortunately, in his first match of the new year, Carter pulled a muscle in the first quarter of an hour. He returned to the pitch after five minutes and hobbled down the left wing. Nevertheless, he still managed to score a goal and almost got a second while Nottingham Forest were making the running. He rushed his recovery by playing the next week, only to aggravate the injury while missing a comparatively easy chance. As a consequence, Carter was forced to withdraw from the RAF team to play the FA, as well as from a couple of Derby County games. At the same time the Sunderland local press were regretting the loss of Raich Carter and envying Derby's use of him.

While playing at Derby, Raich Carter met the Commanding Officer of Loughborough Rehabilitation Centre. The club used to set aside seats at each home game for two coachloads of patients from Loughborough. Raich was soon taking a close interest in the work of the centre. The idea of helping injured airman regain the use of their damaged limbs seemed like a really worthwhile contribution to the war effort. How much support and influence the commanding officer felt able to give on Raich Carter's behalf is not clear. What is certain is that a posting to Loughborough soon came through and Carter was delighted with it. On his arrival at No 3 MRU Raich Carter was told to report to his Squadron Leader at the gymnasium. This turned out to be Dan Maskell, a leading tennis professional and coach, who later became famous commentating for BBC television on tennis. The gym was packed full with 70 or 80 airmen split into classes of eight or ten doing a variety of exercises. One thing which struck Raich immediately was that everyone present, except the instructors, was wearing a plaster cast.

When he had a free moment, Maskell welcomed the newcomer and said, "OK, you start as a patient and get to know the whole routine." So, for a week, Carter spent his time as a patient trying to put himself into the position of someone in plaster and struggling to restore co-ordination between brain and muscles. In between time the new recruit received instruction in anatomy from doctors, much of which was difficult for a footballer to take in at first. However, it was not long before Raich Carter grasped the basic principle of how the various parts of the body worked. He was assigned to a spinal class where many of the new arrivals were in a bad way, both physically and mentally. It was a very rewarding duty to be involved

*The young Raich Carter in the running vest made by
his Aunt Jenny from Uncle Ted's silk shirt.*

Raich Carter pictured in his first year as an England Schoolboy international.

The Northern Schools team which played the South at Bournemouth. Raich Carter is fourth from the right wearing black shorts. (Hull Daily Mail)

We won the cup, Sunderland players carry Raich Carter on their shoulders as they celebrate at Wembley. (courtesy Sunderland Evening Echo)

In action at Roker Park. (courtesy Sunderland Evening Echo)

Raich Carter as Sunderland captain at the toss before a match. (Newcastle Journal)

The Sunderland FA Cup team – except the cup was elsewhere. (back row l/r) Charlie Thompson, Bert Johnston, Jimmy Gorman, Johnny Mapson, Alec Hall, Sandy McNab, (front row) Johnny Cochrane (manager), Raich Carter, Bobby Gurney, Paddy Gallagher, Andy Reid (trainer), (on ground) Len Duns, Eddie Burbanks. (courtesy Sunderland Evening Echo)

Raich Carter as a fireman at the start of the Second World War. He came to regret not joining the services sooner.

Derby's 1946 FA Cup winning team do have the cup. (back row l/r) Jack Parr, Jim Bullions, Jack Nicholas, Vic Woodley, Jack Howe, Leon Leuty, Chick Musson, (front row) Sammy Crooks, Jack Stamps, Stuart McMillan (manager), directors T E Wassel, B Robshaw (chairman), H Walker and JR Cholerton, Peter Doherty, Raich Carter, Dave Willis (trainer), (on ground) Reg Harrison and Dally Duncan. (Derby Evening Telegraph)

Action from Raich Carter's last match for Derby – against Blackpool at the Baseball Ground. (Derby Evening Telegraph)

Raich Carter could have had a career as a First-Class cricketer. He played three matches for Derbyshire while at Derby County. (Derby Evening Telegraph)

in the gradual recovery of these patients. Raich Carter certainly felt the satisfaction of doing something really worthwhile.

At the end of January 1944, Carter signalled his return to full fitness by scoring twice for Derby County in a 4-1 win over Sheffield Wednesday. For the international against Scotland at Wembley on 19th February the England team showed two changes from the previous match. Ted Ditchburn of Spurs received his first call to play in goal while on the left wing Leslie Smith deputised for Denis Compton. This match was played in front of the King George VI and Queen Elizabeth, Princess Elizabeth, King Haakon of Norway, the deputy Prime Minister, Clement Attlee, and General Montgomery. The young Scots team had a good first half which finished with the teams level 1-1. However, an unfortunate own goal early in the second half deflated the Scots' resistance and the England team took control. In the Scots mid-field, Matt Busby had a fine game while Jimmy Hagan scored twice for England. The final England goal to make the score 6-2 came from Raich Carter.

Back at Derby County, the club announced that from 1st March they would have a new manager Ted Magner. He was well qualified for the job having had long experience as an FA coach. It was his foresight and hard work which created the great cup-winning team of 1946. Meanwhile Derby received permission from Sunderland to select Carter in the League Cup competition. With Sammy Crooks as his right-wing partner, Raich Carter was ready to take on Coventry City. He was described as pre-eminent among the forwards of either side and the *Derby Evening Telegraph* stated, "his generalship was allied with such a degree of virility that the whole Derby structure seemed to depend on him."

Towards the end of March, the RAF were able to choose eight internationals in their team to play the Army. They included Ted Ditchburn, Laurie Scott, George Hardwick, Stan Matthews, Leslie Smith and Carter. The combination of representative games and injuries kept Carter out of the Derby team from the end of March until mid-April. With another international against Scotland due on 22nd April it was essential for Carter to prove his fitness, which he did by making a rare appearance for Sunderland against Gateshead. It was apparent that he took care to avoid any risk. He was declared fit for the match at Hampden Park.

Raich Carter's fitness meant that England could field the same forward line as two months earlier. In defence several changes were necessary, however, but the restoration of Frank Swift, Frank Soo and Leslie Compton did not seem to weaken the line up. With the news from the war front improving all the time public interest in football revived and a wartime record crowd of 133,000 turned up at Hampden Park. This was the eve of D-Day and the guest of honour was General Montgomery who held in his mind the secret date of the Normandy landings. It turned out to be a rough, tough match with the Scots desperate to end their traditional foes' run of success. The Hampden roar became a war cry, especially when Jimmy Caskie, the Everton winger, gave them the lead. However, they were silenced by two typically opportunist goals by Tommy Lawton and a third by Raich Carter, all within ten minutes. This just made the Scots' tackling fiercer, especially in the second half when pressure on England captain Stan Cullis caused him to head into his own goal. Nevertheless England held out for a 3-2 win.

Seven days later there was a charity match at Chelsea between an England XI and the Combined Services with Carter being selected for the Combined Services at inside-left while the team was captained by Matt Busby. On 6th May the final England match of the season took place against Wales in Cardiff. This was one of the few wartime internationals which Stan Matthews missed, his place going to Billy Elliott of West Bromwich Albion. Also absent after 13 wartime internationals was Jimmy Hagan, who was replaced by Jack Rowley of Manchester United. These late changes and a stubborn Welsh defence contributed to an uninspiring match in which Lawton and Smith scored for England while Carter hit the bar. The two successes in the Welsh team were Walley Barnes, of Arsenal, and Ronnie Burgess, of Spurs.

A week later another wartime charity match was arranged between Derby County and Huddersfield. On this occasion Raich Carter and Stan Matthews were on opposite sides as the Stoke winger guested for Huddersfield. Also helping them out was Len Shackleton and, between them, they inspired a 4-3 win with Carter getting one of the Derby goals. That match completed a fifth wartime football season for Raich Carter.

During the spring and summer the news from the war fronts was consistently good. By the end of May the Allies were in sight of Rome which fell on 5th June. This was followed by the long awaited 'Second Front' in which a mighty fleet of 4,000 vessels sailed for the Normandy beaches. Operation Overlord, commanded by General Eisenhower, managed to land 326,000 troops in France by the sixth day. By 2nd July nearly a million men had been landed and the Germans were in retreat.

With his duties based in Loughborough and his family settled in Derby there were no opportunities for Raich Carter to play cricket for Sunderland Police in the summer of 1944. During his time at Loughborough a course of physical training and games was arranged for Allied Forces. Raich Carter's contribution was to lecture on football to a party of American soldiers who had never seen the game. He gave a wide-ranging talk about the game but whether the off-side law was fully comprehended is uncertain. It certainly provoked the most questions.

By mid-August the *Derby Evening Telegraph* was able to reveal that Raich Carter would again be available to play for Derby County in the forthcoming season. It went on to say, more enigmatically, that another international inside forward might be secured by the club. It was soon revealed that Peter Doherty, the Irish international, was to play for Derby when his own club, Manchester City, did not need him. Doherty had had a stormy relationship with his club from the outbreak of war. He resented the haste with which Manchester City had cancelled his contract while they doggedly retained his registration. This meant they continued to control his football career regardless of how far he was posted away from Manchester and despite the fact they no longer paid him. Fortunately, his arrival at No 3 MRU Loughborough enabled him to guest for Derby County in similar fashion to Raich Carter's arrangement.

However, few people in August 1944 would have predicted the significance of this combination of inside forward talent in Derby County colours. Indeed, when the history of the club was written more than 50 years later, a chapter was devoted to Carter and Doherty. In fact the telepathic understanding between the two players was immediately apparent in a pre-season practice match. The *Derby Evening Telegraph* wrote, "The way the two great players interpassed and interchanged position was a joy to watch and should give opposing defences a headache. Their deadly marksmanship, too, should compensate for the lack, at present, of a really experienced centre-forward."

This good news for Derby County's prospects coincided with further successes by the Allies in Europe. Both Florence and Paris were liberated late in August 1944. In early September the improving military situation was reflected in the decision to send a Combined Services team to Belfast to play Ireland. None of the 24 wartime internationals played so far had involved an Irish team. There were 50,000 Irish fans to greet a powerful Services team: Swift;

Scott, Barnes, Macauley, Joy, Busby; Matthews, Carter, Mortensen, Mullen. The Irish team included Peter Doherty, so the two new colleagues at Derby were quickly in opposition. And, as it turned out, the match was like a private duel between the two players because, at half-time, the score was 2-2 with both men scoring twice. Eventually the Irish tired and the Services, inspired by Stan Mortensen, took command and won by 8-4. However, the dual finished evenly with both Carter and Doherty scoring four goals. The following week, 16th September, the wartime internationals resumed with a match at Anfield between England and Wales. Because they were all English, not surprisingly the whole of the Combined Services forward line – Matthews, Carter, Lawton, Mortensen and Mullen – were selected for England. In defence, Frank Swift and George Hardwick returned to the side, as did the most versatile player of the war years Don Welsh, at left-half, his third international position. Once again, in wartime internationals, the Welsh proved more obdurate opponents for England than the Scots. At Anfield they matched England in all departments and took a 2-0 lead. Just before half-time Lawton made a goal for Carter and then headed in an equaliser from Mullen's cross.

Later in September, the Combined Services team was assembled to play in Paris just weeks after the liberation of the city. The French were still almost delirious with excitement at the retreat of the German armies. The match against France was played on the excellent turf of the Parc de Princes, which had been used during the occupation as a concentration camp for political prisoners. In fact, the stadium remained surrounded by a high barbed wire fence left by the Germans in their urgent departure. Frank Swift noted that, "More than half the crowd arrived by bike, including many fashionably dressed young women, most of whom were wearing silk stockings." Clearly the Americans had not wasted any time! The services team was captained by Joe Mercer and had the familiar right wing of Matthews and Carter. They won the match 5-0 and Carter scored three goals. The team then flew on to Brussels where they beat Belgium 3-0.

On 4th October 1944 the *Sunderland Echo* revealed that Raich Carter had been selected to play for England against Scotland which meant he would have played in more internationals than any other Sunderland born player. Interestingly, the newspaper was happy to add wartime appearances to full caps from before 1939. The match was at Wembley on 14th October and 90,000 spectators were present. England recalled Len Goulden of West Ham at inside-left after an absence of more than three years. More surprisingly to the modern mind was the selection of Bernard Joy of Arsenal at centre-half. Joy began his career with Casuals as an amateur and, despite his success in taking over at Arsenal from Herbert Roberts, he never turned professional.

The match was a classic example of 'a game of two halves.' The Scots scored very quickly and retained their lead for 56 minutes. The England defence was shaky and the team's performance was desultory in the first half. In the second half the England team was unrecognisable with Lawton leading the recovery: they scored three goals in nine minutes. He scored a hat-trick and had a hand in the other three goals, one of which Carter scored. This match also saw the international debut for Scotland of Darlington's Sgt Robert Thyne. He was surprisingly called up in preference to Matt Busby when Bill Shankly failed a fitness test. Thyne had received shrapnel wounds in France on D-Day plus 7, and, in order to play, had to borrow Shankly's kit. He had played no football for the first four years of the war. This game proved to be a harsh baptism for him into international football.

In October 1944 the Combined Services team were back on the continent for a tour of Belgium. Apart from the captain Matt Busby the party read like a full England team including Swift, Hardwick, Mercer, Matthews, Carter and Lawton. The team won convincingly in Liege and Bruges so that when they reached Brussels their reputation had gathered such impetus that the demand for tickets was like an FA Cup Final. As the proceeds would go to a Belgium charity, the match was a sell out. Thousands of British troops were in the crowd and they cheered the Combined Services on to a comfortable victory.

Not until early November did Carter and Doherty combine together for Derby in a 4-1 win over Notts County. Dally Duncan on the left wing was outstanding, scoring two goals. A week later Notts County were again overwhelmed by Derby's guest forwards Carter, Doherty and Charley Smith, of Aberdeen, each of whom scored twice. For the second half of November Carter took his leave back in Sunderland where he joined up again with Eddie Burbanks for a couple of games in the north east. By December he had returned to Derby where he was part of a forward line containing four guests. Together with Carter and Doherty there were Smith and Colin Lyman of Spurs. As the year of 1944 came to its conclusion, Carter and Doherty were in great form for Derby. Mansfield were beaten 4-0 and 7-1 in successive matches. In the second game Carter and Doherty scored five second-half goals between them and the *Derby Evening Telegraph* reported, "repeatedly bewildered defenders by their brilliant ball manipulation." Alick Grant, in the Mansfield goal, was spectacular and one save which prevented Carter from scoring prompted the star forward to applaud him. A week later in a 4-0 win over Rotherham Carter and Doherty, the *Telegraph* said,"did as they pleased" in breaking down a determined off-side trap. This run of fine form almost took Derby to the top of the league, but they were just held off by Huddersfield.

Chapter Sixteen

The War and Peace in 1945

DERBY COUNTY'S fine form of December 1944 continued into January 1945. The 7-0 victory over Notts County on the 20th was the biggest win of the season and was only the third time since 1918 that every Derby forward scored in a match. It was reported that most clubs had a complex about Carter and Doherty which led them to mark both players closely to prevent Derby scoring. The plan usually failed because Derby's wingers and centre-forward were also capable of scoring. A week later, also against Notts County, Raich Carter scored Derby's first hat-trick of the season. In the next match he went one better, scoring four times.

Despite his fine goal-scoring form for Derby County, Carter was left out of the England team to play Scotland on 3rd February. He had played in the previous ten internationals and the decision was as much a mystery to Carter as it was to everyone else. His place was taken by Bob (Sailor) Brown of Charlton whom the selectors had ignored for the previous five-and-a-half years. The match at Villa Park was won by England 3-2. It was another Brown, Bobby the Scots goalkeeper, who starred in the match by keeping the England forwards down to three goals.

To add to the mystery, Carter was also left out of the RAF team to play the Army on 10th March at Newcastle. According to Argus in the *Sunderland Echo*, Carter was being dropped from both teams because of one off day in the previous RAF fixture. The week after the international at Villa Park, Carter had a 48-hour pass which allowed him to travel to Sunderland and play at Roker Park against Gateshead. His performance was an inspiration to his Sunderland teammates.

The difficulties of playing in wartime were amply shown when he returned to the Midlands. He was due to play for Derby at Leicester but had not arrived by kick-off. Such was his attraction that the match was delayed for 15 minutes. The telephoned message was that Carter was still on his way and Derby started the match with ten men. After a further 20 minutes Derby decided to send on their reserve, who had been standing by.

The crowd cheered the new arrival, thinking Raich Carter had made it, but then groaned in disappointment when they realised he had not. In fact, it was half-time before Carter arrived and therefore took no part in the match.

Carter's good form for Derby continued into March including a close win at Huddersfield with only ten men. He scored both the Derby goals, the local press describing them as masterpieces. The following week Carter was back in the north east assisting Sunderland in an important game at Middlesbrough. However, the opposition had decided he was not going to be allowed to play his part by physically preventing him. So deliberate was their campaign that Alex Hastings appealed to the referee for protection.

While Carter was seeking a recall to representative football by his performances on the pitch, in the press a campaign on his behalf was led by L V Manning of *The Daily Sketch*. He wrote that Raich Carter had been "the key man in every international since 1943. Only a month or two ago Carter was by common consent the man whom Scotland and Wales must beat first, to make a game of it." England teammate Tommy Lawton found the dropping of Raich Carter inexplicable. He wrote, "Raich was the perfect team man. He would send through pinpoint passes or be there for the nod down." When Manning reported the RAF's match against the Army at Newcastle on 10th March he wrote, "there were repeated shouts for Carter and one hopes the injustice done to the player, who made the super England attack during the war years, will be corrected for Hampden. The selectors cannot avoid putting back Carter or let their reasons be known for his sudden and baffling omission against the weight of almost unanimous public opinion."

No reason for the dropping was ever given but Carter was recalled for the game against Scotland on 14th April 1945. Also included for his second appearance was Neil Franklin of Stoke City who was regarded as one of the finest centre-halves ever to have played for England. His career would lead to close links with Raich Carter in the 1950s.

The England selectors did not jettison 'Sailor' Brown after one game; they simply moved him to inside-left in place of Stan Mortensen. The nickname did not come from any nautical connection but from his distinctive rolling gait. Otherwise England were unchanged for the clash at Hampden Park.

On the day of the match Europe awoke to the news of the death of United States President Franklin D Roosevelt. Before the kick-off the crowd of 133,000 stood, bare headed, in the rain, to pay tribute to the lost US leader. The only sound to break the silence of Britain's largest arena was the strains of the 'Last Post.' The crowd then joined in the singing of 'Abide With Me', while a single Lancaster bomber approached the stadium, dipping the wings in salute when it arrived overhead. The flags of Britain, USA and Soviet Union rippled gently at half-mast.

The game opened with a first-minute collision between goalkeeper Frank Swift and Scottish forward Tommy Bogan. Unfortunately the Hibernian player suffered a torn ligament and was carried off. In wartime internationals substitutes were permitted and Les Johnstone of Clyde took over. Naturally Carter was determined to prove the selectors wrong for dropping him. He was therefore delighted to open the scoring for England after half an hour, only for substitute Johnstone to score an equaliser. At halftime the teams were level, and the vast crowd were desperate for a Scots victory during the second half. It never came as England took command and scored five goals. The final goal was from a penalty taken by Leslie Smith. He was chosen to take the kick because he was the only England forward who had not scored. The Scots had suffered the frustration of seeing Frank Swift saving a penalty from his former clubmate Matt Busby. The Scots captain had not wanted to take the kick because he remembered practising penalties against Swift when training with Manchester City before the war. Unfortunately for Busby none of his teammates volunteered. Frank Butler, in the *Daily Express,* asked, "Will there ever be another partnership to rival Matthews and Carter?" He attributed England's supremacy to Carter's class.

By this time German resistance to the Allies was crumbling. General Eisenhower had opened a great offensive on the Western

Front. General Patten captured 24 towns in his advance across the Saar while the 3rd Army progressed rapidly through the Siegfried Line. Early in March 1945 the Allies reached the Rhine as German opposition was reduced to a disorganised rabble. By 24th March General Montgomery's forces had crossed the Rhine on a broad front while the German western defences collapsed. Meantime, on the Eastern Front, the Russians were battering their way towards the centre of Berlin. An Allied victory in Europe was close at hand.

The next international was against Wales, only three weeks after the Hampden Park game. Before the game in Cardiff the England players met at the Great Western Hotel in Paddington on Friday 4th May. Tommy Lawton has described a definite feeling "that something was up." The players were joined by Stanley Rous, the FA Secretary, in the hotel lounge. The radio had been switched on and soon there was a special announcement: Germany had surrendered unconditionally and the war in Europe was over. Bill Baron, the hotel manager, immediately ordered the floodlights outside the Great Western to be switched on. This must have been one of London's first signs of celebration after six years of blackouts. The next day it rained all the way to Cardiff and Ninian Park was saturated, but the Welsh crowd was in festive mood. Nothing could dampen their enthusiasm, especially as their team of largely unknown players (except for Billy Hughes and Ronnie Burgess) put up a spirited fight and came close to upsetting England. Fortunately for the visitors, Raich Carter was in goal-scoring form, confirming that at 31 years old he still could not be left out of England's team. As at Hampden it was Carter's match and he scored all of England's three goals. Ten minutes from the end George Edwards, who had been injured in the first half, losing two teeth, scored a second goal for Wales to set up a grand finale. It was reported that Edwards' goal knocked a leek hanging in the net into the hand of a spectator. The next day, 6th May, was designated VE Day, Victory in Europe.

A week later, Carter returned to the Derby colours at Leicester. As a result of the 2-1 victory, Derby reached the final of the Midland Cup. On 19th May at Villa Park, Derby took a 3-0 lead after the first leg of the final. Carter, very well supported by Sammy Crooks on the right wing, scored all three. Two weeks after that England played France at Wembley. The only England change was the recall of Frank Soo to right half in place of George Smith. It was a very proud Tommy Lawton who was appointed captain of England for this match. The England team had been led to believe the French would provide weak opposition but they quickly found they had been misinformed. The French twice came back to force a fully deserved draw 2-2 and became the first foreign team to escape defeat on English soil. Perhaps England had become complacent after a long, hard season. Several players had just flown back from foreign tours but the French played fine football and the result served as a warning that continental teams could no longer be taken for granted. Carter and Lawton scored for England but few players in the team stood out apart from Bert Williams in goal.

One vivid memory from this period was of a team put together by Carter and Doherty while they were at Loughborough, which played charity matches against local sides. One such match was played at a packed Church Gresley on a May evening in 1945. The result was not important. The significant thing was that Raich and Peter had already played that day for Derby but still turned out again for the local supporters.

A few days before the French match the country was informed that Winston Churchill had resigned and that a general election would be held in July, the first since 1935. In San Francisco a conference of 50 countries drafted the Charter of the United Nations. Two weeks into June, London acclaimed General Eisenhower and granted him the freedom of the City.

For the forthcoming football season, 1945-46, the clubs from the pre-war First and Second Divisions were divided into two Leagues, North and South. Derby County were placed into the South Division which consisted of eight First Division clubs and 14 from the second, while Sunderland joined the North Division. Up to six guest players were to be permitted and it was expected that Raich Carter would continue to guest for Derby whenever Sunderland did not require him. As the war in the far east was still raging there was no question yet of servicemen being released back to their civilian occupations. In any case, Raich Carter's work in rehabilitation would be important to the RAF well after the cessation of hostilities.

Early in August 1945 Derby County were invited by 21st Army Group to play against service teams in Germany. However, Carter did not take part in that tour; instead he could be found playing cricket for the Sunderland Police. In a victory over South Shields he took 4-36, while a week later back at Hendon he hit 65 not out against Seaham Harbour. This innings included a six which went out of the ground and a four which broke a pavilion window. On

6th August it was announced that the FA had warned professional clubs that registered players would only be able to play in the FA Cup for their own clubs. For Derby County this would mean Carter and Doherty returning to Sunderland and Manchester City, provided they were able to make the journeys involved.

Following the dropping of atom bombs on Hiroshima and Nagasaki, the Japanese government accepted unconditional surrender on 14th August. The next day the Allies celebrated VJ Day (Victory in Japan) and the war was finally over.

Derby County joined in the festivities with a 4-1 win over Nottingham Forest. The local press doubted if the Nottingham Forest fans would see a better goal than that scored by Raich Carter. During these summer months Peter Doherty had become increasingly disenchanted with the Manchester City directors, especially when they refused him permission to guest for Derby but agreed that he could play for Manchester United. As a result of this bizarre attitude Doherty asked for a transfer and because he threatened to move to Shamrock Rovers it was granted. Derby made a substantial offer to Manchester City and secured Doherty's transfer. This was a vital step towards creating one of the most distinguished and memorable partnerships in Derby's history.

Sunderland's opening fixture of the new season was away to Sheffield Wednesday. As it was only 35 miles away from Raich Carter's base, he was chosen to play. Sunderland won 6-3, and Carter's shooting and approach to goal were brilliant at times. His first goal was from 20 yards and went into the net like a rocket. The crowd, with all its bias towards Sheffield, burst into a spontaneous cheer for Carter. Just after this game a rumour spread rapidly that Derby were seeking to sign Carter. So persistent was the story that Derby had to write to Bill Murray, Sunderland manager, denying any official involvement on their part. The view in the Sunderland press was that it was inadvisable for clubs to allow their players to guest for other teams. On 1st September Carter again played for Sunderland against Sheffield Wednesday, this time at Roker Park. He was accompanied by his wife, and both expressed a desire 'to get back to the old town' and settle down as soon as he was released by the RAF. Consequently, talk of a transfer to Derby or anywhere else died down. Carter made it clear that he wanted to stay in the game after he retired in three or four seasons time. The question which this prospect raised was, what would the Sunderland directors be prepared to offer? At this stage their views were not known except that they were not prepared to sell him.

The 1945-46 season was a transition between the unofficial football of the war years and the fully-fledged peacetime competitions. The first international of the new season was between Northern Ireland and England, the first semi-official trip to Belfast since before the war. The England forward line showed one change from the previous season with Stan Mortensen restored to inside-left in place of Sailor Brown. In defence there was a first appearance for Harry Kinsell of West Bromwich Albion at left back. The crowd of 45,000 at Windsor Park welcomed an England team with a right wing of Matthews and Carter for the 14th time in wartime internationals. Northern Ireland were captained by Peter Doherty and if they had taken the chances he helped to create, the result would have been different. Instead, a Mortensen goal was sufficient to win the match for England.

Since the beginning of the season Raich Carter had been troubled by an unusual ankle injury. The twinges from the ankle reached a climax with the game in Belfast on 15th September. He returned to Loughborough for treatment but almost immediately was confined to bed for two weeks with tonsillitis. The rest seemed to cure the injury, so it suited him when Sunderland asked him to play against Barnsley because he needed a chance to test it out prior to the international against Wales the following week.

The match at Barnsley is of lasting interest because of one young, small Barnsley fan. He came with his dad and stood on a tin can so that he could see over the spectators in front of him. His name was Michael Parkinson, who went on to become a distinguished sports writer and television interviewer, and he always remembers the display that day of a great inside forward at his work. He recalled how Carter, "Strode alone on to the field some time after the other players, as if disdaining their company, as if to underline that his special qualities were worthy of a separate entrance." Of course, the Barnsley supporters were not impressed. Parkinson continues, "It seemed that he treated the crowd and the game with massive disdain, as if the whole affair was far beneath his dignity. He showed only one speck of interest in the proceedings, but it was decisive. He was about 30 yards from the Barnsley goal and with his back to it, when he received a fast, wild cross. He killed it in mid-air with his right foot and hit an alarming left-foot volley into the roof of the Barnsley goal. Carter didn't wait to see where the ball had gone. He knew. He continued to spin through 180 degrees and strolled back to the halfway line as if nothing had happened. Normally the Barnsley crowd greeted any goal by the opposition with a loud silence, but as Carter reached the halfway line a rare thing happened: someone shouted, 'I wish we'd get 11 like thee, Carter lad.' The great player allowed himself a thin smile, as well he might, for he never received a greater accolade than that."

Raich Carter believed he had a reasonable game and decided he was quite fit for the international. The *Sunderland Echo* was not nearly so impressed with his contribution. It asked if he had turned out because his international appearance was in doubt, then all he did was score a goal with a brilliant shot. However, Carter's journey back to Loughborough was a disaster because he could not get a taxi from the station. With every step of the four-mile walk to camp the ankle became more painful. The next morning when he woke up the ankle was badly swollen. An X-ray showed no broken bones and the orthopaedic surgeon decided the Achilles tendon was injured. Carter, therefore, reported himself unfit for the international against Wales at West Bromwich Albion. He also notified Sunderland that he was injured. The injury only gradually responded to rest and treatment. After three or four weeks inactivity the Unit Orderly Room notified him that he was selected to play for the RAF against the Army in London. Carter had not kicked a ball for weeks and certainly did not feel fit enough for representative football. Still feeling a bit dubious about the ankle he reported to the RAF that he was unfit.

The RAF match with the Army was arranged for a Wednesday in early November and the following Saturday Carter went to watch Sunderland who were playing at Leeds. He had not gone with any intention of playing but was persuaded to do so in order to give the ankle a try out. He was on the pitch but did not feel able to contribute much. His one consolation was that he was not letting down a representative team. However, shortly after returning to camp, he was informed that the RAF authorities did not believe he was unfit and wanted a medical report on his condition. The medical officers were able to confirm Carter's explanation and he heard no more about the matter. But to his great regret he was never chosen to play representative matches for the RAF again.

Chapter Seventeen
Rallying to the Rams

RAICH CARTER'S post-war dilemma came to a head in November 1945. Like so many of his contemporaries in the professional game he had lost six years to the war. As he was approaching 32 years of age he needed to safeguard his future. The only real career option was in football, so he was seeking the best deal he could get. Furthermore, he had to take into account his wife's poor health and his young daughter Jennifer. They were clearly much better taken care of in Derby with his wife's parents in close proximity.

Naturally, Raich had strong ties of affection and loyalty to his hometown club. He would have liked to go back to play for Sunderland, and many at the club would have liked to have him back. Director Ted Ditchburn, writing ten years later, claimed that the board had a plan to build a post-war team around Raich Carter. They took the view that with his great experience and ability he would be a priceless asset in helping a comparatively inexperienced team. However, Carter's search for security meant that he wanted a contract for ten years which would include two more testimonials. He thought he had done a lot for Sunderland and was not asking for the moon. On 10th November it was announced that Raich Carter had been placed on the transfer list. This was done at the player's request, according to the press, but it also reflected the club's unwillingness to meet his terms.

Obviously, from Carter's point of view, a move to Derby County would be ideal. As they had been interested earlier in the year, a bid seemed likely. A national paper suggested that Sunderland were asking for £10,000 thus confirming their reluctance to let him go. Argus in the *Echo* wrote that such a fee for a 32-year-old was unrealistic and in fact the club was awaiting offers. Very little activity took place for a couple of weeks until the Derby chairman Ben Robshaw revealed that his club had made a substantial offer for Carter. Several other clubs were said to be interested and Nottingham Forest had made a bid of £5,000. Sunderland did not seem to be anxious to accept either offer. On 6th December, Robshaw stated that negotiations with Sunderland were proceeding. On 8th, Raich Carter guested for Derby against West Bromwich Albion, only his second game in the last six weeks. The crowd gave him an enthusiastic welcome hoping his appearance was an indication of his impending transfer.

However, the saga continued with Sunderland complaining they did not know Carter was guesting for Derby in that match, and that while he was on the transfer list they would prefer he did not guest for anyone. By 15th December there had been no progress in the negotiations between Derby and Sunderland, but reports said Aston Villa had made an offer of £8,000. However, all clubs knew that the deal would have to be completed in the next week in order for Carter to play for his new club in the FA Cup. After that date his transfer value would probably be halved. It was reported that on the following Thursday Carter had refused to sign for Middlesbrough.

The next morning, Friday 21st December, Raich Carter was leaving RAF Loughborough for 14 days Christmas leave when an airman caught up with him to pass on a message. He was asked to meet the Derby County directors in a hotel in town as soon as possible. When he arrived he was told that his transfer from Sunderland was almost complete but the forms had to be signed before midnight that Friday. It was decided that Raich and club secretary Jack Catterall would leave immediately for Sunderland while the chairman and manager Ted Magner would wait for the final confirmation from the Sunderland chairman. The pair reached York at 8.00 p.m. to catch a connection to Sunderland. They telephoned Derby to check that the deal had been completed. Everything had been agreed. It should have been an hour-and-a-half journey to Sunderland so there would be a reasonable amount of time to sign the forms. However, when they approached the platform they found the area packed out with passengers travelling home for Christmas. They were unable to get near the train which pulled away without them. Vital minutes were ticking away and the next train would cut things very fine, assuming they would be able to get on it.

Therefore, Jack Catterall went out into the station yard and started to negotiate with taxi drivers. Finally he found one who was willing to do the trip and had the petrol to complete it. They set off at top speed through the night to cover the 70 miles to Sunderland. They arrived at the Grand Hotel with an hour to spare. The Sunderland directors were waiting there and Carter signed the forms which made him a Derby County player. Then it was back to the taxi for the return trip to York and from there another taxi journey to Derby. After a couple of hours' sleep Raich Carter joined his new teammates for his debut at Birmingham City. The game itself was disappointing, as Derby lost 1-0. Raich thought his game had been poor because he was weary from his nocturnal travels, but the local press thought he looked the most likely to score for Derby.

Derby had been drawn against Luton Town in the third-round of the FA Cup. For this first post-war challenge for the cup the FA decided ties, in rounds one to six, would be played on a two-leg basis, home and away. This seemed to heighten interest in the competition because attendance figures were at record levels. If the scores were level after the two matches, then ten minutes of extra-time each way was to be played. If the scores still remained equal, then the teams should play on until a goal was scored "which determined the winner and terminated the tie" – an early version of the 'golden goal' rule, used in some competitions more recently.

Derby County quickly recovered from the defeat at Birmingham with two wins over Tottenham. On Christmas Day they won 5-2 at White Hart Lane, and at home on Boxing Day they won 2-0. Raich Carter scored in both games, but his goal at the Baseball Ground was one of the best shots seen all season. The first leg of the cup-tie was played at Kenilworth Road. Carter was partnered by Sammy Crooks who Raich rated as "a splendid little player." Doherty, however, was without his regular left-wing partner Dally Duncan, who was injured. Angus Morrison was moved to the left wing, which allowed Jack Stamps to play at centre-forward. Luton chose Gordon Brice, normally a centre-half, at inside-right in order to bolster up their defence. Although Brice went on to play for Wolverhampton he was unable to shore up the Luton rear-guard, because six goals were conceded. Derby had given them a football lesson, and for most of the game the Luton players were chasing in vain. Doherty was on top form and Carter had a delightfully constructive game. Stamps took his four goals well but they were perfectly created for him. Tim Ward, in midfield, served his forwards splendidly and tackled quickly when required. However, he would not be able to play in the second leg because he was obliged to return to his army base in Germany. The return match was a formality which Derby won 3-0 in unpleasant weather conditions. Raich Carter scored two of the three goals. It must have been a sentimental tie for him because nine years earlier in Sunderland's cup run Luton had to be overcome in two games.

By the time Derby were drawn against West Bromwich Albion in the fourth-round, the whole country was taking a fanatical interest in the cup. The first leg of the next round was due on 26th January 1946. Despite a fabulous display against Millwall between the cup-ties, Carter did not get recalled for the England team against Belgium on 19th January. Jesse Pye of Notts County was chosen ahead of Michael Fenton, who had been called up when Raich Carter withdrew from the Wales game. Such was the interest in the tie with West Bromwich Albion that it was decided to make it all-ticket, very rare at that time. Although both clubs were founder members of the Football League they had only met three times in the cup.

The first leg was played at Derby and it was packed with thrills from the first minute to the last. Doherty was outstanding and scored the only goal of the match. Carter was described by the *Derby Evening Telegraph* as "the danger man" because of his powerful shooting which brought several saves from the West Bromwich Albion goalkeeper Jim Sanders. Unfortunately, just before kick-off, Raich's wife Rose was admitted to Derbyshire Royal Infirmary after being taken ill. It was decided to keep her under observation for a week or two.

Many observers believed that a one-goal lead was not enough to take to The Hawthorns for the second leg. This concern was reinforced by the news that Peter Doherty was unfit, which meant Jack Stamps would play. In the cup-tie, Raich proved to be a great general for the Derby team. It was his uncanny ball distribution and his readiness to try shots that seemed to upset the Albion defence. As a team Derby had rarely played better, and the defence certainly touched top form. Leon Leuty was even better than he was in the first leg, while Jack Parr at fullback played like an international. Raich Carter opened the scoring after 25 minutes but West Brom equalised early in the second half. Within eight minutes Stamps restored the lead, and with 11 minutes left Reg Harrison completed the scoring. The aggregate victory for Derby County was 4-1.

Derby's good form continued in the league when they beat Southampton 8-1. The local press wrote that Carter: "In his own inimitable way and with the greatest ease split the Southampton defence wide apart. He almost made the ball talk." The draw for the cup fifth-round paired Derby with Brighton. The bookmakers immediately made Derby the favourites at 3-1. But they were told not to take Brighton for granted as they possessed two forwards, Bernard Moore and Jock Davie, who were capable of upsetting opponents' calculations.

The first leg was at Brighton on 9th February and Doherty was declared fit to play. The contest was much closer than suggested by the 4-1 scoreline. Brighton defended bravely and their wing halves were not overawed by their famous opponents. In fact, it was not until Carter and Doherty switched positions that Derby got on top with two goals each from the inside forwards. The return leg at the Baseball Ground was much more one-sided. Both Doherty and Carter were playing some dazzling football which brought Carter three goals and Doherty two. Fifty-six years later Moore remembered them "ghosting" their way through the Brighton defence.

The *Derby Evening Telegraph* noted in mid-February that the Derby forward line was dovetailing well since the full-time acquisition of Carter and Doherty. Carter had settled in as schemer in chief, playing deeper than his forward colleagues had, ready to pounce on any loose ball and switch the point of attack. However, when the attack was well developed he was always within shooting range. Derby had played 13 games and won 12 since his signing. Carter and Doherty were undoubtedly the key men in the team and despite their advancing years they had done their job to the full.

The draw for the sixth-round of the cup matched Derby against Aston Villa. They were old rivals, having met eight times in the competition. Such was the public's fascination with the first post-war cup-ties that the government became alarmed by the attendances at second leg games which were played in midweek. In the absence of floodlights the games were played in the afternoon and absenteeism was rife. Britain was struggling to cope with massive post-war problems and could ill-afford any loss of production. The FA therefore agreed that the second legs should be played on the following Saturday.

For Derby County, the main worry was who would play in goal, because Frank Boulton was badly injured at Swansea where Trevor Ford inspired a very physical team. The club's reserves were very inexperienced so Derby turned to the transfer market. In the league their unbeaten run was extended to 15, in matches with Swansea and Leicester, so that Charlton's lead of ten points was cut to three. By the time of the first leg at Villa Park on 2nd March, Derby still had not acquired a replacement goalkeeper.

The attendance at Villa Park was 76,588 and they witnessed a thrill-packed match with enough goals to satisfy the most demanding supporter. The first half was dominated by Villa who twice took the lead through George Edwards and Bob Iverson. Peter Doherty equalised after the first goal but Aston Villa led 2-1 at half-time. In the second half a renewed and relentless Derby took the game to their opponents. The Villa defence came under continuous pressure until cracks began to appear which Derby's star forwards could exploit. In the 62nd minute Raich Carter brought the scores level again but, within four minutes, Frank Broome put Villa back in front. Derby maintained their pressure to equalise for a third time. It took them until the 85th minute when Peter Doherty headed home a Dally Duncan cross. By this time the Villa defence was so demoralised they left Sammy Crooks unmarked, allowing him to give Derby the lead for the first time with just two minutes left. The popular winger was swamped by his ecstatic colleagues.

Soon after the game Derby resolved their goalkeeping problem by signing Vic Woodley from Bath. The former Chelsea and England player would not be eligible for the return match with Aston Villa but could play in the semi-finals, should Derby reach them. There was a huge demand for tickets for the second leg but only 32,000 could be squeezed into the Baseball Ground, compared with the 76,000 at Villa Park. The match on 9th March 1946 was marred by excessively heavy tackling which led to Crooks' injury after ten minutes. He took no further part either in the game or in the rest of the cup run. The *Derby Evening Telegraph* reported that, "although Doherty, in his enthusiasm, practically played himself to a standstill, I regard Carter as the most valuable of the home forwards. It was he who undertook the scheming, acting as a one-man support of the front-line troops and keeping the opposing defence at full stretch by his shrewdly placed through passes."

Although Derby were on top from the start, it was Villa who took the lead after the Derby goalkeeper Billy Townsend fumbled a harmless-looking ball, presenting Broome with an easy chance. Just before the interval Carter completed a long spell of Derby pressure with a headed goal from a Duncan free-kick. That was his 13th goal in 12 games. Derby controlled the second half in which Villa also lost Harry Parkes without adding to the score. The aggregate score of 4-3 meant Derby County had reached the semi-final.

Nationally the match at Derby was completely overshadowed by events at another sixth-round tie at Bolton. At Burnden Park about 70,000 supporters were crammed in to see Bolton take on Stoke City. The combination of overcrowded terraces and a run-down stadium led to a disaster which shook the football world. Thirty-three people were killed and around 500 injured after a barrier collapsed at the Embankment end. Stan Matthews, who played that day for Stoke, was horrified to see body-bags at the side of the pitch. The chief constable ordered the game to be completed but the players just went through the motions. Unfortunately neither the FA nor the clubs took much notice of the Bolton disaster. A wait of 43 years and the Hillsborough disaster were needed before the football authorities took a serious look at how they treated their paying supporters. The poignancy of the Bolton disaster was the fact that the victims had survived the dangers of the war only to die on what should have been a pleasant afternoon.

The draw for the semi-finals paired Derby with Birmingham City and Bolton Wanderers with Charlton Athletic. Derby's game was scheduled to be played at Hillsborough on 23rd March. Derby's unbeaten run of 17 games came to an end at Coventry where Woodley made his debut. The defeat was immediately reversed the following week by 3-0.

Derby County had first reached the semi-finals in 1896 but it was not until their third semi-final in 1898 that they progressed into the final where they lost 3-1 to Nottingham Forest. They returned to the final the following year only to lose this time to Sheffield United 4-1. In 1902 they reached the semi-final again against Sheffield United when it needed three matches before Derby were beaten. The next year they reached the final for the third time only to find Bury in top form and to lose by a record 6-0 margin. There was then a gap of 43 years to 1946 when Derby reached their 11th semi-final. But could they win the cup for the first time in over 60 years? Birmingham City had already completed a league double over Derby. However, that had happened before Raich Carter had time to settle in. Journalist Mark Eaton wrote in the *Derby Evening Telegraph* that Raich was playing better than ever now. He had seen him many times before the war but did not remember him upsetting Derby defences as much as he was demoralising present-day defenders.

The semi-final was all-ticket and the capacity of Hillsborough was limited to 65,000. When Derby's allocation of 21,500 tickets went on sale the queue began to form at 11.00 p.m. the night before, and within an hour of sales beginning they were sold out. The match itself was disappointing, with Derby the better of two poor teams. Carter opened the scoring after four minutes and that remained the score at half-time. The second half was a triumph for Carter who had rarely given a finer exhibition of leadership. He played with confidence and enthusiasm, and with any luck Derby would have added another four goals. Instead, somewhat against the run of play, Birmingham scored an equaliser. Despite having provided practically all the goal-mouth thrills, Derby had to settle for a draw and a replay at Manchester.

The match was played on 27th March at Maine Road. A typical Derby supporter that day was 17-year-old David Orme. He left home at seven o'clock to walk to Derby station to catch the football special. Such was the crush that he counted 22 people in the compartment, ten seated, two lying in the luggage racks and himself among the ten standing between the seats. The stadium was reached by about 11.30 a.m. and by noon the ground was virtually full. The official attendance was 80,407, which is still a record for a midweek game between two English clubs outside of Wembley. Spectators spilled right up to the touchline. Birmingham were at full strength but Derby were without outstanding defender Leon Leuty. Fortunately, Jack Howe, a fullback just returned from service in India, proved an able deputy.

For the first 90 minutes the match was one of cut and thrust with Derby more purposeful and more confident, but there were no goals. The defining moment of the game came after five minutes of extra-time. The dramatic incident began with Dally Duncan cutting in along the goal-line, beating Duckhouse before cutting the ball back to Doherty. Fred Duckhouse charged back in a valiant attempt to intercept but Peter Doherty arrived fractionally first and, as the players collided, he hit the ball past goalkeeper Gil Merrick into the net. Raich Carter was close by, saw the terrific force of the crash and heard a crack which sickened him. There was a huge roar from the crowd which died abruptly as both players lay prone on the ground. Carter rushed over to Doherty, believing him to be seriously hurt.

In fact it was Duckhouse who had broken his leg and Doherty was only mildly hurt. Understandably Birmingham were dispirited by the loss of Duckhouse, and Derby were able to add three more goals including another from the indomitable Doherty. The outcome was that Derby County would meet Charlton Athletic in the first post-war cup final.

Chapter Eighteen

Derby's FA Cup Final

DESPITE Raich Carter's fine form and Derby's successful cup run there was no recall to the England team for the match against Scotland on 13th April 1946. Stan Matthews was also missing but the defence, including Billy Wright for his first international appearance, was at full strength. With 139,500 supporters inside Hampden Park, this was Scotland's time to take revenge for so many wartime defeats by England, although they had to wait until the 89th minute before Jimmy Delaney scored the only goal.

In Derby, the club were faced with the FA's customary miserliness in the allocation of tickets to cup finalists. The 12,000 tickets could have been sold by the club ten times over. Since very few supporters owned a television set, those who failed to get a ticket were dependent on the radio commentary. On a more fanciful note, Derby County had, according to legend, been a victim of a gypsy curse because the club had evicted them from their encampment. The curse declared the club would never win the cup or league. This was meat and drink to the press who took Derby captain Jack Nicholas, to see a modern Romany who conveniently removed the curse. So now both the finalists would start on equal terms.

A more down-to-earth announcement came from Wembley Stadium which said, "Bring your own food to the final as nothing will be on sale." Clearly, this was to be an austerity cup final at a time of rationing and shortages.

An anomaly, caused by the two leg semi-finals, was that Charlton reached the final having lost 2-1 away to Fulham. They progressed to Wembley on a 4-3 aggregate.

The good news for Derby supporters was the recovery from injury of Leon Leuty and Sammy Crooks; however, left back Jack Parr's arm was in plaster and he would not be available. It looked as though this would be labelled 'the veteran's final' because more than half the players were over 30 and the Charlton captain John Oakes, was 42, the oldest person to appear in a Wembley final. The two clubs were to meet in a league game in London a week before the final but so many players were rested by both sides, including Carter and Doherty, that the Charlton victory by 2-1 was not seen as significant. For the final week of preparations the Derby squad were based at a hotel in Harpenden. But there was nearly no final at all because with two days to go a dispute arose between players and directors. The County players had realised that the seats allocated to their wives and close relatives were inferior, uncovered tickets. Led by their determined shop steward Peter Doherty they threatened to strike. This was one confrontation he won easily, the directors giving way and providing the appropriate one-guinea tickets.

For Raich Carter, the unluckiest man in the Derby camp was Sammy Crooks. Although he was fit again the manager decided to retain the forward line from the semi-finals so young Reg Harrison was the choice for right wing. Raich liked Sammy because he came from County Durham; because he was small but still played for England; and because he was a character. He felt sorry for Sammy because he had played for Derby for 19 seasons and this would be his last chance to win the coveted medal. Also unlucky in the final selection were Angus Morrison, who had played 33 games with 19 goals; Parr, who was injured; and Tim Ward who was first choice until military duties posted him abroad.

"I knew we'd win the cup because Raich said so." This was how Reg Harrison summed up the confidence in the Derby camp in the days leading up to the final. Everything was the same for Raich Carter on the day, even the number one dressing room which Sunderland and England used. The lack of novelty took the edge off the excitement. It was impossible to recreate the thrill of the Sunderland cup final. However, one thing was different. In 1937 Raich Carter had never been really certain of victory until the final whistle but, in 1946, he was confident from the start of winning the cup again.

It proved to be a remarkable and thrilling game which could have produced several goals. Derby settled in more quickly and always had the edge but in the Charlton goal Sam Bartram made several fine saves. The football in the final was much better than in 1937 in Raich Carter's view. After 35 minutes, yet another Derby attack resulted in Carter hitting the net but he was judged to be off-side. So, at the interval, the two teams remained goalless, surprising as both teams had averaged more than three goals per game in the earlier rounds. In the second half, Charlton came more into the game but with ten minutes remaining there were still no goals. Then, within a minute, two freakish goals were scored and, remarkably, Charlton's Bert Turner was directly involved in both. The first goal started from a Carter throw-in on the right wing to Harrison who passed to Stamps. From his cross, Doherty headed on to Duncan who shot from about ten yards out. The ball struck the foot of Turner and was diverted past Bartram. From the kick-off Charlton went straight on to the attack and inside-right Sailor Brown was fouled just outside the penalty area. Up stepped the unlucky Turner to take the free-kick and his low, hard shot hit Doherty's leg and cannoned into the net. As a result of these deflections Turner is always credited with being the first man to score for both sides in a cup final.

With just five minutes left it seemed that Jack Stamps had an open goal to win the game. Instead, as he prepared to shoot into the goal, the ball burst. Coincidentally, in a radio interview the day before the match, the referee had stated that the odds against that happening were a million to one. So the whistle ended the 90 minutes of ordinary time and the game moved into extra-time. Derby quickly established their superiority by scoring within two minutes of the restart.

Stamps, their young centre-forward, created the chance when his fierce shot could only be parried by Bartram into the path of Doherty, who scored. The game was put completely out of Charlton's reach by two further goals by Stamps. Alex James, writing in the *News of the World*, summed up the game, "The 1946 Cup Final was a memorable game with a glorious finale. Derby's victory was complete and magnificent." Altogether it was one of the best finals played up to that time and must also be ranked high among those played since the war.

Away from the pitch there were many local stories. Andrew Ward in *Armed with a Football* wrote, "Some men were actually returning home from war that day. They arrived back in Derby wondering how to walk into their houses, greet wives they hadn't seen for a year, perhaps even a child they'd never seen, and make sure they could listen to the game on the wireless. During extra-time Derbyshire farmers remained by their wirelesses while their cows had to wait for milking time. For the Derbeians the occasion was exciting and magnetic, a total release after the black-out years of war. It was their team, their town, their Cup."

For Jimmy Seed, his Charlton players had given as much as they had taken for 90 minutes. But in extra-time Carter and Doherty hit top form and began to play havoc with the Charlton defence. The tired Charlton players were completely overrun and were glad to hear the final whistle. Seed made his way to the Charlton dressing room where the disappointment was not as great as he had feared. In fact, he arrived just in time to hear Sam Bartram say, "Never mind lads, we'll be back at Wembley next year." Seed immediately joined in and declared, "That's right lads, we'll go one better and win the cup." The prediction was made only in order to cheer up the players but, remarkably, they were back the next year and they did beat Burnley. Also, the match went to extra-time and once again the ball burst.

Unbeknown to Raich Carter, the death of his father-in-law had taken place shortly before the kick-off. At the suggestion of his mother-in-law, neither Raich nor Rose was informed of the news before the game. Only when he was back in the dressing room did manager Stuart McMillan, who had taken over at the beginning of the year when Ted Magner surprisingly took up a coaching position on the continent, call Carter to one side to tell him of the bereavement. Carter would also have to break the news to his wife but, because of the transport arrangements, this could not be done until they arrived back at the Harpenden hotel. From there the grieving couple returned to Derby.

As a result of the cup run Derby still had fixtures to complete. Therefore, on the Monday following the Wembley triumph, it was back to basics against Southampton at The Dell. Raich Carter missed that game but was persuaded by his wife and mother-in-law to take part in the huge celebrations on Tuesday when the cup winners were due back in Derby. There were scenes of enthusiasm unparalleled in the history of Derby. Large crowds jammed all approaches to the Police Building to cheer the team on the balcony. The victory coach was unable to make its way through the crowds and was brought to a halt. Eventually captain Jack Nicholas, with the cup, reached the balcony followed by his teammates. They were welcomed by the Mayor, who congratulated the club and the team on their achievement. He was followed by Nicholas who spoke to the crowd and then introduced the team. Most of the team simply thanked the supporters but two, Carter and Doherty, made longer speeches. For Carter, however, it was all the second time round and the thrill of the occasion was not so intense.

The following day, Wednesday, yet another re-arranged fixture was to be played. By strange coincidence the opposition at the Baseball Ground was Charlton Athletic who were still bidding to win the League South title. Derby fielded their full cup final team and again Charlton were well-beaten 3-1. Such was Derby's superiority that at one point in the game they threatened to swamp their opponents. Among the Derby forwards Carter and Doherty were described by the *Derby Evening Telegraph* as the "strolling magicians"as they again had Charlton guessing. In the final match of the season Derby met Chelsea who had Tommy Lawton leading their attack. He had been transferred from Everton for £11,500 in November 1945. The result was a 1-1 draw, with Carter scoring for Derby.

During 1946, Victory internationals were arranged against Belgium and Switzerland. However, they were not full internationals and caps were not awarded. England's game with Belgium had been played back in January but the Swiss game was scheduled for 11th May. Raich Carter was selected for this match after an absence of eight months. The fixture clashed with Derby County's tour of Czechoslovakia and the FA were not prepared to release Carter. It was arranged therefore that he would fly to join his colleagues the day after the international. The Swiss had earned a fixture against England by beating an FA XI in 1945. The promise was that the Swiss would play at Wembley but the match was staged at Stamford Bridge. For this game England chose: Swift; Scott, Hardwick; Wright, Franklin, Johnson; Matthews, Carter, Lawton, Brown and Smith. Bert Johnson of Charlton was chosen for his first unofficial international and his pass led to Carter scoring England's first goal. Two weeks earlier Johnson had been marking Carter in the cup final. In the end England were comfortable winners by 4-1. Carter scored twice and Lawton and Sailor Brown got one each.

Before Carter could rejoin his Derby teammates there was one last international of the 1945-46 season. The French FA invited England to play in Paris on 19th May. This match was England's 36th and final unofficial international between 1939-1946. During the latter half of that period Raich Carter could have been regarded as England's lucky mascot. Only in the final match in Paris did he finish on the losing side. The French won 2-1 and their hero goalkeeper Julien Darui was carried shoulder high from the pitch. The Paris match was Carter's 17th wartime appearance, in which time he scored 18 goals and missed two penalties. Matthews with 29, Mercer with 27 and Lawton with 23 made the most appearances. In the number of goals scored, Carter came second behind Lawton's 24. In terms of strike rate, Lawton, Carter and Welsh all averaged more than a goal a game.

For many players the war marred what would have been six prime seasons in their careers, so there was a certain feeling that the FA were adding insult to injury by declaring the internationals unofficial and not deserving of full caps. It was generally agreed that the standard of play often excelled that produced by the 1930s. There were several persuasive reasons why this could be believed. First, England could call upon an outstanding group of talented players. From the outset of war such distinguished players as Stan Matthews, Raich Carter, Tommy Lawton, Joe Mercer, Stan Cullis, Eddie Hapgood, Denis Compton and Frank Swift were available. Later on, the names of George Hardwick, Jimmy Hagan, Neil Franklin, Wilf Mannion and Stan Mortensen could be added to the list.

A second factor was the fitness of the players. Most international footballers were PTIs either in the Army or the RAF. Also, they frequently played two competitive matches a week, on Saturday for a club and midweek for the Combined Services, the Army, a regiment, a wing or an FA XI. Connected to this factor was the regularity with which international players came together in teams. As Stan Cullis wrote, "We saw an awful lot of each other ... without quite realising it we built an international side like a club team and that was an important part of the success."

Finally, during the war, the FA England selection committee had to be abandoned. Instead the task fell to one man, FA Secretary Stanley Rous. According to Joe Mercer: "The attitude was entirely different. Throughout the war, players played for the team, not to please the selection committee." He added that during his captaincy, from October 1944, the England team started having meetings on the night before matches to consider how they could play best as a team rather than as individuals. Raich Carter had anticipated the need for these team meetings when he spoke to previous captain Stan Cullis about the difficulty in ever getting the ball back from

Stan Matthews. Stanley Rous recalled that picking the team was not difficult, the hardest part was getting the players released from their military duties. The FA must have come to recognise the benefits of having one man responsible for the national team because they requested Stanley Rous to appoint the first England manager and Director of Coaching. The man chosen for this important post was Walter Winterbottom, a former Manchester United centre-half, a trained teacher and a wartime Wing Commander. The appointment was made in June 1946.

Meantime, Raich Carter was due to leave Paris after the international to join his Derby colleagues in Vienna. However, he received a telegram redirecting him to Prague instead. His flight had reached Prague but was unable to land because of a violent storm. The pilot turned back and managed to land at Frankfurt. This was in the American sector of Germany and so Carter, without money, reported to the US Army. They were able to find him a meal and a hotel bed and the next day he completed his journey to Prague. This tour proved to be very unsatisfactory for Derby County. The arrangements to fly to Vienna were cancelled and instead army lorries turned up. The Derby officials refused to allow the players to make such a long journey by lorry so the Vienna section of the tour was abandoned. The Czechs obliged with an extra game in Prague. However, this turned out to be the roughest and most dangerous game in which Raich Carter had every played. The referee was oblivious to any fouls and the Czechs must have been under orders to win at all costs. On their return to England, the club were the subject of an FA Enquiry for not fulfilling the Vienna fixture. The enquiry criticised them for their "selfish refusal" to play in Austria. Ultimately the FA decided Derby would not be allowed to arrange any more continental tours until further notice.

Chapter Nineteen

Derbyshire Cricket and Full Caps Again

BEFORE THE war, Raich Carter's cricketing experience was confined to the Durham Senior League and to occasional games for Durham, a minor county. The move to Derby had brought him into a first class county. In the summer of 1946, he was invited to play for the Derbyshire second team. In an exciting game against Notts' second team early in June, Carter top-scored with 47. This led to an invitation to play professionally for the first XI, which Raich accepted. He was chosen to play in three matches against Worcestershire, Surrey and Northamptonshire.

These matches brought home to him the difference between three-day county championship matches and the everyday club games, or even two-day minor county matches. He found the long sessions in the field exhausting but when given the chance to bowl he took two wickets for 39. However, it was his batting which was most seriously exposed by First Class bowlers. His top score in three games was seven. He admitted that good bowlers would always get him out because of his inability to distinguish between the dangerous ball and the one that could be hit. At 32 it was too late to start correcting his technical deficiencies. He did play again for Derbyshire in one or two benefit matches but no more First Class games. In the meantime Derby County had decided to run a cricket team to play against local clubs. This was the standard where Raich Carter felt in his element and his teammates were his soccer friends. There were one or two guests brought in to strengthen the team including Frank Broome and Sid Ottewell.

Carter also turned out for Chaddesden, his local cricket club. He helped them to reach the final of the Mayor's Hospital Cup. A record crowd of over 3,000 watched his 49 runs in the semi-final against Duffield. Unfortunately, a pulled muscle prevented him from playing in the final which was lost to Rolls-Royce. Derby County players had to report back for training on August 1 but Raich Carter's injury prevented him from playing in the practice matches. The Football League was due to resume its normal peacetime pattern on 31st August 1946. What could be more reassuring than to reproduce the fixtures as they had been drawn up for the 1939-40 season? Derby County's first match, therefore, was away to Sunderland. Derby hoped to field their cup-winning team but there were a number of injury worries. If fit, Raich Carter would captain the team against his old club. He was declared fit and so found himself in the away team's dressing room at Roker Park for his first official league match since the match at Arsenal in September 1939. There were 48,000 spectators to greet him: more than double the number who had attended in 1939. Everyone from the chairman, Ted Ditchburn, to the fans at the Roker End realised that the club had lost a great player, and it was small consolation to win the match 3-2.

In 1960, Arthur Appleton in his book *Hotbed of Soccer* wrote that, "before the War Sunderland fans had, in the main, been slow to value Carter at his true worth, partly because he had developed with other excellent players ... although he was a local boy he was not generally taken to heart mainly, I think, because of his impassive demeanour. His efficiency as a footballer, although recognised by quite a few, was not fully appreciated until he had left – and really emerged as a national figure – during and immediately after the War. Carter was Sunderland's most consistently effective inside forward since Buchan."

Derby had struggled at Sunderland partly because both their cup final wingers, Dally Duncan and Reg Harrison, were unfit. Neither the cunning of Raich Carter nor the dexterity of Peter Doherty could compensate for their absence. In midweek, Derby recalled semi-retired Sammy Crooks to play against Portsmouth. The match was won 2-0, helped by a glorious left-footed goal from Carter. To assist new England manager Walter Winterbottom to select his first team, a match was arranged between an FA XI and a Combined XI. Both Carter and Leon Leuty were chosen to play in the trial. Winterbottom announced his first England team to play Northern Ireland on 30th September 1946 in Belfast. It was: Swift, Scott, Hardwick; Wright, Franklin, Cockburn; Matthews, Carter, Lawton, Mannion, Langton. Only Henry Cockburn and Bobby Langton had not played in any of the unofficial wartime internationals. For this match the FA would award full England caps. Only Carter, Matthews and Lawton had won full caps before the war. The length of time since Raich Carter's previous cap was nine years and 164 days. A second match was arranged against Eire two days later, the first time England would visit Dublin since 1912. Also included in the party were three reserves: Don Welsh, Eddie Shimwell and Tom Finney.

The England party were based in a hotel in Newcastle, County Down. The facilities were excellent and the scenery, which included the Mountains of Mourne, was magnificent. The pool tables were very popular and both Frank Swift and George Hardwick noted that Raich Carter was very effective with a cue, no doubt as a result of many youthful hours in the billiard hall on Fawcett Street. The injury which Stan Matthews had been carrying forced him to withdraw from the team and Tom Finney replaced him.

The match against Northern Ireland was played at Windsor Park, Belfast, but was nearly abandoned. The interest was so great that about 60,000 people turned up, but only 37,000 were admitted. The spectators spilled over on to the playing area, and the kickoff had to be delayed by 15 minutes while order was restored. Frank Butler, in the *Daily Express*, demanded that football crowds should be controlled and that international matches should be ticket only.

Frank Swift watched the game from his goalmouth and described it, a year-and-a-half later, like this, "Our team clicked from the start and the forwards were in magnificent form. Lawton led the line like the genius he is; Raich Carter did practically everything it is possible to do with a football – even to standing, foot on ball, as if marshalling his forces; twinkle-toed Mannion electrified the huge crowd with his amazing dribbles and Tom Finney was more than a match for master Matthews." England scored seven and, in the second half, played exhibition football. Carter's return to official internationals was marked with a first-minute goal. Not even the experienced Peter Doherty, first capped in 1935, could rally his Irish teammates; although they did score twice in the second half!

The next day the FA party went to Dublin, which lived up to Swift's description as "the capital of the land of plenty." They were taken to Government House to meet the Irish premier, the charismatic Eamon De Valera. The meeting made history because this was the first time the premier had agreed to meet members of a foreign football party. In the match against Eire, England were fortunate to win 1-0 with a goal by Finney eight minutes from time. The Irish played with great spirit and determination and made the English team look quite ordinary. Manchester United's Johnny Carey, the Irish captain, was "man of the match," said Swift.

More on the basis of the Belfast performance than that in Dublin, the England team, six weeks later against Wales, showed no changes. The match was played at Maine Road, Manchester, on 14th November 1946. The team selection caused quite a lot of controversy with respect to the retention of Finney at the expense of Matthews. This was a debate which would continue in football circles for the next 12 years. The hard-tackling Welsh defence prevented the England forwards from producing their brilliant movement; nevertheless, each of England's three goals was a classic. Each goal resulted from a four-man movement with Mannion putting the final touch twice and Lawton once.

Within a fortnight the England team was in action again against the Dutch at Huddersfield. England's first change in four games put Harry Johnston at left-half in place of Henry Cockburn. The unfortunate Dutch part-timers were given an 8-2 thumping. Tommy Lawton, playing on his birthday, gave one of the finest displays of centre-forward play. At the banquet in a Harrogate hotel after the match, Karel Lotsy, the President of the Dutch Football Association, made a memorable speech. He said, "In 30 years of football on the continent and in England, I saw today a forward line as I have never seen before." He added that Holland could never adequately repay Britain for the help given to saving the lives of Dutch children during the war.

The England internationals continued that season on 12th April 1947 when the Scots were the visitors to Wembley. Stan Matthews was recalled to the England team to partner Raich Carter on the right wing. George Hardwick passed a fitness test and so captained the team again. The match was considered a trial for places in a Great Britain team to play the Rest of Europe in May. The game arranged by Stanley Rous was to celebrate the return of the home countries' associations into FIFA. The match with Scotland was disappointing from England's point of view because they were fortunate enough to manage a draw. The England attack could do little against a strong-tackling and well-marshalled Scots defence. Archie Macaulay was outstanding in mid-field while the little-known Billy Steel made his debut in attack. Raich Carter scored England's equaliser and nearly got a winner in the dying minutes. He was put clean through by Tommy Lawton but heard a whistle blow and turned his head towards the referee, who had not blown, so Carter continued but shot straight at Bill Miller. This would be Raich Carter's last international against the Scots, 13 years after the first encounter.

Three weeks later England were at Highbury to entertain France. Tom Finney was back on the right wing and there was only one change in defence. Eddie Lowe made his debut at left-half. England were only occasionally at their best but still managed to win 3-0. Tommy Lawton was in fine form but the goal scorers were Wilf Mannion, Finney and Raich Carter. During those weeks there had been considerable speculation and debate about the selection of the Great Britain team. The match was billed as 'the game of the century' and newspapers ran polls to determine their readers' choices for the 11 places. Inevitably there would have to be some compromises in order that each of the four home nations would be fairly represented. In the event the selection revealed a number of anomalies. Firstly, Stan Matthews was chosen at outside right even though Finney currently held that position in the England team. Secondly, George Hardwick was moved from his customary left back position to right back, presumably to accommodate the Welsh left back Billy Hughes. Neither Billy Wright nor Neil Franklin was included so that Archie Macauley of Scotland and Jack Vernon of Northern Ireland could be included. Perhaps the most unexpected selection was that of Billy Steel who had played only ten games for Greenock Morton and one for Scotland at inside-left. The selectors moved Mannion across to inside-right which meant that Derby County's hugely respected and vastly experienced inside forwards, Carter and Doherty, were omitted.

As it turned out, the selectors were rewarded with a clear victory by 6-1. Raich Carter and George Young were the reserves and 134,000 spectators turned up at Hampden Park to cheer on a team containing five Englishmen, three Scots, two Welshmen and one from Northern Ireland. Captaining the Rest of Europe team was Eire and Manchester United's Johnny Carey who led a team including nine nationalities.

A week later a 16-man party left by air to represent England against Switzerland and Portugal. This was the first time the FA had arranged to fly on each section of a foreign tour. This suited Raich Carter because he was a poor sailor but it turned out to be his last tour with England. The team selected against the Swiss showed one change with Stan Matthews preferred at outside right. England should have won the game in the first 20 minutes as they created several chances. Then the Swiss scored and their deep-lying centre-forward tactics became increasingly disconcerting to the English defence. The Swiss defence held out despite a second-half rally by the English attack. The match was played at the Grasshoppers stadium in Zurich where the English players found the pitch cramped. The game was England's first defeat since the full internationals had been resumed and proved to be Raich Carter's last full cap.

For the match in Lisbon, Stan Mortensen replaced Carter and Finney replaced Langton. There were three features of the Portuguese approach to the game: within five minutes they substituted a size four ball, throughout the game they made substitutions without there being any agreement and the whole team failed to turn up to the after-match banquet. The reason was simple: England has won 10-0.

At this point it is possible to examine the commonly believed legend that England's greatest forward line was: Stan Matthews, Raich Carter, Tom Lawton, Wilf Mannion and Tom Finney. As Mannion and Finney did not make their debuts until September 1946, all pre-war matches can be discounted as can unofficial wartime internationals as Finney was not picked during the war. As Carter completed his international career in May 1947 the greatest forward line could only have played together in the seven internationals immediately following the war. In fact, the three inside forwards, Carter, Lawton and Mannion, played throughout this period. The changes took place on the wings where Finney played five matches on the right wing and Matthews played twice; whereas on the left wing Langton played in six games and Jimmy Mullen once. When Matthews and Finney were both chosen on either wing, Carter had been replaced by Mortensen. So the best that was ever achieved was four out of five forwards playing together. Of course, it is possible to argue that an even greater attack was the England forward line which beat the Scots 8-0 in October 1943: Stan Matthews, Raich Carter, Tom Lawton, Jimmy Hagan and Denis Compton.

Chapter Twenty

The Legendary Carter and Doherty

THE COMBINATION of Carter and Doherty had been initiated at RAF Loughborough MRU. Raich had been posted there at the request of the Commanding Officer in 1943, but he had already been guesting for Derby County for some months. Peter Doherty arrived at Loughborough in 1944 and received permission to guest for Derby County. At this stage the future inside forward partners were about 30 years old and had established themselves at the top of the game. Doherty had played for Blackpool before winning the First Division title with Manchester City. He was a Northern Ireland international, first capped in 1935. Carter, of course, had been capped for England and won cup and league titles with Sunderland before he was 24. Both players had also had outstanding club partnerships before the war; Peter Doherty had combined with Alex Herd in the Manchester City team which won the championship in 1936-37; while Raich Carter won the cup the same season, partnering inside-left Patsy Gallacher. When Carter and Gallacher first combined for Sunderland on 29th October 1932, interestingly, Carter was at inside-left and Gallacher at inside-right, and this was how it remained for the rest of the season. It was not until 21st October 1933 that the two inside forwards switched sides. They last played together on 12th November 1938 at Stamford

Bridge, completing about 200 matches in tandem.

Also, during the 1930s, Carter and Doherty would have been aware of each other as their clubs played against each other in the First Division. Doherty recalled later a match at Maine Road at the end of October 1936 in which he admitted that Sunderland had outclassed and outplayed City on the day and won by four goals to two. He said, "The Wearsiders gave a sparkling exhibition of scientific soccer, and Raich Carter had one of his best days – which means, of course, that he was magnificent." Clearly, mutual respect had been established early in their careers. The first time they played together on the same side was on 4th November 1939. In order to raise funds for the Red Cross a match had been arranged between a Football League XI and an All British XI at Goodison Park. The Football League's forward line – Matthews, Carter, Lawton, Doherty and Brook – had a fine game and Carter scored a memorable goal.

Raich Carter's association with Derby County began on 9th October 1943 and his honeymoon with the club began with a hat-trick. During the season 1943-44, however, he managed only 14 games thanks to five international calls and other representative matches. Peter Doherty started at Derby in August 1944 having received permission from Manchester City to guest for the Rams. The two internationals teamed up first in pre-season practice matches. The early signs were very positive as the two players slotted in quickly with each other. Nevertheless, their first official fixture together was not auspicious: a 0-0 draw with Nottingham Forest. It was not long before Derby supporters recognised that in Doherty, Derby County had found the perfect partner for Carter. Early in November a correspondent to the local paper wrote, "Doherty is not only a brilliant player but he is a representative of all that's best in British sport. He is one of the finest inside forwards in football today." During the season reports that Carter and Doherty "did as they pleased" and that "most opposing clubs have a Carter-Doherty complex these days", and "the opposition were given a football lesson, class will tell", confirmed that the combination was flourishing. Further evidence of the team's fine form, especially in the second half of the season, came in the final of the wartime Midland Cup in which Derby played Aston Villa. Over two legs Derby County were winners on an aggregate score of 9-0. During the season Carter played 28 games and scored 29 goals while Doherty played 29 games and scored 35 goals.

Together they scored as many goals as the next 15 players who contributed goals for Derby during the season.

However, it was the season 1945-46 which cemented the legendary reputations of Carter and Doherty at Derby. They completed their transfers to the club and contributed massively to Derby's first (and only) FA Cup victory. During the cup campaign Derby scored 37 goals of which Carter and Doherty contributed 22.

Doherty wrote about Carter that, "He was my twin, a brilliant schemer with a dangerous shot, with whom I was able to dovetail perfectly." He also believed that, "Perhaps there was some telepathic understanding between Raich and me because I have never played with a player that I could find so easily. When I picked it up I was always able to find him and, I think, he would say the same about me. We formed a good habit of knowing where to find each other."

Writing at about the same time in the late forties Carter said, "Doherty was a grand fellow and a great footballer. It was a pleasure to play in partnership with him and there has been no other inside forward with whom I developed such a perfect understanding. We had no pre-arranged plan of action. Our play just dovetailed naturally and instinctively." He added, "Peter Doherty was a perfect example of the true inside forward, combining the roles of both defender and attacker." Although the two players were friends they were also rivals. Almost 40 years after their time at Derby County, Carter admitted, "I hated it when Peter got a better press than me and he was the same – which was good for the game and good for the club." He also insisted that the partnership was intuitive and owed nothing to coaching, which he described as, "a load of codswallop." Later, he moderated his view by saying that coaching was overrated and that you are either born with the ability or you are not. So, Carter and Doherty never planned nor prepared tactics before a game, they "just went out there and played."

Considering its reputation, it is amazing that the Carter-Doherty era was so fleeting. Once they were free from international duties in the autumn of 1946, the combination briefly flowered again. Their return to the Derby team early in October had the expected effect and Brentford were dispatched 3-0 at Griffin Park. Carter, Derby's "supreme strategist," (*Derby Evening Telegraph*) scored the third goal. From Carter and Doherty later in the month at Middlesbrough there was, "almost a surfeit of every good thing except goals," according to the *Derby Evening Telegraph*. In November, against Liverpool, Carter suffered a suspected broken cheekbone. He was admitted to the Derbyshire Royal Infirmary where he underwent a minor operation. He was discharged on Sunday and within a fortnight he played against Chelsea where his generalship, craft and work rate contributed to a 3-1 win. On 9th December he played against Charlton and the way he made the first goal was like "the finesse and simplicity of a chess master." (*Derby Evening Telegraph*). But all was not well with his Irish 'twin.' At the age of 33, Peter Doherty was trying to secure his future by taking over the Arboretum Hotel. The club directors did not agree with the move because they believed it would interfere with his performance as a player. The decision upset Doherty who still keenly remembered the directors' attitude over tickets at Wembley, and he resented the suggestion that he would allow anything to distract him from his responsibilities as a football professional. Although he would have been happy to finish his career at Derby he felt he had no alternative than to request a transfer. He loved the Baseball Ground and the Derby fans but he was transferred to Huddersfield Town in December 1946. The really surprising thing is that Doherty played in only 15 League games for Derby and scored seven times (he played 61 times in wartime league games). The supporters organised a protest against the transfer but it went through just after Christmas. The fee of £9,000 to £10,000 created a record because it brought the total fees paid for Doherty during his career to £27,500 (overtaking sums paid for Hughie Gallacher).

The remaining half of the duo – Raich Carter – continued to delight the Derby fans. He must have taken particular pleasure in a 5-1 victory over Sunderland, on 28th December 1946. Not only did Derby move into the top ten of Division One but also Raich contributed a cracking goal from outside the area. This was revenge, too, for the defeat at Roker Park in the opening game of the first post-war season. Perhaps he had already concluded that Sunderland were silly to have sold him for £6,000 and that Derby were lucky to have got such a good deal.

However, it was time for the cup holders to defend their trophy away to Bournemouth. The ground was wet and heavy and Tim Ward was Derby's makeshift left-winger. He received a pass from Carter straight from the kick-off and Carter was quickly calling for a return pass. But Ward had decided on a long ball down the middle from the touchline near the halfway line. It seemed like a harmless effort until it took a freak bounce and sailed over the head of the advancing Bournemouth goalkeeper. If Ward was looking for congratulations it did not come from Carter who shook his head and said, "They shouldn't allow goals like that." A few minutes later the ball was passed to Ward again and this time he heard a call from Carter for a pass, which he delivered. Carter set off for goal and, with a couple of shimmies en route, the ball was in the net. He turned to Ward with a supercilious look and said, "You see, that's the way to score them!" The remaining 85 minutes were described as a nightmare performance; nevertheless, Derby went through to round four.

The draw matched Derby with Arsenal or Chelsea. A second replay was necessary before Chelsea won the tie. Raich Carter was at the game spying on Derby's next round opponents. Afterwards he said, "I think we have a good chance of beating Chelsea." Both teams were at full strength at Stamford Bridge and after 89 minutes Chelsea led 2-1. But, in the last minute Carter scored an equaliser. The teams would meet again at Derby, their replay dominated by an incident in the first five minutes involving the Derby keeper Alick Grant. He had been warned by Carter and others just before the kick-off that his kicking style, two steps, a hop and a jump, was dangerous on an icy surface. Nevertheless, after a few minutes just such a kick caused Grant to dislocate his shoulder and forced him out onto the left wing for 85 minutes. The goalkeeping jersey was passed to winger Frank Broome who, despite facing Britain's finest striker Tommy Lawton, saved everything. Derby won the match 1-0 after extra-time but were beaten in the fifth-round away to Liverpool. Thus they relinquished the FA Cup in their first unsuccessful cup-tie since 1939.

The background to these cup battles was one of the worst winters for decades. Blizzards and snowdrifts caused water and power failures. It also caused widespread postponement of league and cup fixtures. The only match which survived the icy conditions and the power cuts was the English League's contest against the Scottish League at Hampden Park on 12th March 1947. It was 11-and-a-half years and nine inter-League fixtures since Raich Carter had been selected for the League. There were 84,714 spectators present to see the English League win 3-1. As in his first appearance for the Football League in September 1934, Raich Carter played alongside Stan Matthews. The team also included such seasoned stalwarts as Laurie Scott, George Hardwick, Neil Franklin and Wilf Mannion. Unfortunately, most of the players were snowbound in Glasgow making their return to English league games doubtful.

In fact, Carter was able to rejoin his Derby County colleagues for the fixture with Manchester United. The game resulted in a spectacular Derby victory by 4-3 with Carter, Ward and Broome showing good form. However, in the second half as Derby got on top, the excessively robust Manchester tackling on Carter seemed to upset him so that in his efforts to protect himself the Derby attacks suffered.

Such was the persistence of the bad weather that Derby did not complete their league fixtures until 31st May with a win at Portsmouth inspired by Raich Carter who made one goal and scored the other. The club finished the season in 14th place with Carter and Stamps the leading scorers.

Chapter Twenty-One
New Partner, New Cup Run

RAICH CARTER liked playing for Derby County. He had gained many new friends there, particularly Tim Ward, Peter Doherty and Frank Broome. He would not make comparisons with his hometown club because he felt the circumstances were so different. When he had signed for Sunderland he was very young and inexperienced. There were established stars like Bob Gurney, Patsy Gallacher and Alex Hastings so Carter, the newcomer, stayed very much in the background, although he matured rapidly; whereas when he arrived at the Baseball Ground Carter was a mature international player, instantly recognisable with his strikingly white hair. The atmosphere was free and easy and he could express his opinion on any topic he liked. He was also known to take up a contradictory view just to provoke a friendly argument.

At the start of June 1947 the *Derby Evening Telegraph* revealed that Derby County were prepared to pay their highest transfer fee for Greenock Morton's Billy Steel. Ironically, this was the young Scottish international who had been selected ahead of Carter and Doherty for the Great Britain XI. The £15,000 which Stuart McMillan had to pay for Steel broke the British transfer record.

During July, Raich Carter and Leon Leuty took part in a fitness week at Skegness under the direction of the Central Council of Physical Recreation. Raich was determined not to continue playing beyond the time when he could no longer cope with the pace of the top division. So, when a journalist approached him about his retirement plans, Raich simply told him that he would not outstay his welcome. Next day the press carried stories about his imminent retirement, much to his shock and that of the directors in Derby. On his return to the club he had to have a quiet word of reassurance with the manager and directors. Nevertheless, the question of his future was now at the forefront of Carter's mind. He relaxed by turning out for the Derby County Cricket XI. In an innings against Loughborough he scored 91 runs and lost four cricket balls.

Early in August, Derby County were invited to Edinburgh for the Allison Cup, a charity competition. Derby played an Edinburgh Select XI and the two teams had star-studded attacks. But it was Raich Carter who stood out head and shoulders with his craft and ball control. The *Derby Evening Telegraph* reported that if Steel was worth £15,000 then Carter must be a "pearl beyond price." The Rams, who were 3-1 down at half-time, won the game 5-4. Derby County made many friends in the Scottish capital with their sporting and whole-hearted display on a boiling day.

The burning question from the *Derby Evening Telegraph* at the start of the new season 1947-48 was, "Could Steel take over where Doherty left off?" Early signs were not good as the results were modest and Steel's contribution disappointing. The tide seemed to turn with a home win against Everton on 6th September. It appeared that Steel was beginning to develop a better understanding with Carter even though having four different wing partners in five games had not helped him. Then there was another period of undistinguished form until 27th September when Derby achieved a draw at Roker Park. Raich Carter had a brilliant opening half at his pre-war club when he was the foundation stone on which all the Derby attacks were built. It was clear that Derby needed a new centre-forward and rumours suggested they were favourites to buy Tommy Lawton for £15,500.

Steel scored his first league goal for Derby County in his 11th game on 25th October 1947. By the following Saturday a 4-2 defeat of Middlesbrough led the press to wonder if there was a better inside trio than Carter, Morrison and Steel. The combination of Carter and Steel revealed a long-overdue understanding and they interchanged positions skilfully. The deal for Lawton fell through as he chose to move to Notts County for £17,000.

In the wider world the American Congress passed the Marshall Plan which was to bring massive aid to war-stricken western Europe. At Westminster the Chancellor of the Exchequer Hugh

Dalton resigned his post over a Budget leak and was replaced by Sir Stafford Cripps. A few days later all eyes were switched across the road to Westminster Abbey where Princess Elizabeth and the Duke of Edinburgh got married.

Meantime, Derby County's unbeaten run exceeded two months as they swept Charlton aside 5-1 on 22nd November. The following Saturday the visitors were Arsenal, unbeaten for 17 games since the season started. The Gunners included international fullbacks Scott and Barnes; Macauley and Mercer in midfield; plus Rooke, Compton and Logie up front. In fact, it was George Swindin, their goalkeeper, who saved their day by restricting Derby to one goal. Carter and Steel struck up such a brilliant understanding that people began to make comparisons with the best days of Carter and Doherty. As a result of their 1-0 win Derby moved into joint third place in the League alongside Preston North End, their next opponents.

The match at Deepdale on 6th December 1947 was a game in a million, still rated by many as the greatest ever seen in Preston. Even today Sir Tom Finney says it was the finest game he played in at Deepdale. The match-day programme welcomed Derby as, "Very strong and attractive opposition. They are chock full of star appeal, notably England's silver-haired Raich Carter." By this stage in his career Carter was universally admired by fans and fellow professionals alike. Preston hardly had time to settle down before Derby went two goals ahead. Carter was eclipsing his celebrated England teammate. By the end of 20 minutes Preston had equalised but, with both teams opting for all-out attack, Derby were soon back in the lead with a second goal for Morrison. Just before half-time Preston's determination was rewarded with another equaliser, this time due to the perseverance of Bill Shankly. Morrison's hat-trick was completed after an hour and Derby led 4-3. Then Tom Finney took command of the situation and, in the final 28 minutes, Preston produced a grandstand finale in which they equalised for the third time, took the lead for the first time and completed a thrilling victory by 7-4. During this climax Finney overshadowed the great Raich Carter. The *Derby Evening Telegraph* reported that Carter had worked like a Trojan to pull the bewildered Rams together but that Steel was seldom in the picture.

Over Christmas Derby County completed the double over Blackburn within three days. Such was Carter's dominance in the heavy conditions that the local reporter wrote that, "I can't help laughing at the critics who, year after year, declare that this is Carter's last season." As Derby won their first match in 1948 5-0 over Chelsea, they had scored 14 goals in three games. For this game Steel was back to his best form but questions were beginning to be asked about his inconsistency on the pitch and his lifestyle off the pitch. Some observers felt that Steel only performed when it suited him such as when Scottish FA officials were present or when the match was in London.

However, for the Derby County players, it was Steel's supplementary earnings which caused dissatisfaction. For example, Steel was permitted by the club to write a regular column for the *News Chronicle* which, at that time, was quite unusual. This deal alone was said to double the income he was paid for playing football. But this was not the only additional payment Steel received, for his standard of living was clearly higher than that of his fellow professionals. Undoubtedly he was an unsettling influence, especially to senior players like Carter, Leuty, Stamps and Ward who had been limited to the maximum wage for years.

The new year meant another opportunity to challenge for the FA Cup. The draw for the third-round had produced a local derby with Chesterfield soon made all-ticket. Injury prevented captain Carter from playing but Derby won 2-0 after a hard fight. The fourth-round required Derby to travel to Crewe where the opposition would include goalkeeper Bob Scott who had played for England Schoolboys at the same time as Raich Carter. However, he was unable to prevent the Derby attack scoring three times as Carter and Steel again revived memories of Carter and Doherty. Crewe had done their utmost to contain Carter by marking him very closely. Towards the end Derby had a corner on the left; Carter trotted out towards the right-hand corner flag, 70 yards from the ball. He removed the flag from the ground and handed it to his marker who had followed him all the way, as if it was some sort of reward.

The fifth found of the cup involved Derby in a trip to Teesside on 7th February 1948. Derby played as a team at a windswept Ayresome Park to run out worthy 2-1 winners. Their hero was a young reserve goalkeeper stepping in for his first team debut at the last minute. He rose to the occasion magnificently and Derby realised they had made a real find in Frank Payne. Middlesbrough, who depended heavily on the form of Wilf Mannion, were frustrated because their England inside-left did not have a happy 90 minutes. After a fruitless spell against Ward, Mannion switched over to inside-right where he found Chick Musson in brilliant form. Carter and Steel were completely unselfish in their efforts to bring their wing partners into the game. Derby now faced a sixth-round tie away at Queens Park Rangers. Goalkeeper Billy Townsend's injury looked like being long-term and, as Payne was so inexperienced, it was decided to buy Jock Wallace from Blackpool.

Before the cup was due to resume there was a significant league fixture to be played on 14th February. The match was at the Baseball Ground and the opposition were Sunderland. The game had more than its usual importance for Raich because his old club had just paid Newcastle United £20,000 for Len Shackleton. Raich had always maintained that Sunderland had sold him too cheaply and this was his opportunity to prove it. Sunderland's pre-war keeper Johnny Mapson was still in the team and he was supposed to have told his defenders not to worry about Carter shooting because he could deal with it. How wrong he was: Derby won by five goals to one and Raich Carter scored four of them, including a 21-minute first-half hat-trick. By contrast Shackleton did not impress anyone. He and Jackie Robinson were given a lesson in the art of inside forward play by Carter and Steel who dovetailed perfectly with each other. To add to the celebrations it was Rose Carter's birthday.

In the week before the sixth-round, the Derby trainer Jack Poole banned any practice with a football to prevent an accident like the one which had put goalkeeper Townsend out of the previous round. On the Friday morning before the game, the players organised a fake injury in the gym which Raich Carter agreed to report to Poole. In great panic, the trainer sought out the injured player, Bert Mosley. It was several minutes before he realised he was being conned.

The Derby County directors decided not to permit TV cameras into the cup-tie against Queen's Park Rangers, a decision regarded by most as reactionary. In the middle of February in the same week rumours had begun to circulate that Carter would be leaving soon for a managerial post at Leeds United. Derby manager Stuart McMillan denied any knowledge of such a move.

The Derby team for the cup-tie was unchanged: Wallace; Mosley, Howe; Ward, Leuty, Musson; Harrison, Carter, Stamps, Steel, Morrison. The Queen's Park Rangers' manager Dave Magnall declared that his club were confident of victory and they certainly put up a creditable performance by holding Derby 1-1. In the replay it was clear from the start that Derby meant business as Steel scored after four minutes. Carter played a sound tactical game and the first of his two goals scored from 30 yards was one of the best seen all season. The 5-0 victory meant Derby County would face Manchester

United in the semi-final at Hillsborough on 13th March 1948.

The Rams were unchanged and at full strength but they faced the first of Matt Busby's great Manchester United teams: Crompton; Carey, Aston; Anderson, Chilton, Cockburn; Delaney, Morris, Rowley, Pearson, Mitten. En route to the semi-final they had disposed of four previous cup-winning clubs: Aston Villa, Liverpool, Charlton and Preston. However, Derby were unbeaten for the previous three months so they were confident and rated their chances. On the day it was Manchester United who combined better and were always a shade faster on the ball. Derby could point to the errors made by their goalkeeper Wallace but the neutral observers agreed that United were the better team on the day. Also Stan Pearson netted a hat-trick of opportunist goals in a 3-1 victory. Tim Ward, Derby's main inspiration, thought they had conceded three terrible goals. His disappointment was especially acute because he had missed the 1946 final and now he would miss the 1948 final. Ward had to admit that his great pal Raich Carter had a below-par game mainly because of the close attentions of terrier-like Henry Cockburn.

The match was also significant for Carter because it was the last major fixture he would play for Derby County. Within two weeks he played his last home game for Derby against Blackpool, who were the cup finalists that Manchester United would meet at Wembley. The game on Good Friday attracted 35,000 to the Baseball Ground and predictably Raich Carter scored. Unfortunately, Blackpool escaped with a point thanks to a goal by Stan Mortensen. Also, playing that day was Raich Carter's great international and RAF partner, Stan Matthews. Opinion in the game about the famous winger was divided. Even though he was a friend, Raich Carter said that Stan was, "so much of the star individualist that, though he was one of the best players of all time, he was not really a good footballer. When Stan gets the ball on the wing you don't know when it's coming back. He's an extraordinarily difficult winger to play alongside."

On Easter Monday the return game which Derby won 1-0 was played at Blackpool. Carter scored the decisive goal with a typical 'shoot first and argue afterwards.' Carter's goal against Blackpool was his 50th for Derby County in 83 league and Cup games. This was an impressive strike-rate for a player who was not exclusively a striker. The story was much the same if wartime appearances are added to peacetime because the record then was 106 goals in 148 games. In both cases it represents just over six goals every ten games.

Chapter Twenty-Two
Move into Management

SINCE THE rumours in February 1948 about a Carter move into management in Leeds, the subject had not gone away. In fact, the Leeds' directors had interviewed Carter and a large measure of agreement had been reached. Raich stressed that the manager must have complete control over all football matters. The financial terms of the post were agreed but there was one stumbling block; the club offered only a three-year contract whereas Raich was seeking a five-year deal. The club decided they would not make an appointment until the end of the season. As Raich Carter had been spotted in Leeds, other clubs were alerted to his possible availability.

The next approach came from Hull City who sent seven directors over to Derby to interview him. They were looking for a player and assistant manager. Raich Carter was impressed by the enthusiasm and ambition shown by the Hull directors. He was also attracted by the chance to work with the legendary Major Frank Buckley, the Hull manager. Buckley was a big, broad man with a bald head and a military bearing. He enjoyed wearing plus fours and he demanded the respect of his staff. Raich Carter had one misgiving which was whether he was ready to play in the Third Division. Therefore, he asked for time to think it over. In the meantime other offers came from Notts County, a fresh approach from Leeds and contact from Nottingham Forest. Carter was particularly grateful for a statement from the Derby chairman Ben Robshaw, which said, "We are anxious to do all we can to ensure Carter's future." Obviously, the club would be entitled to a transfer fee if he agreed to play for another club but not if he moved into management. However, no pressure at all was placed on him. The field was quickly narrowed down because Notts County wanted him only as a player, so that was rejected even though it was the most lucrative. Leeds were still disputing the length of the contract so the choice lay between Hull and Nottingham Forest.

It was Wednesday 31st March 1948 when matters came to a head. Derby had an evening game against Liverpool and it was decided to rest Raich Carter because there were so many clubs wishing to interview him. Both Forest and Hull City were offering the post of assistant manager with the possibility of future managership. Hull had the disadvantage of Third Division football but Major Buckley was much older than Forest's manager Billy Walker so the chance of promotion should arrive sooner. Carter was still undecided as he arrived at the Baseball Ground to see the Liverpool game. He was immediately surrounded by the seven Hull City directors and accompanied to the Derby boardroom. A joke by Raich about seven dwarfs, once again after Snow White, seemed to settle the deal and he signed for Hull City for £6,000. The match that evening was the first Derby game Raich Carter had missed since 20th December and the team's long unbeaten run in the League was ended 4-0. The press were sure that Derby were not the same without their 'Maestro.' Without his inspiration the team were like a ship without a rudder. The following day, 1st April, Carter, now a Third Division player, was chosen as England's reserve for the match at Hampden Park. Stan Mortensen and Stan Pearson were preferred at inside forward.

Raich Carter travelled to Hull on the Friday prior to the match with York City on Saturday 3rd April. As he reached the outskirts of the city he noticed posters everywhere advertising the match with York. Each of them had red and white strips across them proclaiming, "Carter Will Play." A lunch had been arranged at the Station Hotel to give Raich Carter the chance to meet the players, and to establish friendly relations with them after all the publicity following the transfer negotiations. He told the press that he had joined Hull City with high hopes of success. He hoped to remain at Hull for many years. His wife and daughter were still in Derby but they would move as soon as a house became available. He said he had played in the cup in Hull before the war. He also played at Anlaby Road for Huddersfield during the war. Undoubtedly he had been the main topic of conversation in the city since signing.

The next day, Carter led his new teammates out on to the pitch at Boothferry Park and received a tremendous reception from 33,000 fans. Carter felt strangely nervous and uncertain in a way he had not experienced since his early days with Sunderland. The game was an interesting one as it gave the new assistant manager his first experience of Third Division football. He was agreeably surprised by the standard of play which was better than he had anticipated. From what he had observed in his first game Carter believed he had made the right decision to transfer to Hull. He thought back to Johnny Cochrane's early days at Roker Park and how the little Scot had built a fine team, blending youth and experience. He felt that a similar potential and enthusiasm existed at Boothferry Park, although it had to be remembered that, when Carter arrived, Hull, like Sunderland and Derby, had never won the cup. Furthermore, they had never played in the top division.

Straight after the York match, which ended 1-1, Carter was on his way home to Derby. He had two commitments to fulfil before returning to Hull. Firstly he had been selected as reserve for England against Scotland the following Saturday, and on the Wednesday after that, 14th April, he had been chosen to captain the Football League against the Irish League at Preston. In the Sunday press next day Carter found himself being blamed for the departure of Hull's assistant manager Frank Taylor whereas, in fact, Taylor's appointment had been terminated before Carter was offered the job. It was evident to Raich Carter that the journalist's story had come from Major Buckley and this made it rather disturbing. But, within a couple of days, another newspaper story revealed that Buckley had resigned as manager of Hull City because of disagreements "in points of policy."

This decision completely changed Raich Carter's prospects. Clearly he was no longer assistant manager to Buckley. There was no contact from Hull so his exact position with the club was unclear. Therefore he made his way to Glasgow to join the England party for the international. Despite the fact that the England goalkeeper Frank Swift was badly injured and was taken to hospital, there was no provision to allow the reserve to take over. In fact, Raich Carter agreed to accompany Swift to Glasgow's Victoria Hospital. Frank Swift later described him as a "very able and considerate nurse."

At this point a message came through from Hull City asking Carter to get in touch with them. When the telephone call came it asked him to return to Hull immediately. However, this was not practicable because on Wednesday he was playing for the Football League in Preston. Therefore it was agreed that Carter should return to Hull straight after Wednesday's match. The match on 14th April 1948 was Raich Carter's last representative game. He had first represented his country in April 1934 so there was a span of 14 years between start and finish. By way of comparison, Tom Finney's international career spanned 12 years; Tommy Lawton's ten years; and Billy Wright's 12-and-a-half years. Not surprisingly, Raich Carter was appointed captain for the match against the Irish.

It soon became clear that Leeds United would secure Major Buckley as their new manager, although their chairman Ernest Pullan resigned over the deal. In the remaining weeks of the season Raich Carter played in three more games for Hull City and watched one match. He made no changes on or off the pitch but simply studied the squad of players he had inherited. On 23rd April 1948 the *Hull Daily Mail* announced to no one's surprise that Raich Carter had been appointed player-manager. He was already in control of the playing policy of the club. He told the press that he, "never expected that promotion would come so soon," and he added, "you cannot command success on the field, you must strive to attain it."

Later in April it was announced that Raich Carter would be able to accompany the Hull City party on their Scandinavian tour as he had not been selected for the FA's tour. The Carters were together in Derby on 3rd May as guests at a function organised by Raich's former clubmates. Jack Howe, the new Derby captain, presented Raich with an inscribed silver cigarette case and also a gift for Mrs Carter. There were many speakers who paid tribute to Carter's contribution to Derby County and to his great popularity at the club. Raich Carter responded by saying how much he had enjoyed his time at Derby and how fantastic the Derby fans had been. He hoped to return to the town one day with the Hull team for a First Division match.

The tour of Denmark and Sweden gave the new manager further opportunities to get to know his squad and to study them in action. The tour was declared a success thanks to the sightseeing, the sunshine and the warm hospitality. Another unusual feature of the close season was the organisation at Wembley's Empire Pool of England's first official five-a-side competition. Carter was chosen, along with Lawton, Matthews, Leuty, Ward and Swift, to play for an All-England team to play Arsenal. Raich Carter's exhibition of skill contributed to a 2-1 victory for England. A further innovation that summer was for Carter and three directors to make a talent-hunting trip to Scotland by chartered plane.

As a result of the new manager's observations it was clear to him that the most pressing need was for a good left winger. He immediately thought of Sunderland, and their consistently good winger Eddie Burbanks. The difficulty was that the player was not on the transfer list so the club had to be persuaded to release him after 13 years and the player also had to be convinced. The fact that Carter and Burbanks had played together in the 1937 cup final probably sealed the deal. The other changes which Raich Carter decided on during the summer were not in personnel but in positions. He realised that there was considerable potential at the club but that to exploit it positional changes were needed. Therefore, Tom Berry switched from left-half to left back, Denis Durham moved from striker to left-half and Ken Harrison crossed over from left wing to right wing.

The Hull players reported to Boothferry Park on 21st July 1948 with the one target of promotion. Carter's aim was to play football of First Division quality regardless of whatever style the opposition might adopt. In his view class would prevail in football even if rough and ready tactics caused the occasional setbacks. Carter was also a strong believer in team spirit as an essential ingredient of success. He quickly appreciated that not only did he have the team spirit on the pitch but also great enthusiasm and support all the way up to the directors.

It was good news for the club that Burbanks was immediately impressed by his new surroundings and that centre-forward Norman Moore was to become a full-time professional. The pre-season public trial was held on 14th August and, as a result, the following team was selected for the first game of the new season; Bly; Fowler, Berry; Greenhalgh, Meens, Durham; Harrison, Carter, Moore, Buchan, Burbanks.

Chapter Twenty-Three

Records and Promotion

THERE WERE great hopes for promotion among Hull City supporters even though, at that time, only one club from the Third Division North would go up to Division Two. The directors had given Raich Carter such a completely free hand that responsibility for the club's progress or setbacks would fall entirely on the manager. There would be no excuses from Carter but, on the other hand, if necessary he was prepared to build the promotion campaign over two or three seasons. The first requirement was to establish a settled team, something Major Buckley had failed to do.

The first League game was away to Tranmere on the 21st August. The feature of a 2-1 victory was the improved teamwork which Raich Carter's guidance had introduced. The first home game was watched by 33,000, a new league record for Boothferry Park. The Hull team was unchanged and Oldham were hit for six, including four goals in seven minutes. Included was Raich Carter's first contribution to the club's score sheet. The next game against Mansfield was won 4-0 and the record attendance was broken again with 34,000 spectators. By the 11th September, Hull City were the only club in the Football League with a 100 percent record, thanks to a 3-0 victory over Wrexham. A week later Hull's 4-2 win over Halifax created a Third Division North record of seven consecutive victories. On 25th September the defeat of Bradford City by 2-0 meant that Hull City had equalled the record held jointly by Everton, Sheffield United and Woolwich Arsenal of eight successive wins. The crowd of 36,500 was also a record and Carter and Burbanks fittingly scored the goals.

In order to hold the record outright Hull City needed to win away at Accrington Stanley at Peel Park. Before a record gate of 13,162, Hull City beat Accrington 2-1 to break the 45-year-old record. Such was the esteem in which Carter was held nation-wide, even the iced cakes in the Accrington boardroom bore his name. In that sequence of nine wins Carter had used only 12 players – Andrew Conway replacing Willie Buchan at inside-left on three occasions. On their way home the Hull players stopped at a hotel in Ilkley where they received the congratulations of the Australian rugby league tourists. As their coach reached the outskirts of Hull it was met by police cars and motorcycle outriders and escorted to a civic reception at the floodlit Regal Cinema.

In a speech to a triumphant crowd of about 12,000 Raich Carter said, "Tonight you are welcoming back a team who have played good football. I can honestly say that I have been very proud and pleased to come to Hull City. We have a long way to go and I hope to see an even bigger crowd here in May." Then trainer George Lax led the players in singing Raich Carter's theme song 'When Your Hair has Turned to Silver.' However, Carter's immediate concern was that three players had been injured at Accrington and his reserve strength was about to be tested at Doncaster. Although the 100 percent record was over, Carter was satisfied with the draw achieved at Doncaster where there was a club record gate of 36,106. It was a reassuring performance for the new manager because it showed that the team was resilient when a crisis arose. It helped him to settle into his new post and to face anything the rest of the season might produce.

Hull City's unbeaten record was finally broken on 16th October when they lost at home before another record crowd of 48,000. The visitors were Darlington who won by 1-0 despite being on the defensive for most of the game. This was followed by a draw at Rochdale which led to an important deal in the transfer market. The Danish international Viggo Jensen, from EFB Esbjerg who had 15 caps, signed as an amateur. It proved to be one of Raich Carter's most popular and crucial signings at Hull. Permission was received from the FA for Jensen to play against New Brighton. He was selected at inside-right with Carter moving over to inside-left. The debut was generally successful, Jensen scoring in a 4-1 victory.

At the end of November, Hull City began their FA Cup run with a first-round tie against Accrington. Raich Carter was not used to such an early start to the cup campaign as his previous clubs had byes until the third-round. Hull City progressed comfortably into the second round where they were drawn to play against Reading. The Reading international inside forward Maurice Edelston made his first appearance in Hull despite being a native of the city and having a father, Joe, who formerly captained City. Raich Carter faced six players in the Reading team against whom he had previously played. The goalless draw meant a replay at Reading, which Hull won without the injured Carter or Burbanks.

The league fixture list had produced a special Christmas package. Rotherham, the only club to pose a serious threat to Hull City's promotion hopes, would meet their rivals twice over the holiday. On Christmas Day a huge crowd of 49,655 turned up at Boothferry Park to see the first clash of the table toppers. The very unexpected selection by the manager was to put himself at centre-forward. This was the first time he had played in that position in a competitive match. With only five minutes remaining Hull City led 3-0 but before the end Rotherham had pulled two goals back. Opinions about the manager's performance varied as some believed he was wasted in the centre-forward role; others thought that while defenders concentrated on Carter, other colleagues were allowed greater freedom. In the return game at Rotherham the Hull defence remained solid in a goalless draw. These two results gave Hull a strong boost to their promotion campaign and also gave them further confidence for their cup run.

The draw for the third-round of the cup involved an away tie at Blackburn. Carter warned his opponents from the second division that Hull City were unbeaten away from home. Despite the absence of both Carter and Burbanks, Hull overcame Blackburn by 2-1 after extra-time. For the League fixtures Carter recovered fitness before Burbanks and took the decision to play on the left wing himself. As he scored a goal with a terrific right-foot drive and the game was won comfortably, the experiment was deemed a success.

The draw for the fifth-round of the cup produced a colourful local derby between Grimsby and Hull. It was not just a clash between two local clubs but the rivalry between the UK's two chief fishing ports. For centre-forward Norman Moore the tie was particularly attractive because he came from Grimsby; he had been transferred from Grimsby and three close members of his family had played for Grimsby. The match turned out to be a great struggle in which Grimsby twice pulled back from a goal behind, only for Hull City to score a third time. Raich Carter decided to play only half-an-hour before the kick-off but his contribution was vital to Hull's success. The draw for the fifth-round meant Hull City would face opponents from the top division, either Blackpool or Stoke, who faced a replay. Raich Carter commented, "We might get a little relaxation by the seaside if we play Blackpool." Then he added with a smile, "At any rate, you'll be seeing the two fast wings – Stan Matthews and myself." In the event, it was Stoke City who emerged as the next opposition to Hull's giant-killing exploits. They were playing well in the top division and had Neil Franklin, the finest centre-half in the country, at the heart of their defence.

The match took place on 12th February at the Victoria Ground and Hull City outplayed their mighty opponents from start to finish and won by two clear goals. The victory was achieved by good football and by great team spirit. Even the masterly Franklin could not stem the tide. The *Hull Daily Mail* reported that, "The ubiquitous Carter must receive much of the praise for the strategy which had such a devastating effect, but all eleven players deserve credit for pulling their weight so well." After the game Raich Carter commented that, "The Stoke officials were loud in their praise of the way we played."

Hull City had the prize-draw for the sixth-round: Manchester United, cup-holders, at home. Raich Carter said that he had been on the losing side against Manchester United the previous year but he wondered, "Has any team won the cup two years in a row in the last 50 years?" However, he went on to remind his listeners, "We have got to win tomorrow. Promotion is our primary aim." In fact, Hull City were surprisingly beaten at Bradford thus ending a Football League record of 13 away games without defeat: not good preparation for the cup tie, especially as two days before the game Manchester United declared Johnny Carey fit, which meant that they would be at full strength. For a fortnight the visit of Manchester United had overshadowed any other topic of conversation in the football-crazy city. On 26th February 1949 a soccer invasion hit Hull as thousands of Mancunians swept in by road and rail. By noon over 13,000 supporters were already in the ground. Ultimately, a ground record of 55,019 was attained. Demand for cup tickets had been enormous and the club received 10,000 written requests which they could not even open, never mind answer. One director, Stan Kershaw, admitted that he had had over 600 letters sent to his home address.

Manager Carter himself chose to play on the left wing again because Jensen and Buchan were doing such a good job at inside forward. Once the cup-tie got under way Hull City imposed themselves and caused United several anxious moments, especially in the goalless first half. The only goal of the game came with 17 minutes left and was surrounded with controversy. The move was begun by United's right winger Jimmy Delaney with a good run followed by a centre to Stan Pearson who beat goalkeeper Billy Bly, but the Hull players and supporters were sure Delaney had taken the ball over the goal-line before centring. Even the United players seemed uncertain about celebrating the goal. Raich Carter admitted that he was not close enough to see whether the ball had crossed the line. The decision had to be accepted and Hull City went out of the cup. Once again, Raich had been involved in a great contest with his marker Henry Cockburn. The local paper wrote that Carter was "subtle, ubiquitous and tireless" but he had less freedom than usual because of Cockburn's attentions.

From the managerial point of view Raich Carter quickly realised that the exit from the cup was a blessing in disguise because the main aim of the season was to win promotion. There were 17 league games remaining and Rotherham were proving to be dogged rivals. They also had the experience of being runners-up in Third Division North in the two previous seasons. At that time, one problem for Carter, with a backlog of postponed fixtures, was the government's ban on daytime, midweek fixtures. This meant the club could not start to work off its arrears until it was light enough for an evening kick-off.

On Sunday 27th February, in the aftermath of the cup-tie, Mr and Mrs Carter were the guests of Canon and Mrs Tardrew at St Mary's Church, Beverley. The sermon was based on 'Lessons from the Cup-tie' and the vicar stressed the value of disciplined training, the need for courage in adversity and the value of team spirit. Although Carter was originally a chapel-goer, he welcomed this initiative by the Church and read the lesson himself. This diversion from football was just one of many invitations which the manager of Hull City received. The success of the team led to Raich Carter touring factories, presenting prizes, opening fêtes and attending charity functions. He had become a public figure whose presence was demanded all over the city. Hull had endured severe damage during the war, second only to London, but had received none of the sympathy which towns like Coventry were given because, for its protection, it was always referred to as a north eastern port. Now the football team had put the city back on the map and had helped to restore the morale of the people.

Raich Carter was really worried that the cup run had damaged the drive for promotion. The backlog of fixtures meant that for weeks in the spring the club would be playing at least two games a week. This additional strain on the players was likely to increase the risk of injury. It was not easy to sign adequate cover in the transfer market. In mid-March victories over Darlington and Carlisle allowed Hull to overtake Rotherham at the top of the table. However, early in April, a home defeat by York by 3-2, after leading 2-0, was worrying. So was the long injury and sickness list which forced Raich Carter to move the versatile Jensen to fullback. In the event, Hull had to be content with a draw against Southport. The pressures on the manager were intensified in mid-April when persistent rumours alleged that a rift had opened between him and the directors. They alleged that some of the directors were seeking to withdraw 'the free hand' which Carter had been given at the outset. It was necessary for Raich Carter to go public to deny all the rumours "as bunkum and stupid." He was at a loss to know how such stories originated. He added that if he did not have a free hand he would not be staying at Hull.

The Easter programme brought Hull City three crucial games, all of which were won with nine goals scored and none conceded. In the next game at Bootham Crescent against York, Raich Carter played despite not feeling his best. Fortunately, it did not show in his play as he was the liveliest forward and, as usual, he was the main target of the opposition. The match was won but Rotherham also won their match. The position on 27th April 1949 was that Hull had 62 points and had three games to play, whereas Rotherham had 61 points and only two games to play. Furthermore, Hull had a vastly superior goal average. In fact, promotion was decided after Hull City's next game at home to Stockport. Victory was assured by five second-half goals, making the final result 6-1 to Hull. Thousands of supporters remained in the ground to find out the result of Rotherham's match. When the news was announced that Rotherham had only drawn then Hull City's promotion was assured (unless Hull lost two games and Rotherham won by over 30-0).

The ovation from the crowd was tremendous, then it turned into a chant for the manager: "Carter, Carter, Carter." A director appeared in the dressing room and called to Raich Carter, "You'll have to go out and speak to them. They've invaded the pitch and the police cordon has collapsed." So Raich led his team up into the crowded directors' box with a towel round his neck and a raincoat over his football shirt. When he spoke he said, "Today is a happy day for Hull City, for the directors, players and myself. I wish to thank you sincerely for your support. We have had a good season and won promotion. I hope you will all come and support us again throughout next season."

As far as one historian, Peter Jeffs in *The Golden Age of Football*, was concerned, for the title of manager of the season there was only one candidate – Raich Carter.

One of his main concerns off the pitch was the welfare side of his players' lives. The club arranged theatre trips and social events to which the players' wives were also invited. Players were encouraged to consult with the manager if there were any personal difficulties with which the club might be able to help. On the other hand, Raich Carter did not believe in any snooping tactics by the club to control the players' social lives. He took the view that if a player did not realise that sensible hours and reasonable socialising were important to their fitness and form, they were not worth bothering with. Another feature of Carter's regime was that he was not keen on post-mortems after matches. He would sometimes give advice at half-time when it could be used in the game, but ranting and melodramatic inquests after the game he regarded as counter-productive. Highlighting players' mistakes, of which they were already well aware, could lead to an atmosphere of recrimination. Carter's style was to have a quiet word during the week with any player who had a recurring problem. Harold Meens, the stalwart centre-half in the promotion season, said that Raich promoted team spirit, involved the players and their wives in everything and made the club like a family concern. The result, he believed, was a team which played for each other.

It was not only a time for Hull City supporters to celebrate. During March and April 1949 two irksome reminders of wartime privations were ended. Firstly the much-resented clothes rationing came to an end. This was quickly followed by the abolition of sweet rationing. During the same period Raich Carter's picture was revealed in two different forms. Early in March Carter's portrait, by local artist Roland Spencer-Ford, was completed. In the newspapers a photograph of the soccer star was used in an advertisement for the hair cream Nufix. In this field Raich was challenging his old soccer contemporary Denis

Compton who was popularly associated with Brylcreem.

One final word of warning was issued to the Hull City manager at the end of a glorious season: the fate of both Doncaster Rovers and Lincoln City, the two previous champions of the Third Division North, was relegation after just one season in the Second Division.

Chapter Twenty-Four

Survival in the Second Division

DURING THE close season Hull City had arranged a tour of Ireland. They beat Distillery in Belfast, drew with Portadown and then moved south where they beat Cork Athletic and Shelbourne. Although he did not know it at the time, for Raich Carter the fixture with Cork Athletic was the forerunner of a successful association. Back in Hull the city's soccer players took on the rugby players at cricket. A crowd of 5,000 turned up and over £200 went to charity. The rugby men batted first but were bowled out for 53 (Carter two for 12). In the footballer's innings Raich Carter scored 46 out of a total of 131 for five wickets.

Early in July, Sunderland Cricket Club were able to recruit Willie Watson, the Yorkshire cricketer, who was playing his football in Sunderland. The aim was to boost the attendance at a Durham Senior League match. The experiment worked, so it was decided to invite Raich Carter to play cricket for Sunderland CC while on his holidays in the town. In typical style Carter hit 45 runs in 25 minutes, including two sixes, to help achieve victory. It was a busy weekend for him because he then travelled back to Hull in a rush to play for Hull City cricket team against Withernsea.

On 20th July Hull City players were due back to resume training after the close season. No new signings had been announced but there was considerable speculation about a large bid to buy Neil Franklin from Stoke. However, the Stoke directors were very reluctant to release Franklin. Hull City's regular centre-half Harold Meens was unfit for the opening second division fixture with Bury so it was decided to buy Gerrard Bowler from Portsmouth, against whom Raich Carter had played in the first division. After beating Bury 3-2 and losing at Blackburn 4-2, Hull City were due to play at Leicester, a ground at which Raich Carter enjoyed producing something extra. This was in order to remind Leicester that they had rejected him at the age of 17. On this occasion he scored in a resounding Hull victory. That day Leicester were captained by 22-year-old Don Revie.

Early in October Hull City played their first ever match with Queens Park Rangers on their first visit to London since the war. In one of his best games for Hull City, Carter scored twice and made a goal for Harrison in a 4-1 victory. In mid-October Hull City reached third place in the league with a win over Preston North End. Late in October, in an East versus West Yorkshire match, Hull City entertained Leeds United, whose manager Major Buckley selected a 17-year-old with a big future, John Charles.

Carter was anxious to strengthen his team and after a long and difficult saga Hull City secured the transfer of Revie for a fee of £20,000, then the third highest ever. Revie went straight in to the Hull team for the visit of Coventry. However, it was Raich Carter who pulled the game out of the fire with two late goals, and his match-winning brilliance overshadowed Revie's debut. Late in November, Hull City beat Barnsley who included the future Tottenham captain Danny Blanchflower. More than three decades later Blanchflower recalled playing against Hull. His manager had told him to keep an eye on Raich Carter. His skipper Gordon Pallister, advised him to keep two eyes on Carter. Blanchflower wrote, "So I shadowed the old fox around the pitch. He accepted me with some grace and patience and gently coaxed me into a spider's web. Raich drew me from mid-field right into my own penalty area. He seemed unconcerned about the ebb and flow play as he kept me idling next to him in front of the Barnsley goal. I was lured into a false sense of security. Then, on one of the rare occasions he received the ball, he turned in a flash and the ball was in the back of our net. That was about all he did, but it was enough."

Early in December, Sheffield United were the visitors to

Boothferry Park. It was Hull's worst display of the season and they were well beaten 0-4. On this occasion Raich Carter was outshone by his old England colleague Jimmy Hagan. The following week Raich Carter made his first visit to Gigg Lane to play Bury. His presence in the team acted like a magnet to the Bury fans who saw a goalless draw.

Just before Christmas, Raich Carter took on the new role of Santa Claus in the Hull City children's Christmas party. It was held in Willerby and the manager entered into the spirit of the occasion wholeheartedly, possibly because it was his own 36th birthday.

January 1950 brought the third-round of the FA Cup and Hull City needed a replay before they removed Southport from the competition. Two league victories revived the club's promotion bid; however, the cup run was short-lived as the Tigers were beaten by Stockport County. Early in February, Hull City had a vital promotion game with Sheffield Wednesday, who were second in the table to Spurs. Hull City needed to avenge a 6-2 defeat at Hillsborough earlier in the season. Carter chose a squad of 14 for the game but there was no centre-forward available. The attendance at Boothferry Park was 50,000 and Hull's emergency striker was Raich Carter. The visitors did well to finish the match with a draw as Hull City hit their best form.

Early in March, Hull faced a tough fixture at Preston where Tom Finney was the chief inspiration. From the outset Hull City were on top and eventually established a 2-1 lead. Tom Finney was well held by veteran fullback John Taylor until the England winger was switched to centre-forward and led Preston to a 4-2 victory. It was apparent that all was not well when Hull's lively winger Ken Harrison was dropped after 84 consecutive appearances. More disturbing was the failure of Revie to live up to Raich Carter's expectations. Originally Revie was seen as the long-term replacement for Carter when he retired as a player. Revie was keen to play alongside Carter to learn new skills and increase his tactical awareness. He was a great admirer of Carter's ability to find space on the pitch, call for the ball and immediately look up before passing it. He also admired the way Carter ordered things on the pitch, although things did not work out too well in practice. Carter generally played a deep schemer role which Revie felt was his best position. Instead, Revie was expected to play further forward where he felt out of position and out of form.

In mid-March Hull City faced promotion rivals Leeds United

One of Raich Carter's first acts as Hull City player-manager was to sign old teammate Eddie Burbanks. (Hull Daily Mail)

The waist might be thicker but the style was the same. Raich Carter in action for Hull City. (Hull Daily Mail)

Walking off at Accrington Stanley after Hull City won their first nine games of the season to break the 45 year-old league record.

A promotion photograph by Reckitt & Colman taken as part of a campaign by a new hair cream Nufix. A free copy was given away with every jar.

Signing for Cork Athletic in February 1952.

Celebrating promotion as Leeds United manager. Raich Carter pours champagne for John Charles. A young Jack Charlton is on Carter's right. (Colorsport)

In managerial pose at Mansfield.

Raich Carter (right) sits in the stands at Boothferry Park with his best man and old Sunderland teammate Bobby Gurney. (Hull Daily Mail)

On the pools panel. From the left, George Young, Neil Franklin, chairman Sir Ronald Howe , Raich Carter, Stan Mortensen, Arthur Ellis.

With wife Pat and his collection of medals.

at Elland Road. Extra interest was aroused by Major Buckley's presence, in charge, at Leeds, and his Welsh protégé John Charles. As a stop-gap centre-forward Raich Carter tried hard to break down the Leeds defence but had a lean time against Charles. Leeds won 3-0 and Hull City slipped down to fifth place. Many believed that Carter's talents were wasted at centre-forward and that a new striker would have to be bought sooner or later. Late in March 1950 a home defeat by Southampton ended any lingering promotion hopes for Hull City.

Early in April, Hull City were faced with two fixtures with the outstanding team in the Second Division Tottenham Hotspur. The much admired Spurs' 'push and run' team would not only win the title and be promoted but they would go on to win the First Division title at their first attempt. The first Spurs v Hull match was played before 66,889 supporters at White Hart Lane. This was the largest gate before which Hull City had ever played and they managed a creditable draw. Three days later the clubs met again and this time Hull City managed a 1-0 victory. Don Revie's form had much improved since he had been moved to right half. Unfortunately, Raich Carter suffered an ankle injury which forced him out on the wing for much of the game.

Hull City finished the season 1949-50 in seventh place with 45 points. The first half of the season was very encouraging but the second half was disappointing. As a consolation, Hull City's close season tour was to Turkey where they won their three matches. When they returned to England it was just in time to benefit from the abolition of petrol rationing after ten years. In the press, Raich Carter found himself proposed for the England party to travel to Brazil for the World Cup. The press argued that every specialist position had cover except Wilf Mannion's. The selectors and manager Walter Winterbottom could object that Carter was 36, to which the press countered that Matthews was older. (Not true, really, as Carter was 14 months older). But Carter was not picked and in June England were infamously beaten 1-0 by the United States. Raich Carter's supporters were able to assert that it would not have happened if he had been out there! As if to reinforce his supporters' case Raich Carter began the 1950-51 season by scoring in eight out of the first nine games.

Once again the new season was preceded by a charity cricket match between Hull City and Hull rugby league clubs. The footballers won and received a huge silver challenge cup from the

Sheriff. There was a crowd of 5,000 and Raich Carter explained his modest score of one by claiming "The ball was not big enough." Hull City's main close season signing was Alf Ackerman from Clyde. He scored twice in the trial match and was selected for the first game of the season against West Ham. The Hull City team was; Bly; Gibson, Berry; Jensen, Meens, Mellor; Harrison, Revie, Ackerman, Carter, Burbanks.

The first two games, in which the Tigers each time fought back from a two goal deficit, finished 3-3 and Carter scored half the Hull City goals. The third game against Swansea was the first win and, because Carter scored again, the press wondered if the team were not too dependent on their captain who could not be expected to go on forever. The winning goal was scored by Don Revie, his first league goal for the club. Carter's goal was his 187th in the league in peacetime, which meant he had drawn level with Tommy Lawton as leading goal scorer. Just behind them came Peter Doherty in third place on 171 goals. Early in September Hull met Doncaster Rovers, who had been promoted from the Third Division. Doherty was Doncaster's player-manager, so the main centre of attention was the battle of wits between the two old clubmates. In the event Doncaster prevailed 2-1, even though Raich Carter opened the scoring.

In mid-September Hull City beat Brentford 3-0. Raich Carter scored two goals which brought his total for the season to ten. This meant for the 11th successive peacetime season Carter had reached the double-figure mark. Another encouraging result early in October was a 4-1 win over an accomplished Southampton team.

The following Wednesday evening, 4th October 1950, Raich was answering questions put by members of the public, and one persistent criticism of his playing style was his loud shouting and gesticulation. Critics over the years had suggested that he was short tempered, arrogant or blaming his mistakes on others. In answer to his immediate questioner he said, "To me, there is nobody at the match. I am concerned only about one thing and that is winning the match. If we don't win I am out of a job." He explained that teammates could be assisted by a timely call which inevitably had to be short and sharp. He also remembered the advice he had received from the shouts of senior players when he began playing professional football with Sunderland reserves. Even in his first international he appreciated the shouted advice he received from Sammy Crooks on the right wing. To another questioner who asked about the pre-match tactical plan Raich replied, "There is only one thing to do – play football and you blind them with science. We go out to no set plan. All we say is, we are going to play football." When he was asked about his views on management he was equally direct. "I pick the team. I get the players I want. If Tom Lawton, for example, was for sale and I wanted him my directors would say, 'O.K., Raich, if that's what you want go right ahead.' I wouldn't take the job if I were going to be dictated to." He added, "I also try to look after players off the pitch. From personal experience I know how important that is."

During October, Hull City's results deteriorated as their injury list grew. In three successive matches the team finished with only ten fit players. At this point Hull City were given permission by Stoke City to speak to Neil Franklin. He was serving a period of suspension until 31st January 1951 for leaving Stoke while under contract and for playing in unaffiliated football in Bogotá, Colombia. The initial Hull City offer of £20,000 was rejected by Stoke who were seeking more than £25,000 (the current record transfer fee at that time was £26,500 for Eddie Quigley). There was no pressure on the negotiations since the suspension still had over three months to run. Early in November 1950 Stoke accepted a bid of £22,500. On Humberside this was seen as the biggest scoop in the club's history because Franklin was generally regarded as the best centre-half in British football. Initially the transfer was a gentleman's agreement until the suspension was lifted. Franklin was delighted the matter had been settled and was pleased to be joining his friend and colleague Raich Carter. On behalf of the directors, Kenneth Percival said, "The fee paid is our highest, but it's yet another indication of our determination to ensure first class football for Hull."

Late in November improved results pushed Hull City up into seventh place in the League. Viggo Jensen completed his two years' residence in Britain in December and therefore was able to sign as a professional. Raich Carter missed seven consecutive matches during November and December because of injury. He scored on his return in the derby against Grimsby on 30th January 1950. The New Year of 1951 brought the third-round of the FA Cup on 6th January. Hull City had a home draw against Everton from Division One. As had so often been the case Raich Carter opened the scoring. Eddie Burbanks was on top form and Syd Gerrie added a second goal which helped to pay off the £11,000 transfer fee paid to Dundee in November. In fact, if it had not been for the brilliance of veteran goalie Ted Sagar, Everton would have lost much more heavily. One innovation in the match was the use of a white football but, more important for Hull City supporters, was the opening on the railway line of the Boothferry Park Halt.

Within a week of the cup victory there was a strong rumour in Hull that Raich Carter was interested in the manager's job at Newcastle. Speaking to the press the manager said, "You can tell the public that I hope to be in Hull for a long time yet. There is no truth in the rumour that I have the intention of going elsewhere." The next fixture was the return clash between Carter and Doherty. Both rival player-managers scored but this time it was a skilful and balanced Hull City who prevailed 4-2. At the end of January Hull City's cup run continued with a 2-0 victory over Rotherham before 50,040 fans. Raich Carter scored his 199th peacetime goal. Further good news came from Don Revie who said he was happy in Hull and wished to stay in the area. He stressed that he had no grievance with the club and did not wish for a transfer. Nevertheless, Carter had been disappointed in his intended successor as Hull's play-maker. He had believed that Revie was an inside forward like himself but now felt he lacked the punch. He was delicate, elegant and accurate but lacked sufficient aggression.

Raich Carter's old England colleague Joe Mercer predicted that Hull City would reach the semi-final of the cup. He said, "In making this suggestion, I pay tribute to one of the finest players and football generals of our time – Raich Carter." The 1st February 1951 meant that Neil Franklin's suspension was completed and the formalities of his transfer could be concluded. Raich Carter enquired if Franklin felt ready to play on Saturday and the unspoken reply was, "Just try and keep me out." Therefore, Franklin's debut was against Blackburn Rovers at Boothferry Park on 3rd February. His previous League game had been on 6th May 1950. There was huge press and public interest in the return of the 'Colombian rebel.' Henry Rose, the sports editor of the *Daily Express*, wrote, "Neil Franklin can banish any fears he may have had about the Hull soccer public's reaction to his return to the English football scene. The 50,000 powered roar, when he stepped on the field against Blackburn behind Raich Carter, his old England buddy, will have left him in no doubt." The match was drawn 1-1, and it was felt that Franklin would need a few more games to settle in. But the next game was the fifth-round cup-tie against Bristol Rovers and Franklin was not eligible. On a heavy pitch, Hull City had no excuses for their 3-0 cup defeat to Bristol Rovers who had cost manager Bert Tann only £350 in transfer fees.

The match at Southampton was a memorable one for Raich Carter. During a 3-2 victory for Hull, their manager and captain scored his 200th peacetime goal (the first had been scored 18-and-a-half years earlier). However, early in March, Carter missed the match at Coventry because of the illness of his wife who had undergone an operation. Hull City's form was inconsistent which meant they did not challenge for promotion. Nevertheless, they did dash the hopes of both Leeds and Cardiff by beating both by two goals to nil. In the matches against Leeds over Easter there was a great duel between Franklin and Charles, who had been moved to centre-forward as an experiment. As a result of Franklin's return to top form the England selectors were known to be watching him. Hull City completed the season with a 5-3 victory over Luton Town. Despite this result the Tigers finished a disappointing tenth in the division.

Chapter Twenty-Five
Resignation and Return

THE CLOSE-SEASON tour in the summer of 1951 took Hull City to Spain. The 15-man party left Hull on 17th May but Raich Carter did not join them. He remained behind because his wife was still recovering from the operation she had undergone in March. Raich was particularly disappointed because he had first been to Spain with Sunderland before the war. From the playing point of view the tour was not a success as Hull lost 4-0 to Atletico Madrid, 2-0 to Bilbao and 5-3 to Barcelona. However, the club had put up with a lot, including the substitution of a five-man forward line at half-time in one game.

Only six weeks after their return the players resumed training for the new season. It was going to be a memorable one for Carter because, on 12th November, he would complete 20 years as a professional footballer. He announced to the press that he would be fit to play for another season.

The opening game of the season against Barnsley was a disappointing goalless draw. Carter found himself closely shadowed by his ex-Derby friend and colleague Tim Ward. He also received an injury to his heel which caused him to miss the next four matches. But, just as he was returning to fitness, Raich Carter shocked the players and the supporters by submitting his resignation to the directors, to take immediate effect from 5th September. The board did not meet to consider the letter until 12th September when they decided, unanimously, to accept the manager's resignation. The directors were not prepared to elaborate on the reasons for the manager's decision while Carter was prepared to explain to the press that it was nothing to do with team matters over which the directors allowed him a free hand. Instead he said it was, "Because of a disagreement on matters of a general nature in the conduct of the club's affairs." He added that he did not have any plans for the immediate future. He said he was sorry to be leaving the club because he had made many friends in the area.

The refusal of the directors to elaborate on the issue, and the vague explanations given by Carter, left shareholders and supporters equally mystified. The news of Carter's departure from Boothferry Park came as a shock to the football world because of the prominent part he had played in the post-war fortunes of the club. His decision to resign was also perplexing because there had been no hint of any discord with the board in any of the many speeches Carter had made when he was guest of honour at various functions around the city.

Although the idea of appointing a player-manager was not invented by Hull City in 1948, the success which Raich Carter had in the role led several other clubs to follow the example. Among the better known exponents were Peter Doherty at Doncaster and Freddy Steele at Mansfield. However, not everyone was impressed with the arrangement. Tommy Lawton, for example, wrote in 1955 that he did not think that the dual role of player and manager worked. He believed it might succeed for a short while and maybe longer in the Third Division but, in the end, it would fail. He said he knew about Carter at Hull and Doherty at Doncaster but he thought it was significant that their success was achieved in the Third Division.

Within a week of the directors' decision to release him Carter received several offers of employment. He said that he would prefer to devote his entire time to management rather than having the extra responsibilities of training and playing. Among those which he was believed to have received were offers from Belfast (Distillery), Crystal Palace, Rochdale and Malta. Later in September Hull City's problems were compounded when Neil Franklin tore a knee ligament.

Early in October relations between the club and its former manager deteriorated when Raich Carter was asked not to train at Boothferry Park. The directors were concerned that embarrassment might be caused by him mixing with his former players. Instead Carter received permission to use the Boulevard, the home of Hull rugby league team. In order to retain match fitness Carter played non-league football at Leconfield, just north of Beverley, where his friend, Squadron Leader George Sizer, was commanding officer at the RAF base. Needless to say, the team became virtually unbeatable.

The Hull City directors tried unsuccessfully to persuade Jack Crayston, who later took over at Arsenal, to become manager. The team were involved in a run of 12 games without a win and only two draws. It seemed as though the directors were involved in an extraordinary form of brinkmanship which put the club's Second Division status at risk. Meanwhile, correspondents to the local press were expressing strong views. On 6th November one wrote, "As sure as Saturday follows Saturday, Hull City will be in the Third Division next season unless something is done now. They can't afford to waste time for we all realise that the position is serious. We don't want new players – the present boys can do the trick but not without a manager. They must have one boss and one boss only. Come on, directors, be bold! Bring back the one and only Raich Carter."

In the meantime, it seemed that Raich Carter had decided to leave league football in order to run a sweets and tobacconist shop in George Street which opened on 19th November. He then asked Hull City to end his contract with them as a player. Carter and his wife had developed a great affection for Hull and wanted to remain in the area. He told reporters that, "I tried to give them good service as regards football and I'll still try to give them good service in my new sphere." He went on to say that, as recently as the current week, one member of the Hull City board has asked him if he would be willing to play for Hull City again. "I told him yes, but it appears that others of the board do not share his views. I was willing to play for the simple reason that I am only too anxious for Hull City." Two days later, 12th November, Raich Carter celebrated the 20th anniversary of signing professional for Sunderland in 1930.

Days later the local press was again full of letters, nine in all, from a larger post bag, demanding the recall of Raich Carter. The directors fixed a meeting for 27th November to discuss the vacant managership. Carter was invited to the meeting with the intention of clearing up any misunderstandings. A friendly discussion resolved the issues and Carter agreed to return as a player. In his statement, chairman

Harold Needler said Carter would resume training immediately and would be available to play on 8th December against Doncaster. He said he personally was delighted that matters had been cleared up. Carter echoed that statement and said he hoped his efforts as a player would assist the club. The next game at Boothferry Park on 1st December was between the reserve teams of Hull and Nottingham Forest. This was Raich Carter's opportunity to prove his fitness and 14,881 supporters turned up to watch him, not quite breaking the record for a Midland League game.

The match against Doncaster was Carter's first league game since 18th August. Eddie Burbanks, Syd Gerrie and Bill Harris were also recalled for this game thus provoking the *Hull Daily Mail* to ask, "Could the old guard bring Hull City victory?" Carter received a great welcome when he led the team out on to the pitch. It seemed that Hull City were transformed by the Carter touch. His brilliant football brain led the way to both Hull City goals. It was the first victory for three months and it paved the way to a much improved second half of the season. In the next game, the league leaders Sheffield United were defeated 2-1.

Hull City's annual meeting on 18th December 1951 was a lively gathering but revealed little new except that the directors were divided over the reinstatement of Carter. Further attempts by shareholders to obtain an explanation for the manager's resignation were parried. Needler claimed he still did not know why the manager had resigned. However, some shareholders took the view that the person who had resigned, Raich Carter, should state the reasons for his action.

Attention was diverted away from the resignation issue by the forthcoming FA Cup third-round match against Manchester United. The relegation battle and the cup competition had to be faced without Don Revie, who had been granted a transfer to Manchester City, and Neil Franklin, who was recovering from knee surgery. Despite the improved form since Raich Carter's return to the team, Hull City hit the bottom of Division Two on 1st January 1952. The next game with Coventry was a crucial relegation contest. It turned out to be a demolition as Hull City, playing with urgency, purpose and teamwork, won 5-0. Despite this return to form, the Tigers were quoted at 500-1 for the cup while their opponents were joint cup favourites with the bookmakers; not really surprising since United were in second place in the top division while City were second from bottom of the division below.

The tie was played at Old Trafford where the crowd was 43,517, fewer than usual, presumably because across the city at Maine Road, Manchester City faced Wolverhampton. The Manchester United team included well-established stars such as Johnny Carey, Allenby Chilton, Henry Cockburn, Stan Pearson and Jack Rowley, plus emerging talents like Roger Byrne and Jonny Berry. Hull City took 3,000 supporters who left the east coast in sleet and hail and arrived in Manchester to sunshine. Within 15 minutes of the start they had a goal to cheer. Raich Carter started the move by beating two defenders; the ball reached Ken Harrison on the right wing who crossed to Syd Gerrie, who drove the ball home. It seemed United were sure to equalise when a penalty was awarded against Denis Durham, but Jack Rowley shot wide from the spot. The furious pace of the game was maintained and it was Hull City who scored the decisive second goal. Harrison was the scorer after good work by Eddie Burbanks. In the second half Hull City defended desperately at times but their victory was deserved as Matt Busby confirmed at the end of the game. The local paper thought this was Raich Carter's best performance since his return to the team. This time, at least, he prevailed over Henry Cockburn.

It was Hull's away form in the league which threatened their second division status. The week after the cup success they lost 3-0 to a Swansea team inspired by Ivor Allchurch. Two weeks later they lost 2-0 at Blackburn where the main uproar from the crowd seemed to be directed at Raich Carter whose ability to annoy home supporters at away grounds remained undiminished. However, between the two away defeats a vital relegation clash with Bury was won 5-0 at Boothferry Park.

Hull City's relegation battle took place in the context of important national events. In October 1951 the post-war Labour government of Clement Attlee was replaced by a Conservative administration still led by Winston Churchill. In February 1952 George VI, who had been recovering from a serious illness, unexpectedly died. Princess Elizabeth received the news of her father's death in Africa where she was on a visit. She was proclaimed Queen Elizabeth II and George VI was laid to rest at Windsor.

Raich Carter was back at his best on 9th February for the match with Luton Town. Bernard Moore gave Luton the lead after four minutes so Carter covered the whole pitch in search of an equaliser, which he eventually scored. But Hull City's away form continued to cause concern, especially after a 6-0 thrashing by Sheffield

Wednesday. Four of the Wednesday goals came from Derek Dooley, who was causing a sensation in south Yorkshire at that time.

The local newspaper reported that Carter must be one of the most entertaining speakers on football after hearing him speak to the Hull British Legion. His main target was the excessive attention which the national press gave to young players – a problem which has obviously not diminished in the last 50 years. He also made comparisons between pre-war teams and contemporary teams. He repeated his concerns about excessive coaching of young players, but was much more positive about the future for floodlit football.

The see-saw season continued into April when Leicester City were the opponents. Arthur Rowley put Leicester ahead in the 66th minute causing Hull supporters to despair. However, inspired by an injured captain, who scored a goal and made the others, Hull City fought back to win 3-1. Also back in fine form was Neil Franklin. The Easter programme brought further away misery at Everton (5-0) and Nottingham Forest (4-0). Fortunately, the tables turned on Everton in the return match at Boothferry Park. The final home game against Brentford would decide the relegation issue. It was Raich Carter's farewell league appearance at Boothferry Park and his old England colleague Tommy Lawton was in the Brentford line-up. It was the Hull City inside forwards, Carter and Irish international Terry Murray, who were the key to victory. Carter laid on great passes and covered an impressive amount of ground, but young Murray patrolled even more territory and had plenty of good ideas. Just to add to the celebrations, Hull City completed their season with their first away win in seven months at Doncaster. Appropriately Raich Carter scored the only goal with 12 minutes remaining.

However, there remained one last flourish to the season: the final of the East Riding Invitation Trophy. This match was played annually by Hull City, and Sunderland AFC were there to mark the occasion of Raich Carter's retirement from football. The gate at Boothferry Park was almost 30,000 and the game was described as a banquet of exhibition soccer. Both teams won the approval of the fans for a bright and clever display, particularly by Bill Harris and Viggo Jensen for Hull, and Willie Watson and Len Shackleton for Sunderland. The result was 2-2 and after the game most of the crowd gathered on the pitch in front of the grandstand. The man who had led Hull City to the Third Division title and had helped save them from relegation was given a rapturous reception. When interviewed before the game Raich Carter said, "After 20 years of first class football it's difficult, almost impossible, to sort out my emotions. Sometimes I feel glad the nervous strain is over – at other times I just can't visualise a Saturday afternoon when I'm not trotting on the field in the familiar rig. But there's one thing for which I'm overwhelmingly grateful, and that is for the support of the tens of thousands who have turned up in all weathers without which I shouldn't have lasted 20 years in the game."

Even if the Hull City had no further need of Raich Carter's services, the city of Kingston-upon-Hull was determined to show its appreciation for Raich's contribution to soccer in the city. The Lord Mayor sponsored a civic testimonial which was set up for Carter. The *Hull and Yorkshire Times* also showed its appreciation by devoting a page to tributes from prominent citizens like the Lord Mayor, the Sheriff, the chairman of the club and the president of the Hull City Supporters' club. In the Hull City Hall at the end of May, presentations were made to Raich Carter from the testimonial fund. His wife also received a gift of a silver service. Carter said that, although he no longer had any connection with the club, he wished them every success and thought they would eventually reach the First Division. He went on to say that the gifts made him very proud. When he came to Hull he had come to do a job. From the gifts he had received it was clear his efforts had been appreciated.

Chapter Twenty-Six

Corner Shop to County Cork

IN THE summer of 1952, after his duties in the shop, Raich Carter was in constant demand to present trophies to schools and clubs. The Hull City players had been introduced to their new manager Bob Jackson who had been successful at Portsmouth. Much further afield in the Argentine the funeral of Eva Peron in Buenos Aires had to be postponed, such was the nation's grief. Nobody at that time saw the events as material for a future successful musical. Raging torrents in Devon in August devastated Lynton and Lynmouth, causing more than 20 deaths. The future Prime Minister Harold Macmillan described the scene as, "Like the road to Ypres."

Into the autumn and sweets and tobacco continued to dominate the lives of the Carters in Hull. In America people had two new heroes to cheer: late in September, Rocky Marciano won the world heavyweight title from Jersey Joe Walcott, while early in November the electors gave Dwight Eisenhower a landslide victory for the presidency of the United States.

There had been some enquiries to the shopkeeper in Hull from football sources, mainly Scottish and non-league, to tempt him back into the game, but nothing had come of them. However, more determined and persuasive officials were on to the Carter trail. Association football had a long history in Ireland, where the Irish FA had been founded in Belfast in 1880, but things became more complex after the creation of the Irish Free State. In the south there was strong competition from the traditional Gaelic sports. Up to the second world war the teams from Cork, which played in the league of Ireland, depended heavily on imports from across the Irish Sea. After 1940 the clubs fielded all-Irish teams and enjoyed great success. Cork Athletic took over from Cork United towards the end of the 1940s and continued to be successful until 1952. Then results deteriorated and support fell, so something had to be done to rejuvenate interest.

Cork Athletic believed that they could succeed where others had failed. They could persuade Raich Carter to play again in Ireland. The club chairman Dan Fitzgibbons and the secretary Doney Ford flew from Ireland to Manchester Ringway, then on to Hull. The Irish press thought it unlikely that the Cork officials would succeed because Carter had home, family and business interests in Hull. But the offer must have been a generous one, otherwise Carter would not have agreed to a meeting in a Hull hotel. He examined the terms on offer which were around £50 per game, plus expenses. Carter could continue to live in Hull and commute to Dublin at weekends for games which were played on Sundays. At that time the English league had a maximum wage of £14 per week during the season. Raich Carter then left the meeting to think things over. At 5.20 p.m. the visitors called at Carter's shop and ten minutes later the deal was signed in the lounge of a hotel nearby. The deal was a short-term one covering the remainder of the season only. Carter was 39 years old and had not played competitive football for nine months. Raich Carter commented on the deal: "I have been getting stagnant in the shop. I've been away from the game for some time now, but I feel I should be OK." Fitzgibbons agreed, "We're delighted to have Mr Carter with us. He's certain to give a big boost to Irish football, particularly in Cork."

The arrangement that had been agreed in Hull would begin on Sunday 8th February. However, he flew over to Dublin a week early in order to meet his teammates who had a league fixture against Drumcondra. It was also necessary for Carter to live in Ireland for two weeks to qualify to play in cup-ties. He made his League of Ireland debut against Waterford at the Mardyke ground in Cork. Raich Carter was familiar with the surroundings, having played there for Hull in a friendly a couple of years before. A crowd of 9,300 attended in heavy showers to see Cork's costly new signing. He needed 20 minutes to sum up the deficiencies of his fellow forwards as well as those of the opposition. Then Carter proceeded to display "his delicacy of ball control, his surgically accurate passes and his two goals." (*Cork Examiner*). The result was a 4-2 victory for Cork Athletic.

The following Sunday, 15th February, Carter made his FA of Ireland cup debut against Drumcondra away in Dublin. The *Examiner* reported that Drumcondra were "bewitched, bothered and bewildered" by Raich Carter, the consummate football artiste. He scored the only goal and finished the game with a plaster across his forehead.

A much more serious injury was in the headlines back in England. Derek Dooley, Sheffield Wednesday's prolific striker, was badly hurt in a collision with the Preston goalkeeper. The fight for the player's life involved an early morning dash for a serum against gangrene. Tragically, it was necessary to amputate Dooley's right leg.

On Sunday 1st March 1953, Cork Athletic defeated Shelbourne 2-0 before a record crowd of 11,300 at the Mardyke. It was a poor game and Raich Carter had a comparatively quiet time. This was not too surprising, as his flight from Manchester was fog-bound and his journey by boat did not reach Dublin until 11.00 a.m. The car journey from Dublin to Cork, in the days before motorways, meant that Raich Carter arrived only 15 minutes before the kick-off. The second round of the cup had drawn Cork against Waterford. All the tickets on sale in Cork for the match at Waterford were eagerly snapped up by supporters. Carter was switched from inside-left to inside-right for the cup-tie and his two goals were vital in a 3-2 victory.

Raich Carter's normal route to Ireland at the weekends was by plane from Manchester to Dublin. The last leg of the journey from Dublin to Cork has been expressively described by Raich himself. "I was driven at nightmarish speed through the Irish countryside to reach Cork in time for the kick-off. The driver, being a Catholic, had to stop off at a church on the way for Mass. Sometimes he would be too late at a village church, so he would jump back in the car and say, 'Never mind, we'll catch the next one,' and off we went at full speed to the next village until a Mass was found."

The following weekend Carter was not available to play for Cork Athletic against Sligo because he had been chosen to represent the League of Ireland against the English Football League on St Patrick's Day, 17th March. He had never thought that one day he would be plotting England's downfall. It was a strange feeling but he was determined to do his best to win the day.

This resolution to do the best he could is clearly illustrated by his preparation for the match. A couple of days before the main game there was a festival match between an Irish select XI and Celtic from Glasgow. One of Raich Carter's former colleagues at Hull, Terry Murray, was in Dublin for that game. Raich Carter had organised a practice session for himself at Dalymount Park where the inter-league game was to be played, and he persuaded Terry to turn up to help him out. Behind one end of the ground there was a school, and before long the boys had recognised the English star shooting into the goal. The irony was that the local boy, who was acting as goalkeeper and ball boy, went unacknowledged. After the practice the two men went on a trip to the seaside which they enjoyed. Murray confessed 50 years later that he "thought the world of Raich."

Back in London the press made Carter's appearance for the League of Ireland the feature of the inter-league match. The papers recalled that, just five years before, Carter was in the Football League team which beat the League of Ireland at Preston. His partner on the wing then was Tom Finney, but this time they would be on opposite sides. The Football League team was a powerful one: besides Finney there were several full internationals like Bert Williams (Wolves), Bill Eckersley (Blackburn), Billy Wright (Wolves), Jack Froggatt and Jimmy Dickenson (Portsmouth), Roy Bentley (Chelsea) and Ivor Broadis (Manchester City). With Raich Carter playing at inside-left, it meant that Billy Wright, who eventually won over 100 England caps, would be marking him. As so often happened in that period the game was ruined by injuries. For the first 23 minutes, inspired by Raich Carter, the League of Ireland more than held their own, roared on by 46,000 Irish supporters. Then Paddy Noonan was injured and did not return to the pitch; shortly afterwards Nelson, a Scot playing in Ireland, also left the field. For nine minutes the Irish played with nine men. Unsurprisingly, the Irish conceded a goal, scored by Bentley, who later added a second.

Cork Athletic had to wait a long time to discover who they would play in the cup semi-final because Limerick and Longford had to play four times before a victor emerged. Eventually it was Limerick who went through and they gave Cork a tremendous fight in the semi-final, with only a last-minute goal preventing a replay. The final between Cork Athletic and Evergreen made history before it kicked off because it was the first time that both finalists were from the city of Cork. The two finalists met in a league fixture on 12th April and the rehearsal for the final went to Evergreen by 1-0.

Four days before the final, Raich Carter was again selected for the League of Ireland; this time the opposition came from north of the border – the Irish League from Northern Ireland. Carter was one of the few to put up any resistance as the Irish League proved too strong and won by 3-0. The cup final took place in Dublin on 26th April 1953 and resulted in a 2-2 draw. Raich Carter's brilliant play contributed to a thrilling match in which he scored the opening goal with an unstoppable drive. He would have been proud of it even in his halcyon days. Four days later the replay was considered to be an even better cup-tie. There were thrills and spills, goals and near misses, and it was all played in a sporting spirit. Cork were the worthy winners because they were the better footballing team. In fact, they would have won by a bigger margin than 2-1 had it not been for the brilliance of the Evergreen goalkeeper Derry Barrett. Carter, who scored the second, nominated Barrett as 'the man of the north.' It was a very moving moment for Raich Carter to receive his cup winner's medal to complete a marvellous comeback. However, he was quick to praise the tremendous play of the other members of the Cork team. It was later discovered that Carter was the first man to win both an FA Cup winner's medal and an FA of Ireland Cup winner's medal.

A couple of nights after the final replay a reception was held for the team on their return from Dublin. They were driven in an open lorry from the station to the largest cinema in Cork, the Savoy. The players were introduced from the stage and the packed audience cheered them to the echo. A special ovation was reserved for the team's inspiration, Raich Carter. As it happened, the film which was due to be shown was about the off-screen life of Charlie Chaplin. In his brief speech of thanks for the warm welcome, Carter brought the house down when he joked about the similarity between himself and the other silver-haired figure.

The following Sunday, 3rd May 1953, Carter made his farewell appearance in the final of the Munster Cup against Limerick. He was given the honour of leading the team out on to the pitch. In the photograph taken by the *Cork Examiner*, Raich Carter sits in the centre of the players, directors and ball boys. The cup was won by Cork Athletic 5-2 so Carter had another medal to add to his collection.

At that time in Cork the players were unanimous in their praise for Raich Carter. They all mentioned his concentration, so intense that he barely spoke before the match. But once in his position, his feet did the talking and, although he was 39, his skill and personality ensured that he was the dominant figure. Also, what was certain was the extra thousands he brought to the Cork Athletic matches. It was even noticed that members of the Gaelic Athletic Association, whose purpose was to support Gaelic sports only, were in attendance when Carter played for Cork. There was also an increase in the number of wives joining their husbands to see the man about whom everyone was talking. The journalist Bill George wrote in the *Cork Examiner*, "Carter was a very big influence on the game here and drew attention to the League. And the £50 he was paid for every match – well, £50 would nearly buy a house for you then."

The man who signed Raich Carter for Cork, secretary Doney Ford, remembered his brief spell, "The man was a sensation wherever he played. He drew record attendances and he was marvellous. He was a model professional who took his contract with us very seriously." Raich Carter wrote of his experience, "The Irish people were wonderful to me. I was treated so well there, like a king, and I remember those days with great affection."

Chapter Twenty-Seven

Following in the Major's Footsteps

WITHIN DAYS of his farewell appearance for Cork Athletic it was announced that Raich Carter would become the next manager of Leeds United. As with his appointment at Hull City, Carter would once again be following in the footsteps of the extrovert Major Buckley. Buckley was now 70 years old and in the five years at Leeds the club's best season was 1950-51 when they came fifth with 48 points. The major's biggest contribution to the club was the discovery of the prodigious John Charles and the redoubtable Jack Charlton. In April 1953 Buckley moved to Fellows Park to manage Walsall. The Leeds United chairman Sam Bolton persuaded Raich Carter to give up the sweet shop in Hull to manage Leeds. From the outset Carter made it clear that he had no intention of playing for Leeds.

The main news item in June came from London where Queen Elizabeth II was crowned at Westminster Abbey. Vast crowds lined the route to join in the celebrations while even larger numbers watched events on their televisions. There was much talk of a new Elizabethan age ushered in by the conquest of Mount Everest. Raich Carter would also have noted the appointment of his former cricket opponent Len Hutton as England's first professional captain. The tourists that summer were the Australians.

All such matters were obliterated from the Carter household by the long illness and death of Rose Carter. For as long as her daughter Jennifer could remember Rose's health had been poor. She had suffered from rheumatic fever in childhood; this left her with a weak heart. She died in Hull before any arrangements had been made for the move to Leeds. She was only 38 years old.

Raich Carter told the local press early in June that he hoped that Leeds fans would get plenty of good football on Saturday afternoons. He was enthusiastic about the new job but asked the supporters for a little patience. Obviously there was a tremendous task to be done at Elland Road but Raich Carter was confident he could tackle it.

In mid-July the rumours which had been around for more than a year, that Leeds would sell John Charles, resurfaced. Both chairman Bolton and manager Carter emphatically denied newspaper reports. The new manager said, "We are trying to build a side, not sell one. We shall not let anyone go if they are of any use to the club." A few days later Carter entered the transfer market to sign his old friend Eddie Burbanks from Hull City. The logic behind the deal was that Leeds had problems with their wingers because of long-term injury and National Service call-ups. It was important to have good wingers in order to give good service to Charles. Burbanks, who was 40, was following his skipper of 1937 for the second time, having signed for Hull from Sunderland. A good omen for the new season was a hat-trick by Charles in a trial match. In the opening league match he went one better, scoring four goals in a 6-0 thrashing of Notts County. After seven games he had 14 goals, and he was the leading goal scorer for all four divisions. The emphasis was very much on attacking football, and Charles was unstoppable.

However, the brilliant opening to the season could not be maintained. Towards the end of September only one point was gained from three games. The undoubted success of Charles at centre-forward meant that he was not playing at centre-half. Drastic action was called for and Carter was expected to enter the transfer market. In the short-term, for the game at Birmingham on 3rd October, four changes were made. The improvement was striking and a useful point was secured.

But the situation with John Charles would not settle and in the middle of October he asked for a transfer. This time Chelsea made an offer of £40,000 (£5,500 more than the British record paid for Jackie Sewell). The offer confirmed the outstanding talent Charles represented, but Leeds had no intention of selling him. The following week Leeds United played a floodlit friendly against Crystal Palace. Raich Carter played in this game and gave a demonstration of soccer skills for the benefit of his players. It was Leeds United's first British game under floodlights and all the players enjoyed the experience at Selhurst Park. Carter's brief reappearance revived memories of the classic style of inside forward play. He seemed to stroll through the game but his apparent nonchalant manner merely cloaked an incisiveness which enabled him to split open defences with pinpoint passes.

Early in November, Leeds United switched on their own floodlights. The guests were Hibernian of Edinburgh who included a number of Scottish internationals like Gordon Smith, Bobby Johnstone and Lawrie Riley. In fact, some observers north of the border believed that the whole of the Hibernian forward line should be picked for Scotland. Raich Carter once again chose himself, this time at inside-left, and 31,500 supporters turned out to make the first floodlit match a great success. What is more, Charles and Carter scored two each in a 4-1 victory. *The Yorkshire Evening Post* thought that Carter's left foot was still one of the best in the game. Charles had not been born when Carter signed professional.

Also in that month England's long-standing and cherished home record against continental teams was destroyed 6-3 by the Hungarians. The Hungarian victory was thoroughly deserved and the skills of Nandor Hidegkuti and Ferenc Puskas were plain for everyone to see. Nor was the England team a weak one as it included Stan Matthews, Billy Wright, Alf Ramsey, Harry Johnston and Stan Mortensen. Of course, Raich Carter had already had a preview of Hungarian potential, having lost to them in Budapest nearly 20 years earlier. Even in 1934 their skill was something to marvel at.

In December 1953 Leeds United were drawn at home against Spurs in the third-round of the FA Cup. The clubs had never met in the cup before. Later on 2nd January Leeds warmed up for the cup-tie by beating League leaders Leicester City 7-1. The Spurs manager, Arthur Rowe decided to revert back to the team which won the First Division title in 1951 – Ditchburn; Ramsey, Willis; Nicholson, Clarke, Burgess; Walters, Bennett, Dunquemin, Bailey – apart from left winger Robb. Raich Carter by contrast announced an unchanged team: Scott, Dunn, Hair; Kerfoot, Marsden, Burden; Williams, Nightingale, Charles, Iggleden, Tyrer. Leeds United put up a great fight and Spurs did not score their equaliser until the 85th minute. The replay at White Hart Lane was played on a mud bath and Leeds again matched their glamorous opponents before going down 1-0.

At the end of January, John Charles and Grenville Hair, both 22-years-old, became two of the youngest players to receive a benefit cheque for £750 on the completion of five years' service. Raich Carter recalled that he received his one-and-only benefit cheque at 23 because his later service was broken by the war and by transfers. At the beginning of March, Birmingham City became the latest club to approach Leeds about the availability of John Charles. The club denied that any serious talks had taken place with Birmingham.

In mid-March, Leeds won their first away match for three months. This was achieved at Carter's old club, Derby County, now struggling in the lower regions of the Second Division. Even more remarkably it was achieved without John Charles, who was injured. At that stage Charles was within two goals of achieving the club record for a season: 35. By the end of the season the record, set by Tom Jennings in 1929-30, was easily broken as Charles reached 42 League goals. He was also top goal scorer for the 1953-4 season for the whole of the Football League. The season finished disappointingly for Leeds United. The final league position, 10th, and the total number of points (43) were both the same as for the previous season when the Major was in charge. The attacking style preferred by Raich Carter had increased the goals scored by 18 but had also led to 18 more goals being conceded. The total goals against was 81, almost two goals per game averaged over the season.

In mid-April, Charles was selected to play for Wales against Austria. The surprise in the selectors' team was that Charles was selected to play at centre-half despite his goal-scoring exploits for Leeds United. When Carter was asked for his comment he said, "I think the selectors have made a big mistake. Even for an outstanding footballer it is expecting too much of him to change his style and technique at will."

Leeds United took 13 players on a close season tour of Holland on which Raich Carter would also play. At Wembley the expected classic 'Finney final' was a disappointment for Preston North End, as West Bromwich Albion won the cup and at the end of May Hungary proved that their victory at Wembley had nothing to do with luck by annihilating England 7-1 in Budapest. This remains the worst defeat suffered by an England team.

In June 1954, both chairman Sam Bolton and manager Raich Carter attended the Leeds Supporters Club annual meeting. The most pressing question from the membership was the club's attitude to approaches for John Charles. Bolton declared that Charles was the last man the club would sell. Carter made a plea for larger crowds at home games so that the club would be financially strong enough to resist transfer bids for their best players.

The World Cup, in the summer of 1954, was played in Switzerland. The Hungarians, known by this stage as the 'Magic Magyars', were odds-on favourites to win the trophy. When they beat the reigning champions Uruguay 4-2 in a classic semi-final, everything seemed to be running to form. However, the West Germans had other ideas and brought Hungary's run of 29 games without defeat to an end 3-2.

Leeds United's opening game of the new season was away to Hull City. The clash of the game was expected to be between Neil Franklin and John Charles. Raich Carter must have found that contest fascinating, and a victory for Leeds was an extra bonus. In the home defeat by Rotherham, Leeds centre-half Jack Marsden was injured and Leeds had to approach the Army to obtain the services of Jack Charlton for the weekend. Charlton had made his debut in the last game of the 1952-53 season against Doncaster Rovers under the management of Major Buckley. Since then his career had been interrupted by National Service in the Royal Horse Guards. Charlton has described how he discovered about his selection for the first team from the team sheets posted on Fridays on the back of the senior dressing room door. Charlton thought it incredible that the manager had not explained why he had been chosen, had not made him welcome on the team bus and had not explained his role or the tactics to be employed. Charlton charged Raich Carter with this neglect but, at the time, Buckley was still in charge at Elland Road.

Leeds United lost their second home game in four days at the end of August 1954, but the young guardsman had fared no worse than the more experienced colleagues around him had. Two more defeats meant that Leeds had made their worst start to the season since the war. In these circumstances, Raich Carter decided to take drastic measures. John Charles, the country's leading goal scorer the previous season, was moved back to centre-half and he was appointed captain. Carter explained, "We cannot afford to lose another game. I want a big, strong, commanding player in my defence – a king-pin of the side." Tommy Burden, captain for four years and a consistent performer, asked for a transfer in order to move back to the west country.

The restructured team, with Charles at centre-half; Keith Ripley, a local youngster, at right half; and Bobby Forrest, a bargain buy from Retford Town, in Charles' old position transformed the club's results. Only one game in the next 17 was lost.

One distraction interrupted the team's revival: a written transfer request from John Charles who wanted to play at a higher level. This was quite different from the newspaper speculation which had previously been the source of transfer deals. Raich Carter's comment on the letter, "I was dumbfounded when this request came in. There is no secret that Arsenal are interested. A record fee could be involved. It's all bound to be controversial in Leeds."

The directors were sufficiently concerned to call a meeting on 29th September to discuss the letter. After debating the request for three hours, Sam Bolton announced that the board had unanimously rejected the transfer request. He said, "Why should we sell a brilliant player like Charles? Our aim is to get into the First Division and we cannot do that by selling our star players." Charles accepted the decision without dissent or recrimination and consoled himself with the improved form his change of position had inspired. Leeds United moved steadily up the table in October and November. Early in December, victory at league leaders Blackburn Rovers meant Leeds were joint top of the table. The improved results were described as a triumph of team spirit and Raich Carter had contributed so much to that spirit.

Raich Carter's major concern during that period was the size of the home gates. "Where are the soccer fans?" he asked. "I understand that over a million people live within 20 miles of Leeds. What's happening to all the men folk? Do they all to go bed on Saturday afternoons? Our critics want us to buy star players but they cost a lot of money. If only we could get some more support."

Charles easily made the switch to centre-forward in the Welsh team to play England. This was his first appearance at Wembley and he scored two magnificent goals. In reply, Roy Bentley scored three times for England. Back at Leeds, the club entered its Christmas programme one point clear of Stoke at the top of the table. This was the first time they had topped the league since they were relegated to it in 1947. Unfortunately, only one point was gained from the two Christmas fixtures with Middlesbrough.

On Saturday 11th December 1954, *The Yorkshire Evening News* announced the engagement of Raich Carter to Patricia Dixon.

An engagement photograph was published and the date of the wedding would be 3rd January 1955 in Hull. Miss Dixon was a former member of staff at Hull City FC. The paper published a wedding photo under the headline 'Raich Carter Marries in Hull.' The bride was a sportswoman in her own right, having represented Yorkshire at netball for four years. The couple did not go on honeymoon because Raich Carter was heavily involved in Leeds United's preparations for an FA Cup-tie against Torquay.

The cup match was a huge disappointment to Leeds fans. John Charles was moved back to centre-forward; nevertheless, Leeds were fortunate to achieve a draw at home and were ripped open in the replay 4-0. In the New Year, Leeds' away form was poor and they lost ground in the promotion race so that, in mid-March, they were in third place. Unfortunately, a final flourish of eight games without defeat, including a 4-0 win over promotion rivals Luton Town, was not sufficient to secure first division status. In an exciting climax to the season any two from seven clubs could have won promotion with two games remaining. Ultimately, three clubs finished on 54 points and Birmingham and Luton were promoted because their goal average was better than Rotherham's. Leeds United, with 53 points, came fourth, their best position since the war. The contribution of Charles to the defence was highlighted by the fall of 28 in the number of goals conceded. Raich Carter summed up the campaign when he said, "Being a fatalist, I realised that this was not our season for honours, but I am highly satisfied by the way my team have completed their programme, especially after that disastrous start."

To complete the season, Carter led his club on a tour of Ireland. Leeds enjoyed victories over Ards, Glentovan and Ballymena before they headed south to Cork. There was a tremendous welcome for Carter and his players from everyone connected with Cork Athletic. A lot of old friends implored Raich to play for one team or the other, but he could not risk a knee which had been badly injured in a floodlit friendly at Elland Road. John Charles scored a hat-trick in a 3-1 win for Leeds over Cork. The highly successful tour was concluded in Dublin with a victory over Drumcondra.

Chapter Twenty-Eight
Leeds Promoted

IN MID-JUNE 1955, Raich Carter had to make an important choice. His old club Derby County made him an attractive offer to take over as manager at the Baseball Ground. Since he was employed by Leeds on an annual basis, he was not contractually bound to Elland Road. Nevertheless, he rejected the Derby offer and signed a three-year deal with Leeds. He told reporters, "Frankly, I do not want to leave Leeds. I am very happy here. I get on well with everyone at the club. Nothing would give me greater pleasure than to get Leeds United promoted."

The players were back in business at Elland Road on 20th July and manager Carter said that they were looking forward to the new season optimistically. They warmed up with the annual cricket match against Holbeck in which Carter hit 40 runs off eight balls and John Charles took six wickets. Despite the emphasis that the manager was placing on giving youth a chance, for the first game against Barnsley the team was a familiar one: Wood, Dunn, Hair; Gibson, Charles, Kerfoot; Williams, Nightingale, Brook, Henderson, Meek.

The pattern of the opening eight games was that the four home games were won, but there were no away wins and only a single draw. It was the familiar problem of not enough goals scored when John Charles was at the heart of the defence. Raich Carter's response on 24th September was to move Charles to a new position of right half. This meant the promotion to centre-half of the demobilised guardsman Jack Charlton. Carter's plan was to give Charles a roving role, supporting attack and defence. The result was a big win over Rotherham in which both Charles and Charlton settled in well with the rest of the team. However, the John Charles experiment did not last long because he was soon needed to lead the attack. The mature and self-confident Charlton was a revelation and retained his position for the rest of the season.

At the beginning of October 1955, Raich Carter was interviewed in *The Yorkshire Evening News* by the Yorkshire and England cricketer Bill Bowes. Firstly Bowes wanted to know why Carter made so many scouting trips to Scotland. Carter replied, "I don't go to Scotland more than other places. I just get recognised there." Next Bowes wanted to know if there was money for transfers? The manager replied, "We do not have money for large transfer fees." Then Bowes asked if there was any local talent? Raich Carter responded, "I am regularly watching local talent. But we have to find a team to get us to the First Division and frankly it's a very hard job."

With Charles leading the attack and Charlton marshalling the defence, Leeds' splendid home record kept them in touch with the promotion race. However, their away performances were undistinguished and it was not until 10th December that they won a second victory away from home at Blackburn. As Christmas approached it seemed that Leeds could narrow the lead held by Sheffield Wednesday, but a disappointing holiday programme produced only two points from three games. Worse was to follow in the FA Cup-tie against Cardiff City on 7th January 1956, which Leeds lost at home. It was the fourth successive season in which Leeds United exited from the cup in the third-round. It was little consolation to John Charles to recall that Cardiff had recently offered £40,000 for him.

In February, Leeds' game with Swansea involved three sets of brothers, five playing for the Welsh club and one for Leeds. John Charles' brother, Mel, was playing alongside the Allchurch brothers and the Jones brothers. As a result of a drawn game neither Charles brother went home pointless. Soon after this result, Raich Carter decided to re-deploy John Charles yet again, this time to inside-right. This was his fourth position for the club and he thrived in his new role from the start. In fact, Dick Ulyatt of the *Yorkshire Post* described it as, "in many ways the best game Charles has ever played for Leeds United." He compared his performance with that of his manager Raich Carter in his prime. At this point late in

February 1956, Leeds United were one of seven clubs in the race for promotion, with Sheffield Wednesday leading the field. Then, on 10th March, Leeds suffered their first home defeat for 34 games. Blackburn's 2-1 victory at Elland Road was followed by defeat at Stoke by 1-0. The Leeds' hopes for promotion appeared to be over for another season. But a win over Plymouth moved Leeds up into eighth place with 38 points while, in second place, Leicester City had just 41 points. Over the Easter holiday the double was achieved over Fulham who included Johnny Haynes, Ron Greenwood and Jimmy Hill. Early in April Leicester City were the opposition and they were dispatched 4-0 in masterly fashion.

When the final away game to Hull City arrived, Raich Carter knew that a win would ensure promotion. The return to Boothferry Park was a sentimental journey for him. Fortunately, he had the encouragement of 15,000 Leeds fans who made the trip to Humberside. They were soon cheering a tremendous left-foot shot by Charles, which gave the visitors an early lead. Hull City, bottom of the division and already relegated, were not submitting without a fight. In the 13th minute they equalised through Tommy Martin. It was not until the 62nd minute, when George Meek was flattened in the penalty area and Charles stepped up to score from the spot, that Leeds took charge. Two late goals by Harold Brook gave Leeds an emphatic 4-1 victory.

Leeds had, therefore, won their last six games in a row and totalled 52 points. They finished three points behind champions Sheffield Wednesday but four points clear of a pack of four clubs equal on 48 points. Thus ended a nine-year period out of the top division. John Charles was the club's leading goalscorer with 29 goals. He also finished third in the annual poll for the Footballer of the Year, a remarkable achievement for a player who had never played in the top flight. The manager was delighted. "They've done well, exceptionally well. One must give credit to the captain and all his men. We've been winning out vital matches because of teamwork. It's gratifying to know that my faith in certain policies has been justified in the end." On their return from Hull, Raich Carter, John Charles and Sam Bolton were photographed with the Lord Mayor and Lady Mayoress at the Leeds Civic Hall toasting Leeds United.

Early in June 1956 the Football League finally accepted that league games, wholly or in part, could be played under floodlights. They also relaxed the maximum wage rule by allowing extra pay for additional games played under floodlights. A couple of weeks later, the newspaper photographers were at the Carter's family home in Headingly to catch the proud father of a second baby daughter Jane and mother Pat. The new member of the family, born on 18th June 1956, was 13 years younger than her sister, Jennifer. When Raich Carter's first wife had died in 1953, Raich bought a house in Sunderland for his first mother-in-law Mrs Marsh where Jennifer went to stay with her grandmother. For Jane's christening at St Chad's in Otley Road, a reunion was organised with friends and family attending from Sunderland and Hull as well as Leeds.

The Leeds United players reported back for training on 16th July. Raich Carter was confident his players could do fairly well in the top division. There were, of course, those who felt that Leeds were a one-man team and that Charles would find things much more difficult against top-flight defences. They could not have been more wrong because, six feet one inch and 14 stone, Charles scored 38 goals at the top level and was the leading scorer in the division. Charles strongly resented the claim that Leeds were a one-man team and emphasised that it was team spirit and teamwork which inspired the Leeds United successes.

For the opening game of the season 1956-57, Leeds faced Everton. Carter decided to rely on the players who had won promotion and they triumphed over Everton 5-1. The star of the day was Harold Brook who scored a hat-trick in 21 minutes; but the downside was an injury to Albert Nightingale which ended his career. Far away in Italy there was a rule change in their league which would have serious consequences for Leeds. The requirement that players in Italy must have some Italian ancestry was abolished. Immediately there was a report that an Italian club was ready to spend a record £70,000 on John Charles. The response of Sam Bolton was that Charles would not be sold, "Not even for the Suez Canal."

Towards the end of August, Leeds United played their first ever floodlit league match. Charlton Athletic were the visitors and Leeds' quick and direct style earned them a 4-0 victory. After the first match of the new season, Leeds had made a creditable start to their First Division fixtures. On 15th September 1956, they gave their best performance of the season, taming the Wolves at Molineux but three days later the main stand at Elland Road was destroyed in little over an hour by a rapidly spreading fire. The blaze could be seen for miles around and the cost of the damage was estimated at between £75,000 and £100,000. Despite the additional destruction of the dressing rooms and club equipment, chairman Sam Bolton told the press that the forthcoming match against Aston Villa would go ahead. Raich Carter said, "The fire is a disastrous thing but we are getting over the difficulties and we are obtaining new kit." The most urgent requirement was 40 new pairs of boots for the entire playing staff. For those selected to play against Villa the order was to wear the new boots as much as possible to break them in before the game.

The encouraging start to the season was maintained and after nine matches Leeds United were second behind Manchester United. Their progress made them one of the most talked about sides in the First Division. It was not until the end of October that Leeds suffered a home defeat when Preston North End won 2-1. Leading the Preston forward line was 34-year-old England veteran Tom Finney. The highlight in November was Leeds 3-2 victory over Manchester United's 'Busby Babes.' Both teams played their part in a really great game. At the end of the month chairman Sam Bolton was busy again denying that Sunderland had offered £50,000 for John Charles. "Sheer bunkum," was Bolton's description of the story, but Sunderland had just paid out to Manchester City for Don Revie.

The draw for the FA Cup third-round again paired Leeds with Cardiff City. Raich Carter was pleased with the home draw despite the experience of the previous season. Leeds remained unbeaten over Christmas against Chelsea and Blackpool and chose an unchanged team for the cup match: Wood; Dunn, Hair, Gibson, Charlton, Kerfoot; Meek, Charles, Brook, Forrest, Overfield. John Charles explained his inside forward role to a journalist, "You are expected to help in attack, fall back in defence and in my case get goals too. The gov'nor used to do all these things but footballers of his mould don't come along every day." Leeds United and their supporters may have thirsted for revenge over Cardiff, but they did not get it because they were eliminated in the third-round for the fifth year in a row. Not much consolation for Raich Carter that his old friend and colleague, Stan Matthews, had been awarded the CBE in the 1957 New Year's Honours List.

One reaction to the cup defeat was to drop Jack Charlton and replace him with local lad Jack Marsden. Charlton's loss of form, he explained in Leo McKinstry's *Jack and Bobby*, was due to the army habits of boozing, girls and late nights, which had clung to him. However, Carter and Charlton were bound to fall out because these strong characters disagreed fundamentally about the running of the club. Charlton regarded Carter as a traditionalist with no real interest in coaching. He also thought the training was repetitive and uninspiring as it consisted of lapping around the pitch followed by a seven-a-side game on the tarmac car park. Charlton was genuinely interested in the coaching side of the game and would soon become a qualified FA coach, but in 1957, as McKinstry wrote, he was still an arrogant, discontented, ill-disciplined young man. What is more, at this stage in his career he was only an average player. Raich Carter had never hidden his scepticism about coaching, and his success in leading Hull City and Leeds United to promotion confirmed his approach to management.

In February there was renewed speculation from Italy that Inter Milan were prepared to pay £72,000 for John Charles. It was a month in which Leeds United's form dipped and the only consolation was a 3-0 home victory over bogey-cup team, Cardiff.

Leeds United's form improved in March and April including their best away win for six years at Portsmouth by five goals to two. There was also a Leeds United–Manchester United clash featuring Bobby Charlton playing for United and brother Jack back in the Leeds line-up. Before the largest crowd of the day, both made important contributions: Jack propped up the Leeds defence with half-a-dozen great cover tackles while Bobby scored a late goal. At the end of their first season back in Division One, Leeds finished a creditable eighth. The champions were Manchester United, eight points clear of Tottenham and Preston. But the top scorer in the division was John Charles, and the European agents and representatives were again preparing to make their move.

Chapter Twenty-Nine
Ticket to Turin

EVEN BEFORE the end of the 1956-57 season, the transfer of John Charles was determined. As late as April, Raich Carter was still maintaining that the club's attitude to the sale of Charles was unchanged. Carter had been in talks with Jesse Carver, manager of Lazio, but no firm offer had been made. The directors had decided that John Charles would be sold for export only. But they had to sell because their finances had been over-stretched by the cost of the new stand.

Juventus were the front runners to secure Charles. The club's 22-year-old president Umberto Agnelli had already checked the player by flying to Belfast for the last of the home internationals between Wales and Northern Ireland. For this game, Charles captained Wales for the first time. Once Leeds announced their willingness to sell Charles to a club outside England, Agnelli and his advisers were on their way to Leeds. An initial offer of £45,000 was rejected by Sam Bolton but negotiation between the clubs was relatively straightforward. Leeds dropped their demand for £70,000 by £5,000 on the understanding that Juventus would play a friendly match at Elland Road. Much more protracted were the negotiations for the personal terms of the player. Charles was the first British footballer to employ an agent to get the best deal available. Just after midnight an agreement was concluded in principle. There were two more stumbling blocks to be overcome before contracts could be signed. Firstly, there was a stringent medical check on the player. The doctor declared Charles to be, "The fittest man I know playing football." Secondly, there was the matter of Juventus' survival in Serie A. The club was in a relegation struggle but, fortunately for the deal, they survived.

Another club in relegation trouble was Sunderland. Earlier in April, they had received the biggest fine in football history for illegal payments. On top of a £5,000 fine, club directors, including the chairman Ted Ditchburn were permanently suspended. This led quickly to the resignation of manager Bill Murray and trainer Bert Johnston. Surprisingly, Sunderland were not vilified for this breach of the rules because everyone knew that illegal payments were widespread and that the real villain was the maximum wage system, which the League imposed. The really good news for Sunderland was that, despite losing to Leeds 3-1 in John Charles' final game before his move to Turin, they avoided relegation. Raich Carter was undoubtedly relieved that he had not been responsible for his old club's demotion. On the other hand, he was saddened by the fate of Ditchburn, who was one of his best contacts back in the old town. The connection between the transfer of Charles, for which he received a legitimate £10,000 signing-on fee, and the inquiry into Sunderland's affairs, was that both events put considerable pressure on the maximum wage system, contributing to its removal four years later.

At the end of April, England announced the names of the players included in the World Cup party. Raich Carter nearly exploded when he could not find Jack Overfield's name on the list. "I don't know what Jackie has to do to get in. He is the best outside left I've seen this season." Overfield was a Leeds-born player, signed from Yorkshire Amateurs in Carter's first year, and had developed into a skilful winger who was a real crowd-pleaser. Early in May, the Leeds players left by plane on a ten-day tour of Holland while manager, Carter, stayed behind to scout for players in Ireland.

Two important government decisions in the spring of 1957 were vital to football league clubs. The first was the abolition of Entertainments tax introduced as a temporary measure in 1916-17. It had cost Leeds United £16,000 in season 1955-56 and was estimated to have cost all clubs about 20 per cent of their gross income since 1952. Sam Bolton described the news as a lifesaver. The second announcement from Whitehall was that the two-year National Service was to end in 1960. Football clubs had all regarded the two-year break in young players' careers as a disturbing and wasteful period. In June 1957 the Leeds City Council refused a loan request from Leeds United. The club denied that there was a crisis at Elland Road and insisted that the new stand would be completed.

Raich Carter began the unenviable task of finding a replacement for John Charles. A record fee for Leeds was paid to Airdrie for Scotland's leading goal scorer Hugh Baird. It required a 60-mile, sight-seeing tour of the Yorkshire villages with Carter at the wheel to convince Baird and his wife that they wanted to move to the area. The local paper described the silver-haired Carter as "American Senatorial" rather than soccer managerial.

Since Bill Murray had resigned from the Sunderland manager's job in the aftermath of the FA enquiry no appointment had been made. Rumours almost inevitably linked Raich Carter with his home-town club but he denied any knowledge of the rumours and said he had not applied for the job. Raich Carter appointed Eric Kerfoot the club captain and paid Jack Charlton a cheque for £750 as a benefit for five years' service at the club. The highest paying supporters were able to say goodbye to the rough and ready accommodation they had to put up with while the new stand was being completed.

The new season 1957-58 began poorly with a 3-0 defeat at Blackpool and the club also lost 2-0 against Aston Villa, which meant the forwards had yet to score. Fortunately, a victory christened the new £180,000 West Stand for the first home league fixture. As a result of the ground improvements, Elland Road was chosen as the venue for the Football League match against the League of Ireland in October. There was a further bonus for the Leeds United fans as Jack Charlton was selected at centre-half for the Football League.

Two home wins steadied the Leeds season and raised confidence for the fixture at Old Trafford. But the 'Busby Babes' were in fine form, winning 5-0. More significantly, perhaps, fullback Grenville Hair left the field injured. He required an operation for cartilage damage and would miss a quarter of the season. This was just the sort of loss which Raich Carter did not need as he strove to fill the "Charles gap."

Early in October, Charles was back in town but in Juventus colours. The friendly match with Leeds United, which was part of his transfer deal, resulted in a 4-2 win for the visitors, with Charles scoring two against has old teammates. Raich Carter continued to scour all over Britain to strengthen the Leeds side in the absence of Charles. Bids for players at both Raith Rovers and Hibernian were rejected, and it was not until mid-November that a further signing was secured: Wilbur Cush from Glenavon, Northern Ireland.

Further moderate results meant that Leeds slipped to 18th place. The stream of injuries and disappointing results caused Raich Carter to make frequent changes which did not necessarily bring immediate improvements. On 30th November, Leeds faced Birmingham, having lost five consecutive matches, and were relieved to gain a point.

In the second week of December, Raich Carter opened negotiations with Blackpool for the transfer of Ernie Taylor. Taylor was an England international and twice cup winner and had formed a close partnership with Stan Matthews at Blackpool. Leeds United and Blackpool had agreed terms for the transfer, so the deal was in Taylor's hands. He brought his wife to Leeds and they stayed the night with Pat and Raich Carter in Headingley. The next day the Taylors left Leeds without agreeing to sign for the club. Since Leeds United were prepared to pay him the maximum wage permitted by the Football League, it was not clear to Leeds fans why Taylor had turned the club down. However, it was very clear to Raich Carter, who used the expression 'greedy bugger' to his wife soon after the visit. Illegal payments were widespread in football, as the Sunderland case had shown, but Raich Carter refused absolutely to jeopardise his reputation by breaking the rules. Earlier, there had been an occasion where a director of Leeds United told Carter that he could make him the greatest manager in the game. Raich Carter's response had been that if it involved anything underhand he was not interested.

A fortnight after the collapse of the Taylor deal, Raich Carter had the satisfaction of a Leeds United victory over Blackpool. This close win was achieved despite the determined efforts of Taylor and Matthews on the right wing. A month later, Blackpool sacked Joe Smith, the League's longest-serving manager. Raich Carter had his critics too when, early in January 1958, *The Yorkshire Evening Post* wondered why it was necessary to make three positional changes to the forward line when only one player failed a fitness test.

For the third consecutive year, Leeds United were drawn at home to Cardiff City in the third-round of the FA Cup. The chances of this happening were calculated at over half-a-million to one. The odds would have far greater if the wager was that each game would finish 2-1 to Cardiff, but that is what happened. Leeds United had not won an FA Cup-tie since 1952, which meant they had the worst cup record in the top two divisions. The Leeds United board met two days later to review the situation but no statement was released. The next league fixture was against the champions, Manchester United, and Leeds produced a much-improved performance to draw 1-1. At the end of January, Raich Carter was able to give a debut to his new Irish acquisition Noel Peyton signed from Shamrock Rovers for £7,000. The diminutive inside forward added pace and tenacity to the attack, which contributed to only the second away win of the season over Bolton.

Just five days later, 6th February 1958, in the slush and ice of Munich airport, the Manchester United team, returning from a European Cup match, was decimated in a take-off crash. The whole nation was shocked by the tragic loss of life: eight players and eight journalists perished. Not only was the United team destroyed, but England too lost the huge talents of Roger Byrne, Tommy Taylor and Duncan Edwards. Raich Carter, absorbed in the relegation struggle, was interviewed a week later and made the comparison between those clubs near the bottom, who had already played a full-strength Manchester United twice, and those who had not yet played them. He wondered how fair this might be when relegation issues were determined. It has to be said that he did not get a very sympathetic reaction; nevertheless, he stuck to his views.

After three lost matches in March, Leeds dropped into one of the relegation positions, but wins over Arsenal and Burnley meant that seven clubs were involved in the relegation battle. It was a very close contest with Leeds on 28 points, one point ahead of four clubs and two points ahead of the bottom club. Leeds were also just a point behind Portsmouth. Over the Easter weekend, Leeds strengthened their chances of survival by gaining five out of six points. On 12th April, they secured a point at Birmingham but the real excitement came after the match, as supporters listened to the results from games where other relegation contenders were playing. The outcome was that Leeds were safe. Great news for Raich Carter, except that Sunderland were not so fortunate and were relegated for the first time after 68 years in the top division.

If Leeds United needed any further confirmation of what they had lost when John Charles left, it came in the news from Italy that Juventus were the champions and that Charles was Serie A's top scorer. It had been anticipated that Leeds would have problems coping without him so it was a shock when Carter became the scapegoat for the failure to replace him. The news that his contract would not be renewed was given to the manager by Sam Bolton on 9th May 1958. The chairman said it was with regret that the decision had been reached and there were tears in his eyes to prove it. Carter wrote in a statement, "This decision has come to me as a great shock. I would like to point out that under my management United went from tenth in the Second Division to eighth in the First Division, and then last season to 17th after the directors had sold the greatest player in the world, John Charles, and have given me far less than half his transfer fee to spend on replacing him. This last season could never be any more than a holding season, once a player like Charles had gone. I am now what you might call 'open to offers.' I have been in football all my life and it is my life."

One story Raich enjoyed telling about his days with Leeds United concerned a decision taken by the board, following the club's promotion to the First Division. It was agreed that the manager should receive a bonus of £500 for his achievement. When Raich suggested to the board that the trainer and the groundsman should also receive a bonus to recognise their contribution, the board agreed that the trainer should have £100 and the groundsman £50, and took both payments out of Raich's £500! However, the £350 was enough to take Pat and Raich on a Mediterranean cruise and bought them their first refrigerator.

Chapter Thirty

From West Park to Field Mill

NO SATISFACTORY jobs in football arrived in the summer of 1958 so the Carters decided to return to Hull. They were sad to leave their lovely house in Leeds but it was necessary to earn a living. Pat Carter's parents still lived in Hull so there was plenty of family support in the city. Eventually, it was decided to go back into the retail trade; and this time, it was a newsagent's shop. The business was situated in Anlady Road, just opposite West Park. The property was in a rather dilapidated condition but a series of articles by Raich in the *Daily Mail* covered the cost of renovation. The family had just about made themselves comfortable and open for business when they were undermined by a printing strike. So there were no newspapers to sell and the business faced ruin. By this time it was late spring of 1959, and the longer the strike lasted the hotter the temperature rose. At the back of the shop there was a spare room and Mrs Dixon, Raich's mother-in-law, had the brilliant idea to turn it into an ice-cream parlour. The situation was ideal because West Park had tennis courts and other sports facilities and, in the summer of 1959, the sun kept shining. So successful was the business in the sale of ice cream and cold drinks that the parlour often stayed open until midnight.

Fortunately, what the newsagents lost on the sale of newspapers was made up from the sale of ice creams. One consolation for Raich was that during the warm afternoons he could nip across the road with Jane and enjoy the park. The disadvantage of the job, once the newspapers returned, was the unreliability of the newspaper boys. When one of them failed to turn up there would be a call from the shop up to the flat to warn Pat that Raich was about to depart with the newspapers on a delivery round. There was one further attraction of being back in Hull and that was the easy access to the coast, which the Carter family made use of every Sunday.

In January 1960, Raich Carter saw an advert for the post of manager of Mansfield Town and decided it was time to have another try at management. Despite his long experience in the game Raich Carter had no idea what the place was like. The Stags, as the club was known, had joined the Third Division in 1931 and remained there until 1958. Then the League decided to form Third and Fourth Divisions out of the two regionalised third divisions – North and South. Because Mansfield were sixth in the Third Division North in 1958, they were placed in the new Third Division. In the season 1958-59, Mansfield avoided relegation to the Fourth Division by one place. When Raich Carter arrived in Mansfield for an interview in February 1960, the Stags were again well down in the relegation zone.

On the day Raich Carter met the directors at the Swan Hotel in Market Place, the town was covered in snow. There was an immediate rapport between the applicant and the directors so the appointment was quickly agreed. Raich Carter was glad to be back in football and told the press, "I appreciate what Mansfield are doing in giving me a job. I hope to repay them in full." The local paper welcomed the appointment and believed it could well be the beginning of a long and more settled period in the club's history. The journalist who spoke to Carter was impressed by his quiet, unassuming personality. The new manager said that football was a difficult business and consequently he was not making any extravagant claims about the future. He thought it would be a tough struggle to avoid relegation.

After his first week in post, Raich Carter said he would prefer if the present Mansfield players retained the club's Third Division status rather than rush into the transfer market for short-term remedies. Mansfield did reward their new manager with an early victory over Shrewsbury, who were led by player-manager Arthur Rowley. However, the new manager soon found how frustrating it was trying to persuade established players to join a struggling

Third Division club. The frustration was more galling because there was so little time available.

Mixed results in March meant that the Fourth Division loomed closer. The local press was surprised by the optimism of the Mansfield supporters which could be attributed to one fact only – the new manager, Raich Carter. The other feature of the new regime which impressed observers was the immediate emphasis on the discovery of local talent.

Despite completing doubles over Accrington and Newport County in April, Mansfield were relegated to the Fourth Division at the end of the 1959-60 season. They finished with 36 points in 22nd position, well behind Tranmere who, with 41 points, were in 20th place and safe from relegation. Raich Carter would use the close season to finalise his scheme to discover and develop the best youngsters in the area.

On 21st July 1960, Mansfield Town players reported back for training. Manager Carter welcomed three new players to the squad: Wagstaff, Phillips and Tarrent, who was signed from Leeds United. Carter was quoted as saying, "I think we have sufficient ability, barring injuries, to do reasonably well." During the close season a lot of work was done at Field Mill by the groundsman and staff, helped by the manager and some of the players. Carter was around to assist, particularly because he was living in the Swan Hotel while waiting for his family to join him. Back in Hull there was the newsagents to be disposed of before the move to Mansfield could be finalised.

A lot of hope rested on the main close season signing Brian Phillips, a centre-half from Middlesbrough. In the pre-season trials, Ken Wagstaff, 17 years of age and signed from Langwith Woodland Imps, showed a lot of promise. However, the hopes for a good start to the season were not forthcoming. Not until the third game, when Wagstaff made his debut, was a goal scored or a point gained. In fact, Wagstaff scored twice before half-time in a 2-1 away victory. Further disappointing results in September caused a financial crisis early in October which led to the resignation of club chairman Dick Childs. Declining attendances caused the club losses which meant they had to turn to the supporters' club for help. For Raich Carter the financial difficulties reduced his scope for new signings to zero. The situation meant the manager's emphasis on building a team out of local talent was now indispensable. This was confirmed by Raich Carter's team selections which, in October, included Wagstaff, Stringfellow and

Smith.

At the club's annual meeting, Raich Carter was in an outspoken mood. He told the meeting that fans who stayed away from home games, "were cutting off their noses to spite their faces." When he was asked if there was any dissension among the players, he replied, "The only dissension they have is that they don't get enough win bonus." One difficulty the manager did confess to was that in the Third and Fourth Divisions clubs did not have full professional staffs training together at the ground. Some players lived and trained elsewhere, while others were only part-timers. Raich Carter had to adjust to these limitations.

Further bad luck struck the club in December when new signing Jimmy Gauld broke a leg in his second game for the Stags. Later he was exposed as the ringleader in a match-fixing scandal which led to the imprisonment of internationals Peter Swann and Tony Kay. The arrival of 1961 did not inspire any improvement in Mansfield's results and a year after his arrival at the club Raich Carter was in another struggle for survival, this time against seeking re-election to the League. Not until March did the tide begin to turn for Mansfield as the Carter youth policy began to work. Stringfellow, Coates and Wagstaff each scored important goals as the Stags won three consecutive away games. Supporters were delighted with the magnificent way the club's youngsters had grasped their opportunity. Raich Carter was especially pleased with the way Wagstaff had adapted to the role the manager set for him. Unfortunately, April's results were inconsistent and the spectre of seeking re-election continued until the final game. The players chose Brian Phillips as their spokesman to approach the manager about an incentive bonus to win the game. Raich's reply was, "You lot got us into this mess and you can get us out of it." That was the end of the matter.

The opponents in the critical match could not have been tougher because Northampton had already achieved promotion to Division Three. However, the young Mansfield team rose to the occasion with a fine 4-1 victory. When all the results were calculated Mansfield and Exeter were equal on 38 points. It was necessary, therefore, to figure out the two club's goal average which revealed an advantage in favour of Mansfield of less than one-fifth of a goal.

With their Football League status secured the directors of Mansfield Town finalised their plans for floodlights at Field Mill. It was hoped that they would be in use by October 1961. During the close season Raich Carter made two modest signings in Scotland on free transfers but just before the new season started in August he paid a club a record fee of nearly £6,000 for Ray Straw. The player, formerly with Derby County, was a centre-forward. Just before the opening fixture Raich Carter outlined his three 'wants' for the new season. He wanted the team to play attractive football; he wanted them to have a fair run of the ball; and he wanted the fans to give the team every possible encouragement. To achieve the attractive football Raich Carter chose a new style forward line including local youngsters Wagstaff and Stringfellow on the wings, together with new signings Straw and Dan O'Hara, a close season free transfer from Celtic, at inside forward. The club also invested in a flashy new version of the traditional blue and amber strip, abandoned seven years before in favour of white shirts and black shorts, to help pull in the fans. It was also the new era of no maximum wage limits for players. Of course this did not have a big impact in the Fourth Division but, at Mansfield, it meant an incentive scheme which could amount to a substantial lump sum at the end of the season.

However, the first task was to overcome Mansfield's first match hoodoo which had meant defeat in every opening fixture for ten years. Ironically, the fixture was against Exeter, who had survived the re-election process. Mansfield were in determined mood and outplayed their west country rivals by three goals to one. A feature of the victory was the fine form of wing-half Peter Morris, another of Raich Carter's youngsters. The local press was confident that the Stags would have a lot better season than the last one. While there were mixed results in the rest of August, Mansfield enjoyed a golden September in which they were unbeaten in seven games and scored 20 goals. Raich Carter had again broken the club's transfer record in buying another striker Roy Chapman (father of former Arsenal and Leeds centre-forward Lee) from Lincoln. In mid-September, Carter explained that, "The floodlights and the signings of Chapman and Straw are all part of a brave attempt to put the club on the map. The directors have taken a gamble but they are committed. One way to find the money is through the turnstiles. We need 14,000 at home gates. The alternative is to part with young players in whom big clubs are interested. But we want to build a team. We don't want to transfer players. But without support we will be forced to."

The club decided to use the home League Cup-tie, with First Division Cardiff City, to launch their new floodlights. This would be the first time in 13 years that Mansfield had faced First Division opponents. Billy Wright, proud possessor of 105 England caps and manager of England's Under 23 team, arrived to switch on the floodlights. The crowd of 10,500 was the biggest for eight years and the opposition was packed with internationals. The game matched the occasion with the Carter-built team from the Fourth Division holding their renowned visitors to a 1-1 draw. Nor were they disgraced in the replay which they narrowly lost by 2-1. The major worry for the Mansfield manager was the insistent offers by bigger clubs for his young stars. Mike Stringfellow was the major interest and the Mansfield directors, in late September, had rejected a bid from Wolves of £20,000. In October, Raich Carter announced that he would not part with his stars. "We are trying to do something for Mansfield." In November, Leicester City raised their offer for Stringfellow from £20,000 to £25,000.

The major problem for the manager, in December, was a lengthening injury list but Carter had travelled thousands of miles since the start of the season to watch dozens of players. Therefore, in the emergency he was able to reinforce his playing staff by buying Sammy Chapman from Portsmouth.

The New Year of 1962 brought a convincing 4-0 win over the League's top scorers, Colchester. However, towards the end of January, the club's determination to retain Stringfellow began to weaken. Nevertheless, the speed with which he departed to Leicester for £25,000, then a record for an 18-year-old, surprised supporters. Perhaps the resignation of Accrington from the Football League convinced the Mansfield directors to enhance their finances. As the season progressed Mansfield failed to improve their mid-table position. However, their final match was a good omen as they beat Darlington 3-0 with their teenagers leading the way.

By this time Pat and Jane Carter were well settled into their home with Raich in Mansfield. The Carters were on very friendly terms with the directors of the club and were generally very happy in Mansfield. When Pat Carter attended her first home match she brought her mother along as well. Both ladies were very smartly dressed for the occasion, which was an evening game. Unbeknown to them, the Mayoress of Mansfield was to be the guest of honour at the match. Pat Carter and her mother arrived early and were greeted grandly by all the club officials. Pat Carter's mother kept telling her how friendly everyone was. Eventually, of course, the Mayoress arrived and the mistaken identity was discovered. Everyone was highly amused and took it in good part.

For the new season the players returned to training on 19th July 1962. Raich Carter watched trainer Sid Carter put the players through their early paces. There had been no spending on transfers during the close season. The first three games were won and Mansfield topped the Fourth Division. Carter's masterstroke was to move Sammy Chapman out of attack into midfield to replace the injured Morris, and to restore Wagstaff to striker, his best position. The club were unbeaten after seven games with 13 out of a possible 14 points.

The unbeaten run lasted until early October, by which time the Mansfield fans had recovered from the lack of transfer activity in the close season. They were further reassured by the arrival of Jimmy Weir and Ian Hall. Hall shared a distinction with Carter: they had both played football for Derby County and cricket for Derbyshire. The club's success attracted the attention of the bigger clubs from the top division. It was not only the players who were being watched but also manager, Raich Carter. The national press linked him with Cardiff City but the manager knew nothing about it. Instead he was taking great pride in the way things were shaping up for Mansfield Town. When he was asked whether he would go if an offer came along he honestly answered that it would depend on the contract. However, he would not just rush off to any offer. Raich Carter still appreciated after two-and-a-half years that Mansfield gave him the chance to get back into the game that had been his life for so long. He knew there was not much sentiment in the jungle of professional football.

At this time Raich Carter became involved in a public dispute with Billy Wright, recently appointed manager of Arsenal. Wright had contributed an article to the *Daily Express* on the role of the modern inside forward in the aftermath of Puskas and the Hungarians. He was particularly critical of inside forwards who were only ball players and dribbled too much. He named Shackleton, Doherty and Carter in his column and implied that they only succeeded because defences in their day always came forward to tackle, whereas in the sixties, defences preferred to retreat as a unit.

Raich was so incensed that he sent the newspaper a telegram in which he said, "Billy Wright's piece. What nonsense! He hasn't a clue!" The *Daily Express* responded by inviting Raich Carter to write an article giving his views. The headline on Carter's piece was, 'Puskas? Give me Doherty every time.' He went on to deny that players like Doherty, Hagan and himself were simply ball-playing dribblers. Players who were so limited had always existed and were never any use to a team. Also, the idea that Carter and Doherty only flourished because defenders came out to tackle them was ludicrous because in the thirties and forties there were all types of defences, including Arsenal's retreating defence. Raich's final comment to Billy Wright was, "There is nothing new in football. All this modern stuff is just a re-hash."

Mansfield's unbeaten away record lasted until the last week in October. It was a top of the table clash at Oldham before 23,700 supporters. The Stags twice took the lead but eventually lost 3-2. The next week Barrow were crushed by 5-0, which made Mansfield the top scorers in their division with 40 goals. November was an even more prolific month for Mansfield goal scorers. Nine were scored against Hounslow in an FA Cup replay. In four home games 23 goals were accumulated and, as a result, Mansfield returned to the top of the division. The goal glut continued in the second round of the FA Cup, which was played at Crystal Palace. Wagstaff led the attack on his 20th birthday and scored both the Mansfield goals in a 2-2 draw. Because Palace's late equaliser had come from a penalty, the Mansfield team lined up to applaud the referee ironically off the pitch. He responded by taking ten names as he passed. Raich Carter predicted that Wagstaff would play for England and the striker confirmed his promise by scoring three goals in the replay, which was won 7-2.

Manager Raich Carter's future at the club was regularly queried. Things had changed so much since August when everyone was despondent through the lack of transfer activity. Supporters were all surprised by how things had turned out, but Carter was not. He was rather phlegmatic about events because he had "seen it all before." He had faith in his experienced men and the knowledge to judge when the youngsters were ready. The local paper declared that, "There's no doubt about it: wherever Carter has been, it's been a success story."

Throughout December, Mansfield and Oldham contested for the top position in the League. The year 1963 brought Mansfield an exciting third-round cup-tie against the reigning First Division champions Ipswich managed by Alf Ramsey. Initially the tie was postponed by snow and, when it was played in what Ramsey described as farcical conditions, Mansfield were beaten 3-2. By then, however, the main item of football news was Raich Carter's departure to Middlesbrough.

The press in Mansfield were generous in their assessment of the manager's decision. "I don't blame Raich Carter. For a man who has known all the thrills and glamour that international and top division football can bring, it must have been agony looking at the squalor and discomfort of places like Spotland. The job at 'Boro not only takes him back near the top but also to his own part of the country."

The Mansfield directors were keen to retain their manager's services but their offer of a salary increase could not prevent his departure. However, Raich Carter assured everyone that the Stags were sure to be promoted. In fact he was right, but only just. Mansfield gained promotion by pipping Gillingham for fourth place on goal average, thanks to being the League's top scorers on 108 goals. Wagstaff (47) and Roy Chapman (34) scored more than 30 goals each and no club since then in the Football League (or Premiership) has had two players each scoring more than 30 goals in a season.

Paul Taylor, the present-day historian of Mansfield, says that, "Raich was a popular manager at Field Mill and is still fondly remembered by those fans old enough to have been around at the time."

Chapter Thirty-One
Transferred to Teesside

ON FRIDAY 11th January 1963, only hours after Bob Dennison left Ayresome Park, Raich Carter's appointment was announced. Dennison had spent nine years seeking promotion to the First Division without success. Twice he had managed fifth place but currently they were tenth. Ten days later Carter was photographed being welcomed to Middlesbrough by secretary Harry Green. The local press described the new manager as, "A man who exudes confidence." When asked how he felt about his new job, Carter said, "I've come back to Yorkshire, I helped to win promotion for a team from the East Riding, Hull, then a team from the West Riding, Leeds. I'm hoping to do the same for a team in the North Riding. I'm not really worried about the South Riding." He was keen to promote the club and encourage spectators back to the games. He made his ambitions public, which were the second promotion place, a First division club and a Wembley cup final.

Unfortunately, Raich Carter arrived in Middlesbrough in one of the worst winters on record. Snow arrived on Boxing Day and remained well into March. Middlesbrough's third-round FA Cup-tie at Blackburn scheduled to be played on 5th January was postponed more than a dozen times and did not take place until 6th March 1963. The club were able to play a league match early in February because it was at Plymouth, where conditions were less severe. This was Raich Carter's first opportunity to pick the team.

He described it, "It's as you were": Emmerson; McNeil, Jones; Yeoman, Nurse, Horner; Kaye, Gibson, Peacock, Orritt, Povey. The match was an action-packed thriller after six weeks of no action. Middlesbrough prevailed 5-4 and Ian Gibson was outstanding. However, a week later, when the first game at Ayresome Park for two months was played, conditions were farcical. The pitch was waterlogged and the players could not keep their feet. At the end of February Raich Carter had to make it clear that, "No player who can assist the club to win promotion will leave. That is definite and includes Alan Peacock." The plea, which named a striker, recalled the battles Raich Carter had had to keep John Charles at Leeds and Ken Wagstaff at Mansfield.

In a speech to the local Rotary Club, Carter said that he was always conscious of the favour life had done him in enabling him to enjoy and earn his living through professional football for so many years. The game had been one of the great joys of his life. The long-delayed cup-tie triggered some fine performances by the 'Boro team. The Blackburn match was drawn and the replay meant Middlesbrough could play three matches in a week. First of all there was a league fixture against Chelsea, the leaders, at Ayresome Park; then, in a thrilling game, 25,000 spectators were wonderfully entertained in a 1-0 victory for 'Boro. Next came the replay with Blackburn which was a blistering end-to-end tie, with Middlesbrough deserving to prevail by 3-1. Raich Carter commented, "What about that wonderful crowd? No wonder we won with support like that."

The next round brought Raich Carter face-to-face with the club who ditched him and the player who disappointed him. Leeds United, now managed by Don Revie, were the fourth-round opponents. Revie was Middlesbrough born and Leeds were the form team. He predicted "a cracking game." Manager Carter at his desk, despite laryngitis and a temperature of 101°C, announced an unchanged team. On the day Leeds were workmanlike and efficient enough to win the tie 2-0.

Following the cup defeat, Middlesbrough's league form was disappointing for a month so that any chance of promotion was lost. The tide began to turn after Easter and the season was completed with an unbeaten run of nine games. As a result of this late surge the club finished a commendable fourth in the league table. Late in April the local press commented that Raich Carter, "was never the type to panic as a player and he remains unperturbable; calm and unruffled, that's Raich."

In the close season, George Eastham shook the football world with his High Court test case against the 'retain and transfer system' operated by the Football Association and the Football League. On 4th July 1963 the court found in favour of Eastham and declared the system illegal. The long-term implications for footballers' contracts were profound. The feudal system which the League had maintained for so long was terminated. Also in trouble was the government of Harold Macmillan following the resignation of Defence Secretary John Profumo after the Christine Keeler scandal. The Prime Minister himself survived in office only for another three months.

Raich Carter's most important job in the summer was to secure the transfer of winger Bobby Braithwaite. The fee of £12,000 was a record for an Irish club. At the same time Ian Gibson, the club's record signing, had been seeking better terms for the next season. In late June Gibson made a shock transfer request and when the players reported back for training on 22nd July, the situation had still not been resolved. The sales of season tickets for Ayresome Park were the best for four years but, at the shareholders' annual meeting, Raich Carter said that he was not satisfied with the gates: "The fans are letting me down." He then appealed to the people of Middlesbrough for their support.

The club arranged a pre-season friendly against Raich Carter's old club, Mansfield. The League's leading scorer for season 1962-63 with 41 goals, Ken Wagstaff, was up against his former boss. In the game the 'Boro showed a tremendous new spirit and Mansfield were dismissed 4-0. Just before the new season commenced Middlesbrough signed a new goalkeeper Eddie Connachan from Dunfermline. He made an immediate debut in the team to play Plymouth Argyle: Connachan; Knowles, Jones; Orritt, Nurse, Horner; Kaye, Gibson, Peacock, Harris, Braithwaite. Middlesbrough made a bright start to the season, winning four of the first five games, scoring 18 goals and conceding only four. However, by the end of September the club's form deteriorated as both Alan Peacock and Bobby Braithwaite suffered long-term injuries. Rock bottom was reached when 'Boro lost at home in a League Cup replay to Fourth Division Bradford Park Avenue. Some pride was restored towards the end of October when local rivals Sunderland were beaten 2-0 without the help of Peacock, who had failed a fitness test. Raich Carter remained optimistic through this spell and the local paper referred to him as "the ebullient manager." He must have been popular, too, in Redcar, where he and his family had settled, because twice within seven days he was guest of honour at two local cricket clubs. For the rest of 1963 the Middlesbrough results continued to be mixed and consequently they fell behind in the promotion race. The bad news from Sunderland was that the career of former 'Boro star striker, Brian Clough, was over. He had failed to recover from a serious knee injury.

In January 1964, Middlesbrough were ejected from the FA Cup at the first hurdle by two goals to one at Brentford. As with the League Cup, defeat came at the hands of a club from a lower division. In February, Peacock, now restored to full fitness, was sold to Leeds United for £55,000: once again, Raich Carter had his main striker transferred as he tried to build a team around him. The manager was consoled with about half the fee to buy a replacement. In the same month Jim Townsend arrived from St Johnstone to fill the gap. His goal scoring capabilities turned out to be disappointing. In mid-March Peacock was back in his native Teesside and, to rub salt into the wound, scored in a 3-1 Leeds victory. The remainder of the season was a mediocre period for Middlesbrough. For Raich Carter there was nostalgia in the final home game against Cardiff City. The visitors had in their attack John Charles at centre-forward and his brother Mel at inside-right. Also alongside them was another Swansea old boy, Ivor Allchurch, but the nostalgia was irrelevant to the 'Boro players, who won the game 3-1.

The season 1963-64 must be viewed as a disappointment for Middlesbrough because they dropped back to tenth place in the League. The promotion places went to Leeds United and Sunderland who were 20 points clear of Middlesbrough. The only crumb of comfort for Raich Carter and his team was that they conceded 33 fewer goals than the previous season.

In the middle of May, Middlesbrough sold their very promising 19-year-old fullback Cyril Knowles to Spurs. Bill Nicholson, the Spurs manager, had been keeping an eye on him for some time and paid 'Boro a cheque for £45,000. Knowles would become a great favourite with the fans at White Hart Lane. As with the sale of Peacock, Raich Carter was able to use only about half the receipts to buy James Irvine from Dundee United. At the end of June, Jackie Milburn, the Ipswich manager, arrived on Teesside to make an offer for Mick McNeil. With nine full caps for England and 193 first-team appearances for 'Boro, the 24-year-old was already an experienced professional. The decision to sell a second fullback that summer must have been a difficult one but the offer of £18,000 was accepted.

In July, Raich Carter gave a long interview to Cliff Mitchell of the *Middlesbrough Evening Gazette*. He gave injuries and poor away form as the reasons for failing to challenge for promotion in the previous season. He blamed the away results on defensive mistakes, although over the whole season only two clubs had conceded fewer goals. The manager was confident that the youngsters, who were pushing for first team places, had great potential. He dismissed reports of match fixing by saying he had never had any experience of it.

The 'Boro players reported back for training on 22nd July. The captain Mel Nurse told the press that no team in the Second Division would be trying harder than Middlesbrough in the coming season. Sadly, everyone in the game was shocked by the tragic death of Tottenham's John White, struck by lightning on a golf course late in July. There was better news from Roker Park, where Brian Clough was to attempt a comeback in a pre-season friendly against Middlesbrough. Raich Carter announced his confidence in his young players to build a team the supporters would admire. It would be easy to win promotion if you could go out and buy Jimmy Greaves and Denis Law, but the money was not available.

Middlesbrough won an exciting friendly against Sunderland 2-1 and Clough survived a leisurely 45 minutes. Once again 'Boro made a decent start to the season with two wins and two draws, which put them in third place in the league. However, by the end of September they were down to 13th place, and out of the League Cup by 2-1 at Charlton. The only redeeming feature of the month was the emergence into the first team of 18-year-old Don Masson.

In mid-October, with one third of the season over, Middlesbrough were three points above the bottom club in 15th place. They had been beaten at home by Crystal Palace and the look on the manager's face was sufficient to tell that he was not happy with the players' performance. An unbeaten spell of five games in November brought the club back up to eighth place. The win at Rotherham was particularly impressive and Raich Carter was delighted with the team's display. He said, "It was the greatest fighting performance 'Boro had given since I took over as manager. This is what I have been longing for." The local press had never known the manager to be so enthusiastic. Further encouragement came from a 4-1 victory over Swindon in which Masson scored twice with thunderbolt shots. The 'Boro players received a tremendous ovation from the crowd at the end of the game.

In December, injuries to both fullbacks came to haunt the club.

But Raich Carter was able to point to an eight-game period in which only two games were lost, despite a long injury list. At the end of December, Middlesbrough lost to Newcastle but the manager's comment was, "We can never be sure of finishing a game with 11 players." He also made a plea for two referees because in an incident, unseen by the official, one of his players was flattened in the penalty area. The offence must have been blatant because Carter rarely made public criticism of referees.

As the New Year of 1965 arrived Raich Carter made a personal call for football to be cancelled a week before Christmas until the New Year. The reason was that his birthday was on 21st December, his wife's on the 24th followed by the Christmas celebrations. If the team lost in that period all the celebrations would be spoilt. Unfortunately, his Christmas was ruined by Newcastle who completed a double over Middlesbrough over the holiday. The next 14 weeks were a nightmare for the club, its manager and its supporters. There were no league victories and little consolation from an FA Cup run to the fifth-round in which Oldham and Charlton were beaten. The club had been tenth before the first Newcastle match but slipped to 20th by the end of February. Just as worrying was the plunge in attendances which had begun the season averaging 23,000 but which had reached an average of 11,000 in February and March. For the home game with Plymouth Argyle in mid-February, the gate was the lowest in the Second Division which was probably the first time it had ever happened. Plymouth won 3-1 and 'Boro were "so bad it hurt", said the *Middlesbrough Evening Gazette*. In an attempt to stem the tide, Raich Carter strengthened his squad by buying Ian Davison, a wing-half from Preston, for £16,000, and Dick LeFlem, a winger from Wolves, for a similar amount.

However, there was little improvement in the results and a 5-3 home defeat by Rotherham in mid-March caused Raich Carter to comment that, "I have never known professional footballers to make so many mistakes." A week later Middlesbrough beat Swansea in a vital relegation match. It was tough, tense and nerve-ridden and it was their first league win for three-and-a-half months. At the bottom of the table only two points covered five clubs with Middlesbrough in 18th place. It was not until the penultimate match at home to Leyton Orient that 'Boro finally escaped from the threat of relegation by winning 2-0. They finished 17th in the table but they had only two points more than relegated Swindon. The only consolation for Raich Carter was the potential of his very young reserve team who had scored 102 goals in the season just completed.

At the Football Association annual meeting at the end of May 1965, a proposal by Swindon Town, seconded by Manchester United, that substitutes for injured goalkeepers be permitted, was passed. The move had the wholehearted support of Raich Carter although he thought it did not go far enough. He believed that a substitute should be allowed for any player regardless of position. Raich had had so much experience of games being ruined by one team being reduced to ten or even nine players. Nor did he think that teams who were responsible for an injury to an opponent should benefit from their tactics. He also believed that supporters should be able to watch a game between two teams of eleven players. Raich also supported a move from two up and two down to four up and down. This would mean more interest in the outcome of the League for the whole season. In these two respects, plus his enthusiasm for floodlit football, Raich Carter showed himself to be a forward-looking student of the game. His views in other areas, especially coaching, remained more traditional.

One of the curiosities of the 1964-65 season had been the appointment of George Hardwick, one of Middlesbrough's greatest players, to the post of manager of Sunderland, while Raich Carter, a great Sunderland star, was managing Middlesbrough. Both managers had struggled successfully to prevent their clubs being relegated. However, Hardwick had taken over 15 games into Sunderland's first season back in the top division with the club in bottom place, and had got them up to 15th place. Carter was in his third season and managed only 17th place. Hardwick was sacked after 164 days in the job but Carter had another chance to make good.

The World Cup organisers had picked Ayresome Park with Roker Park as venues for the 1966 group matches. This gave Teesside a definite boost and meant that the ground would be substantially upgraded. Raich Carter hoped that the playing performances of 1965-66 would match the improvements to the stadium. The manager also announced changes on the pitch. His own approach would be modified so that he would be more involved in planning and tactics, even though he remained convinced that there was no substitute for ability. There was also going to be an appointment of a team coach within a few weeks. The players returned to training on 19th July and found they faced a stricter and tougher programme then in the past.

Despite a lively performance in beating Newcastle in a pre-season friendly, Middlesbrough made a modest start to the season.

Two draws were followed by a crushing 6-0 defeat at Huddersfield. This proved to be Mel Nurse's final game before being sold to Swindon. He was immediately replaced by Dick Rooks, signed from Sunderland for about £20,000.

It was not until the eighth game that Middlesbrough won their first match although they had played in five draws. There was limited satisfaction from a 4-2 victory over Fourth Division Colchester in the League Cup. Middlesbrough supporters must have had mixed feelings over the selection that week of Alan Peacock to lead the England attack against Wales. The former 'Boro centre-forward was said, "To have come out of the wilderness."

For the first time in the club's history, the Middlesbrough team travelled to their away match at Plymouth by plane. The game was played on 25th September and 'Boro fought back from a two-goal deficit to record their seventh draw. This result left them in 17th place in the league table. In October the succession of draws was replaced by two wins and three losses. The club's interest in the League Cup was also ended by Millwall in a replay.

The major event for Middlesbrough in November was the signing from Newcastle of Stan Anderson. The ex-schoolboy and full international and Sunderland idol was offered the role of player-coach. He made his debut against Cardiff City and captained the 'Boro team from right half. There was no fairytale ending to the story because Cardiff won a thrilling game by four goals to three. At the beginning of December Middlesbrough promoted Harold Shepherdson from trainer to assistant manager. He had already been appointed as England trainer for the World Cup in 1966.

The Anderson arrival then inspired an unbeaten run of four games in December, lifting the club to 14th place. The New Year of 1966 brought a huge increase in the injured list with ten players unavailable for the home game with Derby. Further dismay was caused by another transfer request from Ian Gibson just before the FA Cup-tie at Tottenham and in the middle of a relegation battle.

The forwards were a big disappointment in a 4-0 cup defeat at White Hart Lane on 22nd January 1966. For the first 20 minutes Spurs were matched but two controversial goals in two minutes settled matters. The next week 'Boro lost to the league leaders Manchester City by 3-1, and the following week they lost by the same score at home to Huddersfield. The club slipped to 20th place in the league and the board decided to part company with Raich Carter on 12th February. The chairman said that with 15 games still to go it gave enough time for a new appointee to pull the club free from relegation.

The *Middlesbrough Evening Gazette* summed up events in this way: "The name of Raich Carter has invariably been associated with success. This catastrophic chapter in his career must have come as a big blow to him. Most people will feel sympathy but they might think the club didn't have much option. Initial prospects were not bad, success was predicted but it did not work out that way. Raich Carter was a 'natural' footballer who wanted his players to 'play it by ear.' But not all of them were good enough and he had to change his mind and go in for more tactics and coaching. Raich has no complaints against the club. He knows the manager's chair is the hot seat. He knows success has evaded him in Teesside. He felt there was a hoodoo in the club: nothing seemed to go right for it."

Not much went right for Shepherdson and Anderson either when they took over for the remaining months of the season. With one game to play, the club was one position above the relegation places. The fixture was away to Cardiff City who were one place below Middlesbrough in the table. A draw would be enough for 'Boro to survive, while only a win would save Cardiff. The result was a 5-3 win for Cardiff. Middlesbrough were consigned to the Third Division for the first time in their history.

Chapter Thirty-Two
Back to Hull Again

RAICH CARTER'S final comment on his departure was, "This Middlesbrough have been a bad club for me. They have knocked me for six." He probably also had in mind his sending-off there back in the 1930s. One thing both Raich and Pat Carter would miss was their home in Redcar. They were only a mile from the coast and used to visit the beach as often as possible. Raich was in the habit of walking along the beach from Redcar to Saltburn and back several times a week. Pat thought that he did all his thinking on those solitary walks. She very much enjoyed her time there with the eight miles of beach, ideal for daughter Jane, with the lovely views and the atmosphere of boats and fishermen. Also, in 1965, they had been joined by Raich's elder daughter, Jennifer, who moved to Redcar from Sunderland following the death of her grandmother. Now all four of the family were on the move again once more to Hull, where Pat's parents still lived. In fact, the house hunting ended in Willerby, just outside Hull, to the home in which Pat still lives with Jane.

The house was bought, but there was the immediate problem of how it was to be paid for. By this time Raich was 52 and job offers in football were no longer arriving. Nevertheless, there was a temporary source of income from journalism because Raich had considerable experience in that field. One of his most interesting ventures was the football magazine, *Raich Carter's Soccer Star*. It was first published on 20th September 1952 after Raich had resigned from Hull City. The magazine was published from 150, Cheapside, London, and Raich Carter was listed as its editor. The plan was to make the publication the national weekly magazine of soccer. By 20th November, Raich wrote about the amazing progress that had been made in the first eight issues. In January the magazine was 16 pages long, and Raich was writing in his editorial about how much work was involved in the project. Soon Raich was combining journalism with his duties with Cork Athletic. By this time the magazine had an Associate Editor Eric Linden. In August 1953 Raich had to admit that his responsibilities prevented him from attending his editorial desk as he would like, so a second Associate Editor was appointed. In October 1954 Raich stepped down to Associate Editor alongside Robert Bolle. The following July 1955 the Raich Carter name was taken off the title and in October Bolle became the sole editor. *Soccer Star* carried on without Raich until 1970 when it was incorporated with *World Soccer*.

Therefore, jobless and with a house to pay for in Willerby, Raich was pleased to report matches for the *Sunday Mirror*. The games chosen for him unusually involved Hull, Sunderland or England, teams in which he had a particular interest. His first report was on 20th February 1966 and featured a Hull City fightback against Queens Park Rangers in London. His match reports continued until 3rd April when he was at Hampden Park to watch Scotland against England. He was impressed with an England team that could score four goals in the tension of Scotland's massive stadium. He predicted that England were ready for the World Cup that summer and that Bobby Charlton, a world-class player, was capable of inspiring a victory in the competition. One of his articles, which appeared in October 1966, discussed his pleasure in watching the great left-footed players. Raich referred to them as "cuddy footed" because that was the term used in Sunderland 40 years earlier to describe his own footballing ability. He recalled Sam Weaver, Denis Compton and his clubmate, Jimmy Connor, as prime examples of the 'cuddy footed' species. He also paid tribute to Ferenc Puskas of Hungary and Real Madrid, whose left foot destroyed Eintracht Frankfurt in the European Cup final at Glasgow. He must have revised his opinion since his dispute with Billy Wright five years before.

While this part-time journalism helped to tide the Carters through their first six months back in Hull, it was no substitute for a full-time contract of employment. In fact, for the first 18 months after the move away from Middlesbrough, the Carters lived mainly off their capital. Then Raich received a call from the Cooperative department store to manage their sports section. Raich took the job as the money was needed but he never enjoyed the experience. He hated being confined all day inside a shop. Within a year the sports department was closed down and Raich was out of a job again. By this time he not only had a mortgage to pay off but he was about to become a father again. In fact, Pat Carter heard about her husband's redundancy from a doctor in the hospital where she was being treated during her pregnancy. Thirteen was becoming a lucky number for Raich Carter because there were 13 years between his daughters Jennifer and Jane and now there were 13 years between Jane and her brother, born in 1969. While Raich Carter had never been fond of his full name, Horatio, he was happy enough with its abbreviation. So the new member of the family was christened Raich.

Just when the Carters were desperate for a regular income, salvation came in the form of an invitation from the Pools Panel for Raich to join the panel. This body had come into existence in January 1963 during the infamous 'big freeze' when hundreds of matches were postponed. Since the country still wanted to enter their coupons, it was decided by the pools promoters to set up the Pools Panel to determine the outcome of games which could not be played. Raich joined George Swindin, the former Arsenal goalkeeper, Neil Franklin, his old friend and colleague at Hull, Arthur Ellis, the world-class referee, Stan Mortensen, another friend and rival, and Ian McColl, Scottish player and manager, on the 1969 panel. In the chair was Sir Ronald Howe, former Metropolitan Police Commissioner and head of CID. The meetings were held at that time in the Connaught Rooms, London. Every Friday for the next six football seasons, Raich left Paragon Hull station for Kings Cross. Once the panel members had booked into the hotel they were confined in luxurious 'imprisonment.' They did not find this confinement too irksome because they were extremely well paid. Speculation estimated they received more than £1,000 between them when the average weekly wage was about £14 per week.

One of the rules for members of the panel was that they and their families must not take part in the pools. This was no problem for Raich for he confessed, "I've never filled in a football coupon in my life." Most weekends for the panel members, their duties were over when football was seen to be 'on' all over the country at five minutes past three. In fact, in the early days, their expertise was only required if 25 or more games were postponed. Therefore, by early evening on most Saturdays they were well on their way home. In December 1970, *The Sun* printed an article by Frank Nicklin under the headline 'The Seven Just Men.' It featured the absence of Raich senior from young Raich junior over the Christmas festivities if the weather was bad.

This was a generously paid, part-time post for Raich but it did not solve his longer-term career prospects. The answer came when a credit collection business came up for sale. Raich decided to buy it and that was the end of his search for a position outside football. He remained in the business for the next 20 years. He enjoyed his round, which took him to regular customers who always had something to chat about, which was often football. Extra security came when Pat went back to work with the Trawler Owners' Association. By that time, young Raich was six years old.

In his spare time, Raich had two passions: his garden and Hull City. It was the garden which had convinced Raich that the house in Willerby was the right one. In fact, the building was a bit dilapidated but the garden had tremendous potential. Raich junior reckons that his Dad took him to his first Hull City game when he was three years old. The youngster was immediately hooked and has been a Tigers fan ever since. He could claim to be Hull City's biggest fan, as he has not missed a home game in 12 years. Young Raich loved going to Boothferry Park with his Dad but it used to take him nearly an hour to reach his seat. They would arrive at the game at 2.00 p.m. but so many people wanted to stop and shake Raich's hand that it was 2.50 before they reached their seats. Young Raich had the added excitement of being introduced to the great players when they visited the ground: Matthews, Finney, Lofthouse and Charles, not to mention sitting next to Elton John. When young Raich was 11 and attending Hymers College he even persuaded his Dad, aged 67, to play for the Dads v the Lads. Raich senior watched all his son's junior games and described his son as, "Not bad. He enjoys it."

The next occasion when Raich was thrust back into the limelight was at the time of the 1973 FA Cup final. Sunderland were back in the final for the first time since 1937. Consequently, the press were anxious to hear the views of the man who led the club to their first FA Cup victory. Asked by *The Sun* journalist John Sadler how he would have coped with the demands of present-day football, Raich replied, "Brilliantly." At this time, Raich was coming up for 60 but the paper said that he, "Still had the distinguished hair, still had the impish sense of humour, still had the appearance and style that insists that this man is someone special." The *Daily Mail* also called on Raich to organise a meeting with the current Sunderland captain, Bobby Kerr. In the article the paper produced, it was clear that Raich dominated the conversation. In fact, Bobby was struggling to put a word in as Raich produced his full range of anecdotes.

In 1976 Raich was invited to Boothferry Park to kick-off Ken Wagstaff's testimonial game. It was an appropriate choice because Wagstaff was Raich's discovery at Mansfield and he was arguably the one goalscorer to have recaptured the public's imagination since Raich's own days.

The Football Association celebrated the 100th FA Cup Final in May 1981. Raich was invited to the banquet at the Royal Garden Hotel the evening before the cup final, as a past captain of a cup-winning club. The following day the captains were guests at the final and took part in a short ceremony before the game, when they were each presented with a commemorative plate which had the names of all the winning clubs around the edge. Pat Carter gave up her place as Raich's guest at the game so that young Raich, aged 12, could attend. The Football Association also decided to immortalise the all-time greats from the first 100 finals. They chose one cup finalist to represent each of the 11 positions plus one substitute. Twelve solid silver cigarette cards depicting each of the chosen players were struck. A limited edition was produced selling at £260 a set, which have now become collectors' items. The FA's chosen team was: Trautmann (Manchester City); Spencer (Villa), Hapgood (Arsenal); Blanchflower (Spurs), Wright (Wolves), Moore (West Ham); Matthews (Blackpool), Carter (Sunderland/Derby), Milburn (Newcastle), Charlton (Manchester United), Finney (Preston); substitute Edwards (Manchester United). Jackie Milburn, who played in three finals and scored the then quickest cup final goal in 45 seconds, was Bobby Charlton's uncle. Jackie was taken to his first big football match at Roker Park when he was 13. He remembered that when Raich Carter ran out that day he looked immaculate, with his hair combed perfectly in place and his stockings showing precisely the right number of inches of white turnover. Jackie's companion told him, "If you ever want to be a professional footballer you must look like him." And Jackie never forgot that.

Towards the end of 1981, Jack Milburn and Raich Carter were brought together again along with a crowd of soccer celebrities. The occasion was the BBC's 'This is Your Life' programme presented by Eamon Andrews. The subject was Milburn It was half an hour of pure nostalgia as Bob and Jack Charlton, Billy Wright, Tom Finney and Bert Trautmann joined Raich in paying tribute to the Newcastle legend.

In 1985 Sunderland were again at Wembley to contest the League (Milk) Cup final against Norwich City. The *Daily Mail* decided to bring together Sunderland's three Wembley captains: Raich Carter, Bobby Kerr and Barry Venison. Of course, Kerr and Carter knew each other because the paper had brought them together 12 years before. Also, they had both won their finals and both agreed with Venison that Sunderland would maintain their 100 per cent record at Wembley. Raich recalled for the younger skippers the period he played in. "Hard up men from the Sunderland area used to scratch for sea coal along the coast near Seaham. They would return on hair-raising bike trips with their bags to sell the coal to come and watch us. I used to tell the team, 'These are the people we play for. Give it everything.'" Kerr agreed that Sunderland supporters were amazing people. Venison, like Carter, a Sunderland supporter born and bred but two generations younger and without any experience of worldwide slump, just sat back and listened. Unfortunately, his team lost 1-0 to Norwich.

By this time the Raich Carter family had grown because daughter Jennifer had married Peter Josse and they had a son Peter Josse Junior. The next anniversary in football's history was the centenary of the Football League, which was commemorated on 29th November 1987. Raich was one of the guests and he was driven to Manchester by his son-in-law Peter. Among the other star guests were his old friend and colleague Neil Franklin, his prize asset at Leeds, John Charles, plus Nat Lofthouse and Bobby Charlton. After lunch the toast was to the next hundred years of the Football League. At that time there was no hint of a Premier League.

In 1992 Sunderland were back at Wembley in the FA Cup final against Liverpool. Raich was nearly 80 years old and there were only two other surviving members of the 1937 cup-winning team, Bob Gurney and Johnny Mapson. Sunderland offered each of them two tickets for the final. However, there were no arrangements for the veterans to travel to Wembley. Raich was so upset by his old club's attitude that, rather than risk the trouble of travelling to London, he declined the offer of tickets. The Supporters' Club supported the veteran's complaint. Their spokesman said, "They created history for this club and should have been well looked after." Bob Gurney did accept his tickets and was not at all impressed with the way the club dealt with their guests that day.

On 4th July 1992, Raich suffered a mild stroke which reduced his mobility and forced him to give up his credit business. As a result of his illness he received a hamper at Christmas from the League Managers' Association. Pat Carter telephoned Olaf Dixon to thank the association for their kind gift and happened to mention in the conversation that she had heard that Bill Foulkes had sold his medals and she wondered how one went about such a sale. Pat's motive was to get a valuation for insurance purposes and to know whether extra security measures were necessary.

However, someone in the press completely distorted the story and announced that Raich was seriously ill, that he needed medical treatment which he could not afford because he was broke. The whole article was nonsense because Raich was in a private medical scheme. But it caused havoc and distress to the family. First the telephone started ringing from friends and fans from all over the country offering support. Then the letters began to arrive from well-wishers, many of whom enclosed cheques. This continued for several weeks so that it was necessary for Raich and Pat to go to another paper to get the story quashed. It had taken Pat three weeks to write to everyone to explain the mistake and to return their cheques which came to around £2,000. Pat Carter said, "Of course, the reaction of the public is heart-warming. Raich is deeply touched to know he's still remembered as a great player and manager. Raich didn't earn much as a player but he looked after his money." Raich joked that so many flowers came for Pat she thought she must have died. Raich also had a call from Kenneth Wolstenholme, which gave them a chance to chat about the old times. So, out of the ordeal some pleasure did arise.

It was for the charity CAP, which supports autistic people, that Raich made what proved to be his last visit to Sunderland. 'A Night of Nostalgia' was held on 4th May 1993 at the Swallow Hotel, Seaburn, Sunderland. Alongside Raich were his two pals from 1937, Bob Gurney and Johnny Mapson. Other guests included Sunderland legends from the post-war period such as Len Shackleton, Charlie Hurley and Jim McNab. Also in attendance was practically the whole of the 1973 FA Cup winners and their manager Bob Stokoe.

On 3rd September 1993 Raich suffered a second stroke, which completely incapacitated him. He was in hospital and then a nursing home until February 1994. He wanted to come home and it was arranged for that to happen.

On 21st December Raich celebrated his 80th birthday. Distinguished journalists from the broadsheets were ready to write birthday tributes. David Miller, of *The Times,* wrote that Carter defined English football for the generation either side of the Second World War. "His football was a concept, an ideal, the fulfilment of ordinary men's dreams. Carter meant more to his generation than Glen Hoddle did to his and Carter had only a quarter of Hoddle's caps." His daughter, Jane, told Miller that, "Sunderland was where his heart always was, his happiest time. He's glad he played when he did with and against so many fine players." Frank Keating, of *The Guardian*, also wrote a warm tribute. He said that Raich, "Was a sublimely skilful, attacking, inside forward. He enthralled through the longest career of any in the white number eight England shirt – nearly 14 years from his callow precociousness of 1934 to 1947, by which time his hair had long gone famously and prematurely grey."

The decision to bring Raich Carter home in February 1994 meant that Pat and the family had a full-time nursing commitment. The consolation was that Raich was much happier back home. The arrangement lasted for ten months until 9th October 1994 when he passed away peacefully. His death recalls one of his most quoted comments about footballers: "When they become too old to play they should be sent to the Knacker's yard and shot like old horses." His reasoning was that there was nothing to compare with playing the game, especially not coaching it.

At the request of the chairman of Hull City Martin Fish the funeral cortege of Raich Carter slowed to a halt at Boothferry Park to be met by a respectful guard of honour of 350 fans and the entire management and playing staff of the club. Among the mourners was Raich's old England colleague Wilf Mannion and the last surviving member of the 1937 FA Cup-winning team Johnny Mapson. Bobby Kerr was also among the mourners representing the 1973 Sunderland cup winning team. Floral tributes came from Raich's old clubs, from the Professional Footballers' Association and from the Football Association of Ireland, recalling his playing time at Cork Athletic. Pat Carter said that the whole family had been touched by the warmth of people over the last week and this had been a great comfort. The funeral on 15th October was exactly 62 years after Raich made his debut for Sunderland against Sheffield Wednesday.

In February 1998 Pat Carter was diagnosed with cancer. So the question of Raich's memorabilia arose in her mind again. The collection was locked away in a bank so no one was able to get any pleasure from it. As Raich had three children it would not be simple to divide up the trophies. If the collection were broken up amongst the family, future generations might not appreciate its value. Pat wanted them to be kept together somewhere they could be seen and enjoyed by people interested in Raich Carter. Therefore, Pat decided to approach Christie's in April with a view to their sale. The auction was arranged to take place in Glasgow in June 1998 to coincide with the World Cup in France.

Pat's decision had been backed by her daughter, Jane, her son, Raich Jnr and by her step-daughter, Jennifer. The family did not need the money but believed the collection should be on public display. Pat's tough decision soon aroused considerable interest on Wearside. There was some debate in the press about who should make a bid on behalf of Sunderland – the city council or the football club. The council decided to launch a fund to buy the collection and made a grant of £5,000 itself. The former chairman of Sunderland AFC Tom Cowie pledged £10,000. The council were keen to display the collection at the proposed new Raich Carter Sports Centre in Hendon, so it was sensible to negotiate with the club so that a single offer could be put to Pat Carter. The city were also able to secure a grant of £8,350 from the Victoria and Albert Museum. In June 1998, an amicable agreement was reached between Pat Carter and the council for the collection to be withdrawn from the Christie's Auction. The bulk of the collection went to the Sunderland City Council but a late approach by Derby County to buy four items from Raich Carter's time at the Baseball Ground was accommodated. Derby County had just unveiled plans to open a Hall of Fame museum and they expected the 1946 FA Cup winning team to fill one of the centrepieces of their display. Back in Sunderland the collection was prepared for its first public display, which was held between November 1998 and April 1999 at the City Museum. Prior to the collection being opened, a special reception was held at the Sunderland Civic Centre attended by Pat Carter, to say a special thank you to everyone in Sunderland who had contributed to the fund, which had ensured the collection went to the City.

The ultimate, magnificent, tribute to Raich Carter came in October 2001 with the opening of the splendid Raich Carter Sports Centre. The new complex was built with a grant of £4.9 million from the Lottery Sports Fund and is situated in Hendon very close to where Raich was born and grew up. Pat Carter and the family attended the official opening, which was performed by Trevor

Brooking, chairman of Sport England. Pat said that, "Raich would have been very moved to see a centre bearing his name open in the area where his roots were. Raich's heart was always in Sunderland. To see the children here with his name on their t-shirts – they can't know how much that means to us. We even met a nine-year-old at the centre who was actually called Raich Carter. And it was amazing to look through the windows and see the very lampposts where Raich would have practised as a youngster."

The collection of Raich's memorabilia now had three venues; the City Museum; the Stadium of Light and the Sports Centre in Hendon.

Chapter Thirty-Three
The Two Mr Carters

THERE CAN be no doubt that Raich Carter was a great footballer. Several records give an indication of his considerable natural ability. First of all, in May 1937 at the age of 23 years, Raich Carter had an England cap, a League champion's medal and an FA Cup winner's medal, which meant he had won all the honours available then to a player in England. Secondly, during the war, he won a place in a powerful England team and scored 18 goals in 17 internationals. Thirdly, in 1946, Carter became the only player to win an FA Cup winner's medal both before and after the war. In that year too he was one of only three players to represent England both before and after the war. Fourthly, in 1953, Carter became the first player to gain a cup winner's medal on both sides of the Irish Sea. Lastly, he had one of the longest England careers, spanning 13-and-a-half years.

Another source of evidence of Raich Carter's talent comes from verdicts of his fellow professional players. Walter Winterbottom both played against Carter for Manchester United and managed him when he was appointed England's first team manager. He has written that, "Raich Carter was a most gifted footballer. He also had an acute tactical awareness of positional play around him." Another tribute, of which Raich would have been particularly proud, came from his hero, Charlie Buchan, the Sunderland and England international, who became an eminent sports journalist. Buchan wrote about Carter, "His wonderful positional sense and beautifully timed passes made him the greatest inside forward of his generation: he stood out in every game he played in. He was that rare combination, a ball artist and a marksman."

Of those of his contemporaries who played with and against Raich before and during the war, and therefore saw him in his prime, Lawton, Matthews and Mercer have written tributes about his prowess. Tommy Lawton said, "Raich Carter, as a player, would be there for me in any team of immortals. I know of no other man who measured up so well as the complete footballer." Stan Matthews recalled that, "Carter was deadly with his left and right foot inside the box. He read the game well and liked to make long passes. Carter was a great player." Joe Mercer noted that for six-and-a-half years he had played and had captained teams which were among the best Britain had produced. They included men like Raich Carter, "who was the best all-round effective player I have ever seen." Willie Watson, England's double international at football and cricket, has given one of the best descriptions of Carter's style: "I never knew how good Raich was because you can only judge a player when you've seen him under pressure. I never saw him under pressure. He carried space around with him like an umbrella." Bill Dodgin, manager of Southampton, Fulham and Sampdoria, told about how he advised the young Johnny Haynes, who was always trying to beat every defender, "I told him the greatest footballer I'd seen was Raich Carter and he always made the ball do the work. So why didn't he try that for a change? Soon he was knocking about those marvellous 45-yard passes."

Not surprisingly, Raich Carter's friend and former colleague Peter Doherty was equally flattering in his assessment. "The Wearsiders gave a sparkling exhibition of scientific soccer and Raich had one of his best days – which meant, of course, that he was magnificent. We were outclassed and outplayed." Sir Tom Finney, speaking in 2003, told me that Raich Carter was, "Highly rated, one of the greats whom it was wonderful to play alongside." Sir Tom also recalled Carter being, "kind and encouraging to younger players like myself." Frank Swift, one of England's outstanding goalkeepers, wrote that in his team of all-time greats, he would chose Raich Carter at inside-right to partner Stan Matthews. "Raich is the one man who understands Matthews' style of play. In addition, he has one of the hardest shots with either foot I've ever seen. His secret is the most uncanny art of anticipation." This list of admirers is long and includes Neil Franklin, George Hardwick, Stan Cullis and Charlie Mitten.

Alongside Raich Carter's supporters and his fellow professionals, there are many admirers among the authors and journalists who watched him play. For example, Michael Parkinson has written, "Great inside forwards are made in heaven. They are fashioned out of gold and sent on earth to win football matches and weave the stuff that memories are made of. They are the architects who design a game. My first clear memory of football is of a great inside forward at work. His name was Horatio Carter."

James Herriot, whose series of books about a Yorkshire vet became the very popular TV series 'All Creatures Great and Small', wrote that, "Raich was simply the best. He could score goals from 35 yards with either foot. He was just a natural." The playwright Alan Plater wrote, "Raich dominated games. These days he'd be called a left mid-fielder but, in truth, he reinvented the game as he went along. He didn't play the game, he presided over it. When Hull had two international inside forwards, Raich wore the number 11 shirt, took all the corners and throw-ins on either side of the field and also turned up on the goal-line when necessary to help Bly, the goalkeeper. He did all those Italian jobs – libero and catenaccio and such, years before the names were introduced and without sweat. He was the greatest of his kind and he knew it."

John Arlott, writer and commentator, in a preface to a history of Sunderland AFC, described the elegance of Jimmy Connor, which lingered in his memory, "A picture of unhurried style with, at the end of his run, a steely shot. Then came the years of that footballing genius, Raich Carter – football brain, tactician and opportunist, both maker and taker of goals."

When Raich Carter died in 1994, he had not been directly involved in football for 28 years. Yet in no sense was his wonderful career forgotten, as can be seen from the newspaper headlines. *The Sun* proclaimed, 'Legend Raich is Dead;' the *Daily Express* in similar vein, 'Legend Raich is Dead at 80;' the *Daily Mirror* simply, 'Carter Dies:' *Today*, 'Soccer Legend is Dead' and the *Daily Mail*, expansively, 'Farewell to an England Soccer Legend.' The *Hull Daily Mail*'s headline was, 'Genius with Golden Touch,' and went on to quote Stan Matthew's tribute to Raich, "A football artist with perfect ball control who could outwit any defence." The *Derby Evening Telegraph* led with the headline, 'Death of a Legend.' The paper added, "Carter's goals tended to be definitive. even as the ball was on its way, he knew the goalkeeper had no chance." The *Sunderland Echo* also had the headline on page one, 'Death of a Legend' and described Raich as, "widely acknowledged as one of England's greatest inside forwards." *The Daily Telegraph* led its obituary with the headline, 'Virtuoso with Unbruisable Self-confidence.' *The Times* obituary was simply headed, 'Raich Carter,' and it went on to say that he was one of the great inside forwards of English football who would undoubtedly have played many more times for England had he not lost six years to the war. Finally, *The Guardian* headline said, 'Autocrat at Inside-Right.'

So, clearly, there was only one Mr Carter, the player, the legendary football international. So how could a mistaken identity arise? The headline, 'The Two Mr Carters' dates from the *Hull Daily Mail* in February 1949. The article claimed that there were two Mr Carters because it seemed that Raich had a dual personality. This double-sided personality really reflects the context in which Raich was encountered. On the field of play or in the manager's dugout or on the training ground, there was a minority who found him arrogant and too fully aware of his own special talent. When the charge was put to him directly, Raich joked, "I used to be arrogant but I've matured and grown more tolerant; now, I'm just conceited." As a captain or as a manager he was a disciplinarian, a man of exacting standards who shouted his orders to fellow players and expected an immediate response. He was not always popular as a manager because he was too honest with his players; he did not suffer second-rate play lightly. Not everyone could take that. When Carter was at the helm there was never any doubt about who was calling the shots. He could be a rough taskmaster. In answer to a question about his Derby days, he denied that he was selfless in his teamwork with Doherty. He maintained that both he and Doherty strove for individual glory. "I may have been arrogant. I wanted to be recognised as a better player than Peter, better even than Matthews. I couldn't have put up with being just an ordinary player." In effect he had the intelligence to put his natural gifts to maximum use. But on the field he could not tolerate those whom he did not think should be professionals.

There were also public occasions where his lack of modesty was evident and his wide range of opinions would be aired. He could be a good speaker on such occasions but, if the company included someone with a strong Oxford or Cambridge accent, Raich would exaggerate his own accent so that broad Sunderland vowels were expressed. On one such occasion Raich was on a panel of sportsmen answering questions from the public. One other member of the panel represented Derbyshire tennis. His voice was posh and he referred to certain sportsmen as 'Damn professionals.' Raich was provoked by this and eventually said, "My contention is that the main difference between amateurs and professionals is that professionals pay tax on their earnings."

When Raich was manager at Mansfield there was a full-length painting hanging behind his desk. It was a portrait of himself, in his England kit, with his foot on the old leather ball. When he left for Middlesbrough it was the first thing to leave his office. Ian Hall, a player with Derby and Mansfield and later author of *Derby County Superstars*, has described him as a man of immense self-belief who oozed authority. He even told the referee what to do!

However, away from the pitch and the managerial office, an entirely different Mr Carter emerges. This was a man who had forgotten the shortcomings of a teammate and who was out to cheer and encourage. He is said to have had a wicked sense of humour and to have enjoyed a practical joke. When asked about his great contemporary and England teammate Stan Matthews, he answered, "Yes, you could see he could play a bit", said with a twinkle in his eye as he recalled their great times together. Those who became his friend, like Tim Ward, felt fortunate to have got to know him so well.

To the second Mr Carter a mention of Sunderland in the 1930s could produce a note of humility. He idolised the working men of his home town. He said, "The thing that used to amaze me was the level of support we used to get in those days when most of the men were out of work. Heaven knows where they got the money from, many couldn't afford shoes let alone admission money." He went on, "Throughout my career, I was always conscious of the supporter. When you've travelled to a ground in a bus and seen them walking along with their scarves in their thousands, you could not but go and try to win for them." In particular he recalled a cup match at Tottenham in 1938. It was a tough, even game with no goals after 80 minutes. Then Raich received a perfect pass from Burbanks and shot left-footed into the goal. He was elated as his teammates crowded round to congratulate him but, as soon as he began to walk back to the centre circle, jubilant Sunderland supporters began to sing the 'Blaydon Races.' He had heard the familiar tune many times before but never quite like this. "My God! I thought. My goal has given them this feeling of exhilaration. Then I cried. The tears came into my eyes and rolled down my cheeks."

Clearly, Raich Carter was a sentimental man; or maybe he was a rare sports hero who experienced genuine empathy with the spectators? He realised that football was a relief from the drudgery of everyday life. Victories in particular brightened the lives of spectators.

This was the Mr Carter known to his family and friends, the man who was reported to be quiet and unassuming in the Mansfield press. In Willerby he was the friendly, easy-going man with the immaculate garden, so widely liked and admired that people travelled from all over the country to pay their last respects at his funeral. He was also 'a soft touch' when he met up with an ex-teammate like Patsy Gallacher, who had fallen on hard times. Raich knew that he had been fortunate to be given a special gift and he thanked God for it. "I always wanted to express the talents bestowed on me. I wanted to thrill people. Wherever I played I wanted to leave something special behind so that they would always remember Raich Carter."

Bibliography

Raich Carter	Footballers Progress (Sporting Handbooks) 1950
Peter Doherty	Spotlight on Football (Art & Educational Publishing) 1947
Tommy Lawton	Football is My Business (Sporting Handbooks) 1946
Tommy Lawton	My Twenty Years of Soccer (Heirloom Modern World) 1955
Stan Mortensen	Football Is My Game (Sampson Low) 1949
Frank Swift	Football From The Goalmouth (Sporting Handbooks) 1948
Charles Buchan	A Lifetime in Football (Phoenix House) 1955
Geoffrey Green	The Official History of the FA Cup (Heinemann) 1949
Ivan Sharpe	40 Years In Football (Hutchinson & Co) 1952
Willie Watson	Double International (Stanley Paul) 1956
Neil Franklin	Soccer At Home And Abroad (Stanley Paul) 1956
Jackie Milburn	Golden Goals (The Soccer Book Club) 1957
John Charles	King of Soccer (Stanley Paul) 1957
Billy Wright	One Hundred Caps and All That (Robert Hale) 1962
Anthony Davis	Stanley Matthews CBE (Cassell) 1962
Arthur Appleton	Hotbed of Soccer (Rupert Hart-Davis) 1960
Brian James	England v Scotland (Pelham Books) 1969
Bryon Butler	
Ron Greenwood	Soccer Choice (Pelham Books) 1979
James Walvin	The People's Game (Allen Lane) 1975
Douglas Lamming	The Who's Who of Hull City (Hutton Press) 1984
Jack Rollin	Soccer at War (Willow Books) 1985
Roy Mason	Sunderland Number Ones (Northdown Publishing) 1988
Bryon Butler	The Football League: First 100 Years (Colour Library Books) 1988
Tony Francis	There was Some Football Too: 100 Years of Derby County (Derby County FC) 1984
Nicholas Fishwick	English Football and Society (Manchester University Press) 1989
Peter Jeffs	The Golden Age of Football (Breedon Books) 1991
Ivan Ponting	The FA Cup Final (Tony Williams Publications) 1993
Paul Harrison	The Elland Road Encyclopedia (Mainstream) 1994
Bob Graham	The History of Sunderland AFC (Wearside Publishers) 1995
Andrew Ward	Armed With a Football (Crowberry) 1994
Joe Mercer	The Great Ones (Oldbourne Book Club) 1964
Alan Brett	
George Hoare/	
Alan Brett	Sunderland AFC 1879-1973 (Chalford Publishing) 1996
Andrew Clark	Newcastle v Sunderland (Black Cat Publications) 1995
Malcolm Macdonald/	
Martin Jarred	The Leeds United Story (Breedon Books) 1992
Jim Hossack	Head Over Heels: A Celebration of Football (Mainstream) 1989
Nick Varley	Golden Boy – biography of Wilf Mannion (Aurum) 1997
Jack Charlton	The Autobiography (Corgi Books) 1996
Roger Hutchinson	Into the Light: Complete History of Sunderland AFC (Mainstream) 1999
David Bond	The Hull City Saga (Breedon Books) 1999
Harry Glasper/	
Chris Kershaw	The Boro Bible: Complete History of Middlesbrough FC (Middlesbrough FC) 1999
George Hardwick	Gentleman George (Juniper) 1998
Bryan Horsnell/	
Douglas Lamming	Forgotten Caps Internationals of the Two World Wars (Yore Publications) 1995
David McVay/	
Andy Smith	The Complete Centre-forward (SportsBooks) 2000
Richard Coomber	King John (Leeds Utd Publishing) 2000
Paul Agnew	Football Legend: Biography of Tom Finney (Milo Books) 2002
Leo McKinstry	Jack and Bobby (Collins Willow) 2002
John Gibson	Wor Jackie (Sportsprint) 1989
Michael Parkinson	Football Daft (Stanley Paul) 1968
David Miller	Stanley Matthews (Pavilion) 1989
Anton Rippon/	
Andrew Ward	Derby County Story (Breedon Books) 1998

Horatio Stratton Carter
born: Hendon, Sunderland, 21/12/1913
England Schoolboy international 1926-27, 1927-28
Apprentice electrician
Amateur Whitburn St Mary's, Sunderland Forge
Trial for Leicester City December 1930 – rejected
Signed amateur forms for Sunderland AFC July 1931
Signed professional for Sunderland 12 November 1931

Sunderland AFC

Season:				
1932-33	League	24 ap	6 goals
	FA Cup	5 app	0 goals
1933-34	League	29	17
	FA Cup	3	2
1934-35	League	38	11
	FA Cup	3	1
1935-36	League	39	31
	FA Cup	2	0
1936-37	League	37	26
	FA Cup	8	3
1937-38	League	39	13
	FA Cup	5	1
1938-39	League	39	14
	FA Cup	5	2
1939-40	League	3	3
	abandoned – war		

Total 279 appearances – 130 goals

FA Cup victory 1936-37

Third round	16 Jan 1937	Southampton	(A)	3-2 (Carter unfit)
Fourth round	30 Jan	Luton Town	(A)	2-2
replay	3 Feb		(H)	3-1 (Carter 1)
Fifth round	20 Feb	Swansea	(H)	3-0
Sixth round	6 Mar	Wolverhampton W	(A)	1-1
replay	10 Mar		(H)	2-2
replay	15 Mar			4-0 (Carter 1)
		at Sheffield		
Semi-final	10 Apr	Millwall		2-1
		at Huddersfield		
Final	1 May	Preston NE		3-1 (Carter 1)
		at Wembley		

Wartime appearances

Season	1939-40	Huddersfield	11 app	6 goals
		Hartlepools Utd	6	0
		Sunderland	3	2
	1940-41	Friendlies only (for Sunderland Police, FA XIs,		
		Civil Defence & Sunderland)		
	1941-42	Sunderland	27	23
		(League Cup final losers to Wolverhampton W)		
		Huddersfield	3	5
		York City	1	0
	1942-43	Sunderland	24	15
	1943-44	Sunderland	5	2
		Derby County	14	13
		Nottingham F	1	0

1944-45	Derby County		28		29
	Sunderland		3		3
1945-46	Derby County				
	(War League)		10		13
	Derby C				
	(FA Cup)		11		12

Total 147 appearances – 123 goals

FA Cup victory 1945-46

(two-leg basis)

Third round	5	Jan 1946	Luton Town	(A)	6-0	(Carter 1)
	9	Jan	Luton Town	(H)	3-0	(Carter 2)
Fourth round	26	Jan	West Bromwich A	(H)	1-0	
	30	Jan	West Bromwich A	(A)	3-1	(Carter 1)
Fifth round	9	Feb	Brighton & HA	(A)	4-1	(Carter 2)
	13	Feb	Brighton & HA	(H)	6-0	(Carter 3)
Sixth round	2	Mar	Aston Villa	(A)	4-3	(Carter1)
	9	Mar	Aston Villa	(H)	1-1	(Carter1)
Semi-final	23	Mar	Birmingham C		1-1	(Carter1)
			at Hillsborough			
	27	Mar	Birmingham C		4-0	
			at Maine Road			
Final	27	Apr	Charlton Ath		4-1	
			at Wembley			

Transferred from Sunderland 21-12-1945 £6,000 approx

Derby County

Season:	1946-47	League	33 app	19 goals
		FA Cup	4	2
	1947-48	League	30	15
		FA Cup	5	2

Total 72 appearances – 38 goals

Transferred from Derby County 31-03-1948 £6,000 approx

Hull City (Player-manager)

Season:	1947-48	League	4 app	0 goals
	1948-49	League	39	14
		FA Cup	5	3
	1949-50	League	39	16
		FA Cup	4	0
	1950-51	League	32	19
		FA Cup	3	2
	1951-52	League	22	8
		FA Cup	2	0

Total 149 appearances – 62 goals

Cork Athletic

Season: 1952-53   13 appearances   9 goals

Cork Athletic won the FA of Ireland Cup, drawing 2-2 with Evergreen in the final and winning the replay 2-1.

Career Record

Full Internationals

v					
Scotland	3-0	Wembley	14 Apr 1934	
Hungary	1-2	Budapest	10 May 1934	
Germany	3-0	White Hart Lane	4 Dec 1935	
Ireland	3-1	Victoria Ground, Stoke	18 Nov 1936	(Carter 1)
Hungary	6-2	Highbury	2 Dec 1936	(Carter 1)
Scotland	1-3	Hampden Park	17 Apr 1937	
Northern Ireland	7-2	Belfast	28 Sep 1946	(Carter 1)
Eire	1-0	Dublin	30 Sep 1946	
Wales	3-0	Maine Road	19 Oct 1946	
Holland	8-2	Leeds Rd, Huddersfield	27 Nov 1946	(Carter 2)
Scotland	1-1	Wembley	12 Apr 1947	(Carter 1)
France	3-0	Highbury	3 May 1947	(Carter 1)
Switzerland	0-1	Zürich	18 May 1947	

Total 13 caps – 7 goals over a period of 13 years 34 days (second longest to Stan Matthews for an outfield player).
The gap between sixth and seventh caps was nine years 164 days and the third longest ever.

Wartime internationals

v				
Scotland	2-1	St James' Park, Newcastle	2 Dec 1939	(Carter 1)
Wales	5-3	Wembley	27 Feb 1943	(Carter 1)
Scotland	4-0	Hampden Park	17 Apr 1943	(Carter 2)
Wales	1-1	Ninian Park	8 May 1943	
Wales	8-3	Wembley	29 Sep 1943	(Carter 2)
Scotland	8-0	Maine Road	16 Oct 1943	(Carter 1)
Scotland	6-2	Wembley	19 Feb 1944	(Carter 1)
Scotland	3-2	Hampden Park	22 Apr 1944	(Carter 1)
Wales	2-0	Ninian Park	6 May 1944	
Wales	2-2	Anfield, Liverpool	16 Sep 1944	(Carter 1)
Scotland	6-1	Wembley	14 Oct 1944	(Carter 1)
Scotland	6-1	Hampden Park	14 Apr 1945	(Carter 1)
Wales	3-2	Ninian Park	5 May 1945	(Carter 3)
France	2-2	Wembley	26 May 1945	(Carter 1)
Northern Ireland	1-0	Belfast	14 Sep 1945	
Switzerland	4-1	Stamford Bridge	11 May 1946	(Carter 2)
France	1-2	Paris	19 May 1946	

Total 17 appearances – 18 goals
Raich Carter's wartime international goals placed him second to Tommy Lawton's 24 in 23 games. In 17 internationals Carter was on the losing side only once, in the last game.

Football League Representative matches

v				
Irish League	6-1	Oval, Belfast	19 Sep 1934
Irish League	1-2	Bloomfield Rd, Blackpool	25 Sep 1935
Scottish League	3-1	Hampden Park	12 Mar 1947
League of Ireland	4-0	Deepdale, Preston	14 Apr 1948

League of Ireland Representative matches

v				
Football League	0-2	Dalymount Park, Dublin	17 Mar 1953
Irish League	0-3	Dalymount Park, Dublin	22 Apr 1953

Career total 696 appearances 387 goals

Cricket

3 First Class appearances for Derbyshire, 4 Minor Counties appearances for Durham, including matches against the West Indian and Australian touring sides.

Index

Index

Index

Index